A

NORTHERN SUMMER;

OR

T R A V E L S

ROUND

THE BALTIC,

THROUGH

DENMARK, SWEDEN, RUSSIA, PRUSSIA,

AND PART OF GERMANY,

IN THE YEAR 1804.

BY JOHN CARR, ESQ.

AUTHOR OF THE STRANGER IN FRANCE, &c. &c.

PHILADELPHIA:

PRINTED FOR

AND PUBLISHED BY ROBERT GRAY,

ALEXANDRIA.

1805.

TO THE HONOURABLE

SIR JAMES MACKINTOSH, KNT.

RECORDER OF BOMBAY.

SIR,

WHILE you are imparting new light to those regions, so gloriously illuminated by the genius and the virtues of the late Sir William Jones, will you allow a Traveller to express his thoughts to you in contemplating your character and situation? I cannot but felicitate that race of my fellow-creatures who are placed within the protection of your judicial care; yet, in recollecting how many listened to you with delight in this country, I feel your distance from it, in one point of view, a source of national regret. Conscious that these sentiments are sincere, I am encouraged by them to request, that you will honour with indulgent acceptance, a book, whose author has endeavoured to unite amusement and information.

Doubtful of his success in each of his purposes, he is anxious to conciliate favour, by introducing his performance to the Public under the shelter of your name: a name that awakens universally the respect due to the beneficent exertions of knowledge and irresistible eloquence.

DEDICATION.

That health and felicity may attend you, in those scenes of arduous duty where your gracious Sovereign has stationed you; and that you may return to this favoured island, and long enjoy in it all the various rewards of honourable service, is the ardent wish of him who is,

SIR,

With the truest esteem,

Your faithful and obedient servant,

JOHN CARR.

No. 2, GARDEN-COURT, TEMPLE,
1st JUNE, 1805.

CONTENTS.

CONTENTS.

THE AGREEMENT.

THE ground which my pen is about to retrace has not very frequently been trodden by Englishmen. Northern travellers of celebrity, who have favoured the world with the fruits of their researches, have generally applied their learning and ingenuity more to illustrate the histories of the countries through which they have passed, than to delineate their national characteristics. Nature generally receives our last homage; we never wander from the contemplation of her simple charms, but we return to them with pleasure. As the attempt, although aiming at originality, is not of an aspiring nature, I feel the more confidence in stating, that the object of the following pages is to describe those features which principally distinguish us from our brethren in other regions, and them from each other.

I hope that the execution of my wishes will at least be without the fault of fortifying those prejudices which so unhappily divide nations that ought to be linked together by mutual love and admiration. Whilst I wish to amuse, I am desirous to facilitate the steps of those who may follow me, by giving the detail of coins, and post charges, and some little forms which are necessary to be observed in a northern tour. My descriptions follow the objects which they pencil, and partake of the irregularity of their

B

appearance. I write from my feelings; and as I propose that my Reader shall travel with me, it is reasonable that he should share some of the inconveniences as well as the enjoyments of the excursion. Before we smile together in the beautiful islands of Sweden, we must be content to bear with resignation the gloom of her almost interminable forests of fir.

If he will not commence the Tour upon these terms, and agree to support without disappointment those vicissitudes of amusement and of languor, that seldom fail to diversify all the roads both of literature and of life, much as I shall lament the separation, it will be best, for both parties, that we should not wander together over another page.

A

NORTHERN SUMMER;

OR

TRAVELS ROUND THE BALTIC.

CHAP. I.

TIME OF SETTING FORTH—A WESTERN TOWN—HARWICH—THE POOR
NORWEGIAN'S TOMB—HELOGOLAND—FLOATING MERRY FACES—
HUSUM—A STUHLWAGGON—THE FAIR—THE WONDER—NOVEL AP-
PLICATION OF A CHURCH—WALTZES—A SHOCKING SECRET.

IT was on the 14th of May, 1804, that, impelled by an ardent
desire of contemplating the great and interesting volume of man,
and by the hope of ameliorating a state of health which has too
often awakened the solicitude of maternal affection, and of friendly
sympathy, the writer of these pages bade adieu to a spot in which
the morning of life had rolled over his head, and which a thousand circumstances had endeared to him. I cannot quit England
without casting a lingering look upon my favourite little town of
Totnes, where, as a characteristic, family alliances are so carefully preserved, that one death generally stains half the town
black, and where Nature has so united the charms of enlightened
society to those of romantic scenery, that had a certain wit but
tasted of the former, he would have spared the whole county in
which it stands, and would not have answered, when requested to
declare his opinion of the good people of Devon, that the further
he travelled westward, the more persuaded he was that the wise
men came from the east.

The angry decrees of renovated war had closed the gates of the south; the north alone lay expanded before me. If she is less enchanting, thought I, perhaps she is the less known; and wherever man is (women of course included) there must be variety: she has hitherto been contemplated, clad in fur, and gliding with the swiftness of a light cloud before the wind, upon her roads of shining snow. I will take a peep at her in her summer garb, and will endeavour to form a nosegay of polar flowers.

There is always a little bustle of action and confusion of ideas, when a man, about to slip from his friends, is in the *agonies of packing up*. My mind alternately darted from my portmanteau to the political appearances with which I was surrounded; and, with all the vanity which generally belongs to a traveller, I resolved to commemorate the period of my flight, by a cursory comment upon the state of my country, which, by the time the last strap was buckled, was simply this: A great man had succeeded a good one in the direction of its august destinies, and another being, who may be considered as the wonder of the west, was preparing amidst the blaze of brilliant novelties to mount the throne of a new dynasty; amongst them was a threat to cover the shores of England with his hostile legions. Nine hundred and ninety-nine Englishmen, out of one thousand, had started into martial array, on the sound of the haughty menace—patriotism, with the bright velocity of a wild-fire, ran through the valley and over the mountain, till at last it was discovered that we might be invaded whenever we pleased. Ministers were more puzzled by their friends than their enemies; where streams were expected to flow, torrents rolled headlong; and, whatever may be our animosities, we are at least under an everlasting obligation to the French, for having enabled us to contemplate such a spectacle of loyalty. How I happened to leave my country at this time, it may be proper to explain: Devonshire offered, to her lasting honour, twenty thousand volunteer defenders of their homes and altars, nine thousand were only wanted or could be accepted; in the latter, a spirited body of my fellow townsmen, who honoured me by an election to command them, were not included; after encountering (and it was equal to a demi-campaign) the scrutinizing eye of militia-men, and the titter of nursery-maids, until awkwardness yielded to good discipline, and improvement had taught our observers to respect us, we found that our intended services were superfluous, and I was at full liberty to go to any point of the compass; so, after the touching scene of bidding adieu to an aged and a beloved mother, whilst she poured upon me many a half-stifled prayer and benediction, I hastened to the capital, where, having furnished myself with the necessary passports and letters of introduction to our embassadors from the minister of foreign affairs, a circular letter of credit and bills from the house of Ransom, Morland, and company, upon their foreign correspondents, and with a packet of very handsome letters of private introduction, which were swelled by the kindness of Mr. Grill, the Swedish consul, and a passport (indispensably necessary to the visitor of Sweden) from the baron Silverhjelm, the enlightened and amiable representative of a brave and generous nation, I proceeded to Harwich, and at midnight passed under the barrier arch of its watch-tower, which was thrown into strong picturesque varieties of shade, by its propitious light, which from the top flung its joyous lustre over many a distant wave, so gladdening to the heart of the homeward mariner.

In the morning we went (I had a companion with me) to the packet-agency office, where we paid four guineas each for our passage to Husum; 1l. 11s. 6d. for provisions on board (seldom tasted); after which, douceurs of 10s. 6d. each remained to be paid to the mate, and 7s. each to the crew, and 5s. a-piece to a personage who contributes so largely to human happiness, and particularly to that of Englishmen, the cook; we also paid ten guineas for the freight of a chariot belonging to an acquaintance at Petersburg, 2s. per ton on the tonnage of the vessel, and 1s. in the pound upon the value of the said carriage; this accomplished, I had nothing further to do, but to amuse the time until four o'clock in the afternoon, when the foreign mail from London arrives.

The church-yard lay adjoining to the inn: in this solemn spot, we are not always enabled to indulge in those serious and salutary reflections, which it ought alone to inspire; the quaint or ridiculous effusions of the village schoolmaster, and the sexton, those prolific mortuary laureates, too often awaken an irresistible smile; by commemorating the ravages of death in some pious pun or holy conundrum; a perversion which well merits the interposition

of the ecclesiastical officer whose power extends over these regions
of the dead. I had not wandered far, before a fresh plain slab attracted my notice, and, by its inscription, informed me that it was
raised to the memory of captain Christensen, of Krajore in Norway, who fell by the bite of his dog, when mad; the tale was
simply, but touchingly, told, and drew from me the following
lines:

> Ah! hapless stranger! who, without a tear,
>   Can this sad record of thy fate survey?
> No angry tempest laid thee breathless here,
>   Nor hostile sword, nor Nature's soft decay.
>
> The fond companion of thy pilgrim feet,
>   Who watch'd when thou would'st sleep, and moan'd if miss'd,
> Until he found his master's face so sweet,
>   Impress'd with death the hand he oft had kiss'd.
>
> And here, remov'd from love's lamenting eye,
>   Far from thy native cat'ract's awful sound;
> Far from thy dusky forest's pensive sigh,
>   Thy poor remains repose on alien ground.
> Yet Pity oft shall sit beside thy stone,
> And sigh as tho' she mourn'd a brother gone.

Soon after we had quitted the tomb of the poor Norwegian, the
mail arrived, and at five o'clock a favouring breeze bore us from
the lessening shore. Now, as I am one of those unhappy beings
who, like Gonzalo in the Tempest, would at any time give one
thousand furlongs of sea for an acre of barren ground; and as
there may be many more who may find the rocking of the ocean
somewhat unfriendly to the regularity of appetite; let me advise
them to lay in some anchovies, lemons, oranges, and a little brandy:
and as we are upon the subject of travelling economy, let me also
recommend the packing up of a pair of leather sheets and a leather
pillow-case, in addition to their linen ones; the former will prevent the penetration of damp, and repel vermin. As we passed
Orfordness-castle, the sun was setting in great glory; and several
ships working to windward, and alternately crossing each other,
presented the most graceful figures: it was such a scene as the
chaste spirit of Vernet might have hovered over with delight.

The next day, we saw the topmasts of our brave blockaders off the Texel, It was painful to contemplate the effects of a dire necessity which forces us to harass a people, who in their hearts cherish no animosity, but against the tyranny which separates them from us. A noble frigate from the squadron passed us under a croud of sail, " breasting the lofty surge;" she proudly dashed through the foam of the ocean, and to the eye of Fancy looked like the palace of Neptune. Her appearance reminded me of the nervous, spirited, and Chatham-like exclamation of a celebrated wit, upon the same subject: " an English man-of-war is " the thing after all: she speaks all languages; is the best ne- " gotiator, and the most profound politician, in this island; she " was Oliver Cromwell's embassador; she is one of the honestest " ministers of state that ever existed, and never tells a lie; nor " will she suffer the proudest Frenchman, Dutchman, or Spaniard, " to bamboozle or give her a saucy answer."

On the third day, a very singular object presented itself; it was Helogoland, a vast lofty perpendicular rock rising out of the ocean, and distant about forty-five miles from the nearest shore: it is only one mile in circumference, yet upon its bleak and bladeless top, no less than three thousand people live in health, prosperity, and happiness. The hardy inhabitants subsist principally by fishing and piloting, and are occasionally enriched by the destroying angel of the tempest, when the terrified observer, looking down upon the angry storm, might, in the moving language of the clown in the Winter's Tale, exclaim, " Oh! the most piteous cry of the poor " souls, sometimes to see 'em and not to see 'em : now the ship " boring the moon with her mainmast, and anon swallowed with " yest and froth." But to the honour of the brave Helogolanders, they never augment the horrors of the enraged element. Humanity and honourable interest impel them gallantly to face the storm, and snatch the sinking mariner, and the sad remains of his floating fortune, from the deep: they never suffer the love of gain to excite any other exclamation than that of thanks to God; not that the storm has happened, but that the ocean has not swallowed up all the wreck from them. How unlike a body of barbarians who infest the west of England, and prefer plunder to the preservation of life, and who have been even known to destroy it, whilst struggling with the waves, for the sake of a ring or a bauble, and who

are accustomed in the spring of every year to speak of the last
wreck season as a good or a bad one, according to the violence or
moderation of the preceding winter![*]

The Helogolanders are a fine healthy race of people, remarkably fair, live in small huts, and sleep on shelves ranged one above
another, and are governed by a chief who is deputed from the government of Denmark. They are obliged to victual their island
from the shore. What a spot for contemplation, to view

> " Th' ambitious ocean swell, and rage, and foam,
> " To be exalted with the threat'ning clouds !"

We entered the river of Husum about four o'clock in the morning, in a stiff gale attended with rain. The clouds in the west were
dark and squally, with here and there a streak of copper colour;
in the east the sun was gently breaking. Whilst I was contemplating this picturesque appearance, and occasionally regarding
the anxious eye and gesture of our Danish pilot, who by the aid of
buoys and floating poles conducted us with admirable skill through
a narrow, and the only navigable, part of the river, which lies between two long lofty sand-banks; the effect of the scene was encreased by an owl of yellow plumage, endeavouring to reach our
ship : the poor bird we supposed had been blown off the coast ; his
wing touched the extremity of the boom, but, exhausted with fatigue, he dropped breathless in the water. A sailor, who was looking over the sides, with a quaint imprecation of mercy, pitied the
dying bird.

The shore as we advanced looked low, flat, and muddy, surmounted here and there with a solitary farm-house and wind-mill;
but the river presented a scene of considerable gaiety. Boats put
off from the little islands which appear on either side of the river,
filled with hardy men, women, and boys ; the ladies wore large
black glazed pasteboard bonnets, glittering in the sun : they were
all going to the great fair at Husum. We cast anchor about four
miles from that town, whose tall spire appeared full in our view :
a large boat filled with these good holiday folks came alongside,
and received us, baggage and all. As we proceeded up the river,
which became narrower as we advanced, and which seemed more

---

[*] I allude to the wreckers of Hope Cove, near Kingsbridge.

like thin mud than water, through which we heavily moved by the assistance of punting poles, I waded through the tedium of the time by contemplating my companions, most of whom, with myself, were covered over below with the hatches to avoid a heavy shower of rain. They were all in their holiday dresses; the men in blue or brown druggets, and large round hats, and the women in coarse striped camlet gowns, in which red was the prevailing colour, with those vast shining bonnets before described, and slippers with high heels without any quarters: we were crowded together almost to suffocation. Our company was more augmented than improved by pigs and poultry, and the various produce of the farm, amongst which I noticed some delicious butter. In the party was a fine blooming young Scotswoman, who had married a Helogolander; her expressive dark eyes flashed with delight, to find herself seated near an Englishman : in her look was legibly written the inextinguishable love of our country.

Upon our landing, we were immediately addressed by a Danish centinel who was upon duty at the quay, and whose dress and appearance were very shabby; he dispatched one of his brother soldiers with us to the burgomaster, to notify our arrival and produce passports, thence to the secretary to procure others to proceed.

A little money here had the same virtue which it possesses in almost every other part of the globe, by producing unusual energy in these subordinate ministers of government, and enabled us to sit down to an early dinner at an English hotel, during which, I was a little surprised at hearing one of our fellow-passengers, who was immediately proceeding to Hamburgh, frequently vociferate, " Is my waggon ready ? What a country, thought I, must this be, where a waggon is required to convey a man, and one too who was little bigger than his portmanteau! Observing my surprise, he informed me, that the carriage of the country was called a Stuhlwaggon; upon its driving up, I found that its body was very long and light, being formed of wicker work, and fixed to thin ribs of wood; the bottom was half filled with hay, a cross seat or stool was fastened by straps to the sides, and the whole mounted upon four high slender wheels; it runs very lightly, and is admirably adapted to the heaviness of the roads, which are very deep and sandy.

C

Soon after dinner I strolled through the fair, which was filled with peasantry from various parts of Holstein and Slesvig. The women, in their rude finery, reversed the ambition of their fair sisters on the other side of the water; they were strongly buckramed to the top of the neck, and exhibited no traces of the bosom; but, to soften the severity of this rigid decorum in front, they presented such a projecting rotundity behind, that, to eyes which had been accustomed to gaze upon the symmetry of English fair-ones, appeared truly grotesque, and awakened many a smile.

The church, which is large and ancient, was upon this occasion disrobed of the sanctity of its character, and in its fretted aisles booths were erected, in which books and haberdashery were exposed to sale, and where I found some coarse copies of engraving from some of the pictures of Westall, In several places upon the continent, I witnessed, with no little degree of pride, a striking predilection for the works of this distinguished artist. Almost every article which was exposed for sale was called English, although I am satisfied that many of them were never fashioned by English hands; but the charm of the name has an influence every where; its sound is attractive, and the very pedlar of the fair finds his account in its forgery.

A custom-house officer waited upon us at the inn to inspect our luggage, but the dexterous introduction of a dollar into his hand convinced him in a moment, from the mere physiognomy of our trunks, that they contained nothing contraband. Let him not be blamed; for his penetration was admirably correct.

Before the river of Husum was choaked up with mud, the town was a place of considerable commerce. It is now principally filled with tradesmen and farmers; and the removal of the packets to this place from Tonningen has circulated a considerable quantity of money amongst the inhabitants. It is rather a large town; lime-trees grow before the houses, the roofs of which run very high, and present the appearance of steps; these vast attics are never used but as lumber-rooms, and have a very disagreeable effect. There is a palace with gardens belonging to the duke of Holstein; but they are unworthy of further notice.

The gaiety of the day terminated with great sobriety. There were many light hearts, but I believe not one aching head. In the evening, a crazy violin and drum allured me into a public room, in which the merry peasants were dancing waltzes. Heavens! what movements! A Frenchman, who resolves every thing into operatic effect, would have felt each particular hair stand erect, had he contemplated the heavy solemnity of the performers. The females looked like so many tubs turning round, and their gallant partners never moved their pipes from their mouths.

Upon quitting this scene of phlegmatic festivity, I strolled to the quay, where the skippers were landing the carriage, which a fine sprightly powerful fellow of an English sailor, with scarce any assistance from the smoking crowd who had assembled to view it, put together in little more than an hour. The alertness and activity of the British tar afforded a striking contrast to the sluggishness of the Danish seamen who surrounded him. As soon as the carriage reached the inn, we proceeded to the post-house, and ordered four horses, being one more than we were compellable to take by the Danish post-law, but no more than the weight to be drawn and the depth of the roads rendered necessary. The post was to Flensborg, distant five Danish or twenty-five English miles, and for which we paid eight dollars, one marc. Of the coin and post regulations I shall speak in the next chapter.

Thus having prepared every thing for our departure the next morning, we returned to the inn; where in one of the front rooms we had not been seated long, before a pretty pale and interesting girl, whose age could not have exceeded thirteen, entered with a trembling step, and presented one of the gentlemen present with a note—the contents of it unfolded such a secret as must have shocked the soul of the most depraved libertine—it was written by her mother. We detained her miserable and devoted child until we had raised a little subscription for her, and dismissed her with an involuntary exclamation of abhorrence against the parent.

In the first step which an Englishman makes out of his own country, he is sure to meet with something to satisfy him that he cannot find a better.

CHAP. II.

THERE is scarcely a duller thing which an ardent traveller or reader can encounter, than the little detail of money matters which occur on the road; and I shall therefore, with all due dispatch, dispose of it upon the present occasion.

In Slesvig and Holstein, the only Danish money received is the Danish specie dollar, and the notes of the banks of Slesvig and Holstein, as also those of the bank of Norway. The specie dollar contains sixty skillings, or so many English pence, of the cur- rency of Slesvig and Holstein, and at par is equal to five shillings English. The rix dollar of the currency of Slesvig and Holstein contains only forty-eight skillings; of course four specie dollars are equal to five rix dollars current money. The money is divided into skillings, marks, and dollars :

> 16 skillings make 1 mark.
> 3 marks   1 rix dol. Slesvig and Holstein cur.
> 3 marks 12 skil. 1 specie dollar.

It will be advisable not to take up more money than will be suf- ficient to last as far as the island of Fynen or Funen; as the only money there received, and so on to the capital, is the currency of Denmark Proper. It will be most convenient to take rix dollar notes instead of coin. It may be as well here to state the post re- gulations. If the number of travellers exceeds three, they are compellable to take four horses.

In Holstein and Slesvig, as far as Hadersleb, a horse is twenty skillings of that currency, per mile Danish, which is equal to five miles English; the other charges are per station or post: thus,

> 4 skillings Slesvig cur. for shrivepenge.
> 4 ditto   for fetching horses from the field.

4 skillings Slesvig cur. to the ostler.
4 ditto   to postillion.

It is usual, however, to encrease this latter charge to one rix-dollar per station. With respect to this charge two drivers are only considered as one.

Having procured all this essential information, the carriage appeared at the door, surrounded by a crowd of gaping peasants, who gazed upon it as if they expected to see us mount in the air with it. As soon as we had passed the town-gate, we instantly dropped into a deep sand, through which we ploughed our way at the rate of two miles and an half in an hour, and beheld on each side of us nothing but a dreary waste. Had not the cheering beams of the sun refreshed and supported us all the way, we must have suffered pretty severely under the pressure of a distemper which foreigners confine, and very justly, to Englishmen. Our driver was mounted on the near shaft-horse, drove four-in-hand in rope harness, and carried, more for show than service, a prodigious long lash whip. He was dressed in scarlet, with yellow facings, and wore a brass plate on his hat, on which was stamped "Christⁿ 7." From a string, which was suspended over his right shoulder, depended his french-horn, somewhat battered by long exercise, which he applied to his mouth with the most frightful consequences whenever we met a traveller, and with which, whenever we ascended a hill, he never failed to serenade our ears and those of his cattle, who, deafened by long use, or having no taste for the concord of sweet sounds, seldom turned their auricular organs towards this hoarse croaking tube. Thus did we move in all the majesty of a menagerie upon the point of entering a town on a fair-day.

Two or three times in the course of each post, our driver begged to have a little snap money. Snaps is one of the earliest and most frequent words which a traveller will pick up in Denmark. In plain English it signifies a refreshing glass of spirits. We always found our account in granting this request.

The Danish driver is merciful to his horses. To equalize their labour, in the course of the station, he changes the situation of each of them. A whimsical fellow of this condition amused us not a little, by every now and then peeping into the carriage, or as he called it the *waggon*, to see that we and the luggage were all safe; these men, whenever they stop to refresh themselves, feed their horses with large slices of barley bread. We passed some neat farm-houses, having the barn with two large folding doors in the centre, the offices belonging to the farm on one side, and the farm-house on the other; the whole, upon a ground floor, and under one roof.

As we approached Flensberg, the country became more agreeable, and we observed the wonderful activity with which nature was every where exerting herself, in a climate which so much confines her to time: it was then the 30th of May; and the ground had been covered with snow only three weeks before, and some bitter winds very sensibly informed us that winter had not as yet retreated very far.

At a very clean inn, where we dined, we found some excellent red dried beef, sweet butter, good bread, baked like English tops and bottoms, and miserable *vin du pays*. In our dining-room the best china and glass tumblers made a gala show upon the tester of the bed, which gave a double capacity to the room. I was highly pleased to observe, that whilst the postillion took very good care of himself, he did not neglect his horses.

At eight in the evening we reached Flensborg, having accomplished twenty-five English miles in nine hours; a tedious time, sufficient to make any traveller peevish who had been accustomed to the velocity of an English mail. It was solely owing to the great depth of the roads; for upon better ground, our horses " were not hollow pampered jades of Asia, which cannot go but thirty miles a day."

As soon as we had entered the inn, our driver presented us with a small printed paper, that directed the traveller to state his opinion of the conduct of the former, which is afterwards submitted to the postmaster; and, by an ordinance of government, if any cause of complaint arises, the postillion is punishable.

Upon a traveller's reaching the end of a Danish post, it will be lucky for him if he does not find his patience put to a trial, by having to wait in general an hour for horses to forward him, which, at the time of his arrival, are nibbling the blade in some distant field. Our inn was the post-house, which every where affords the best accommodations.

Flensborg is a large commercial town, very neat and pleasantly situated. It is well supplied with excellent water from foun-

tains, which are placed at certain intervals in the centre of the
principal street: the houses are like those at Husum, with the
addition of strong braces of iron. The view from the quay, the
river, and the opposite village, is very beautiful; the language
thus far is German, and the religion of the country throughout is
Lutheran. The English chariot was still the object of admiration; smiths thronged the yard to examine the springs, and wag-
gon-builders to contemplate the wheels and body. The patent
boxes of the former excited uncommon astonishment. At the
corner of the yard, the last beams of the setting sun threw an
agreeable tint upon a variety of interesting faces, all waiting for
intelligence—the friend, the lover, and the merchant; for the
postman had just arrived, the

> ————————Messenger of grief
> Perhaps to thousands, and of joy to some;
> To him indiff'rent whether grief or joy.
> Houses in ashes, or the fall of stocks,
> Births, deaths, and marriages, epistles wet
> With tears, that trickled down the writer's cheeks,
> Fast as the periods from his fluent quill,
> Or charg'd with am'rous sighs of absent swains,
> Or nymphs responsive, equally affect
> His horse and him, unconscious of them all.

When I had retired to my chamber, the constant dashing of
the fountain in the court-yard, the frequent crowing of a little
hoarse bantam cock, two cats making violent love, and a party of
foraging fleas, united their powers most successfully to keep
"tired nature's sweet restorer" from my lids the greater part of
the night. In the morning, at five o'clock, we entered the great
road to Copenhagen, from the city of Slesvig, and proceeded
along the shores of the Baltic, through a sandy and dreary country; our progress was now encreased to five English miles an
hour. We found the population very thin, the land but little cultivated, and the solitary cottage, which appeared to cover more
misery than industry, had rarely a little garden by the side of it.
The only vegetables which we met with were small stinted asparagus and parsnips, both of which the good people here boil in
their soup. The few houses which we saw on the road side were,
however, neatly built, with a light brown brick, and thatched.

The steeple and the body of the church were every where divided
from each other; whence their separation arose in Denmark can
be no more accounted for, I should suppose, than their conjunc-
tion in England.

Upon strolling into one of the church-yards, I remarked that
their monuments were principally composed of a frame of an oblong square, divided by cross pieces of wood painted black, and
the spaces between filled with stones.

The country about Abenraac, a small fishing town, where we
changed horses, was very pretty, and much resembled that beautiful slope of wood in Lord Borringdon's park at Saltram, which
parts the high road to Plymouth. The country from Abenraac
to Hardersleb is hilly, woody, fertile, and romantic. The cattle
were every where tethered, or fastened by a cord, to a circle of
pasture.

At Hadersleb, whilst dinner was preparing, we went to the
bank, to exchange our Holstein and Slesvig money for the currency of Denmark Proper, previous to our embarking for the
island of Funen. Here the exchange, which is governed by that
of Hamburg, is always in favour of the traveller going to Copenhagen. For one hundred and thirty-five rix dollars Slesvig we
procured one hundred and fifty-six current dollars and six skillings, which was at a premium of seventeen pounds per cent. in
our favour. Upon our shewing the banker one of the new dollars
from Bolton's mint, he appeared to be much gratified with its
beauty, and begged that we would permit him to exchange it; a
little favour which we gladly granted him.

On our return, we found a good dinner, in a long room, painted
of a leaden blue colour, having the floor well sanded, three little
windows decorated with festoons of muslin, an old-fashioned
chandelier threatening peril to those who passed under it, and
two ancient portraits of a king and queen of Denmark, who looked
very smirkingly upon each other.

I must not omit to introduce the reader to the kitchen, in which,
in Denmark as well as in Germany, the fire-place is raised about
two feet and a half high from the floor, and very much resembles
that of a blacksmith's forge; the meat is baked, or, as they call
it, roasted, in a sort of cheese-toaster, and having undergone the
previous operation of three parts boiling: such is a Danish inn.

The traveller in this country would do well to confine his supper solely to bread, butter, and eggs. The wine every where is very poor, and the beer detestable.

The peasantry appear to be clean and happy. It was pleasing to see, early in the morning, as we travelled, groups of young milkmaids, whose cheeks glowed with the bloom of health, balancing their pails with great dexterity, and knitting and singing as they went.

As we could save several tedious miles by crossing the Little Belt at its broadest part, we proceeded to Aversund instead of Snoghoi, where we found the country very undulating and beautiful, but the roads rather heavy. Nothing can be prettier than the situation of the post-house, with its gardens sloping to the water, to which a bright sun, distinctly marking out the little island of Arroe to the south, and the greater one of Funen in front, distant about eight English miles, added new charms. The boatmen, with uncommon dexterity, in about ten minutes hoisted, by means of tackles, our carriage entire and luggage into an open boat, and having a fair breeze, we crossed the Little Belt in about an hour and a half, and landed at Assens.

A stranger cannot but be surprised to see a kingdom so composed of islands. The province which we had just left, notwithstanding the desolate appearance of some parts of it from the main road, is, on account of the independent spirit of its peasantry, the most valuable of the crown of Denmark.

	Rix Dollars.	Mark.	Skills.
The passage for ourselves and carriage was	3	0	8
To assistants getting the latter into the boat	0	0	12

At Assens we, for the first time, experienced the change of a large feather-bed, instead of a blanket and sheet. To an untravelled Englishman nothing can be more singular. In the morning, as the horses were putting to, a singular procession passed us. A young woman in gala, whose hair was stiffened almost to the consistency of stucco with powder and pomatum, on which was raised a high cap of lace, decorated with a profusion of artificial flowers, and with a large nosegay of spring and artificial flowers in her bosom, and a book in her hand, and turning in her

D

toes most abominably, passed in the most stately manner up the
street, preceded by three girls in mob caps, decorated with little
bits of silver and gold lace, and in red jackets, each with a book
in her hand, and followed by two old women, holding books also.
The fair heroine of this singular group moved to me as she passed. She was proceeding to the church, where her bridegroom
was counting the lagging moments of her absence. The old and
the young peeped out of the doors and windows as they passed.
Heavens keep me from any thing like pomp or publicity on the
marriage day!

In this island, as I have before intimated, the coin is provincial,
thus:

    16 skillings make 1 mark.
    6 marks   1 rix-dollar Danish currency.

And one skilling of Holstein and Slesvig is equal to two of the
currency of Denmark Proper.

              The post regulation as under:
1 horse per Danish mile   2 marks Danish currency.
For fetching horses per pair   6 skillings Danish.
To the ostler   4 ditto.

At Odensee, which is a large respectable town, an episcopal
see, the richest in Denmark next to that of Copenhagen, and the
capital of the island, we dined; there was nothing singular in our
repast, but that the first dish was manna soup.

There is a public school here, where a small number of boys
are educated and maintained gratuitously, and a gymnasium for
students of sixteen years of age. The cathedral is an ancient
pile of brick, and is remarkable for nothing more than containing
the tombs of John and the sanguinary Christian II, who seized
upon the crown of Sweden by the right of conquest, and, in a
cold-blooded massacre, put six hundred of the flower of her
nobility to the sword. That scene of slaughter is exquisitely displayed in the beautiful tragedy of Gustavus Vasa, published, in
1738, by Henry Brooke, esq. and with which I am sure my reader
will be delighted.

————Think upon Stockholm
When Cristiern seiz'd upon the hour of peace,
And drench'd the hospitable floor with blood;
Then fell the flow'r of Sweden, mighty names!

Her hoary senators, and gasping patriots.
The tyrant spoke, and his licentious band
Of blood-train'd ministry were loos'd to ruin.
Invention wanton'd in the toil of infants
Stabb'd to the breast, or reeking on the points
Of sportive javelins.—Husbands, sons, and sires,
With dying ears drank in the loud despair
Of shrieking chastity.

The thatch of the cottage in this island, and in most parts of the north, is bristled at the top with cross braces of wood, to keep it together, and has a very inferior appearance to the warm compact neatness of the English thatch. The road from hence to Nioborg is good, partly paved, and the country on all sides very picturesque. The lambs, in the flocks which we passed, had one foot fastened to the body by a piece of string. A custom so painful to the luckless objects was intended to fix them more closely to their dams, and, by abbreviating their exercise, to fatten them.

I was much surprised at not seeing, either in Denmark or any other part of the north that I visited, a single member of a very ancient family, the most useful, the most ill-treated and depised of any that moves upon all-fours—an ass.

About nine o'clock in the evening we arrived at Nioborg, which is a small but handsome fortified town, containing about nine hundred inhabitants, and determined, as the wind was fair, to cross the Great Belt that night. We were there obliged to shew our passports ; the captain of the passage-boat, on account of the lateness of the hour, threw many difficulties in the way of our determination, which, however, the tender looks and eloquence of a French girl at the inn, aided by a little bribery on our part, effectually removed. Here the wheels of the carriage were obliged to be taken off, and after a delightful sail of about two hours and an half, we effected our passage, which is twenty English miles, and landed at Corsoer, in the metropolitan island of Zealand.

As I passed over this mighty space of water, I could not help reflecting with astonishment, that in the month of February, 1658, it formed a bridge of ice for the hardy troops of the warlike and ambitious Charles X, who, contrary to the advice of his council of war, marched over it to give battle to the Danes. During this tremendous passage, a part of the ice gave way, and a whole squa-

dron of the guards were immolated, not one of whom were saved,
an order having been given that no one should attempt to assist
his neighbour in such an emergency, upon pain of death. After
passing the Little Belt in the same way, Charles Gustavus Adolphus obliged the Danes to make the peace of Roschild. This enterprise may be ranked amongst the most marvellous achievements, and a recurrence to it will furnish ample means of occupation to the mind of the traveller during his passage over these
portions of the sea.

It was midnight by the time we quitted the vessel; the wind
was very fresh, and the moon occasionally darting in full efful-
gence from a mass of black clouds, illumined the front of an ancient castle of little strength, near the quay, which is the occasional
residence of the crown prince. Upon the ramparts the cloaked
centinel kept his solitary watch; it was a " nipping and an eager
air;" and the scene, more than any other which I saw in Denmark,
impressed the imagination with the similitude of that

> " In which the majesty of bury'd Denmark
> " Did sometimes march."

The good people at the post-house were in bed; but, after many
a rap at the door, it was at last opened by a figure, who most completely corresponded with the bard's description of Bardolph.
With Shakspeare we might have exclaimed,

> " Thou art an admiral; thou bear'st thy lantern
> " In thy poop—but 'tis in the nose of thee——
> " Thou art the knight of the burning lamp."

As the night was very sharp, we made our way to the kitchen,
to catch a little warmth from its expiring embers; but here we
found we were distressing the coyness of a comely young cook,
who had just quitted her bed to prepare something for our supper,
and who was very uneasy until we had left her territory. After a
comfortable repast, Bardolph lighted us to bed.

CHAP. III.

DANISH CHARACTER—GIN—ZEALAND—TURNPIKE-GATE—MILE STONES
—INTELLIGENCE OF WOMEN—THE TOMB OF JULIANA MARIA—HUS-
BAND INTRIGUING WITH HIS WIFE—MARGARET OF VOLDEMAR—THE
MOURNING MOTHER—COPENHAGEN—A DANISH DINNER—TOMB OF
THE HEROES OF THE 2D OF APRIL, 1801—THE BATTLE OF THAT
DAY—LORD NELSON—THE BRAVE YOUNG WELMOES.

IT is scarcely necessary for me to observe that the government
of Denmark is despotic. The Dane is a good natured, laborious
character; he is fond of spirits, but is rarely intoxicated; the severity of the climate naturalizes the attachment, and his deportment in the indulgence of it is inoffensive.

At breakfast at Corsœr, a respectable Dane entered the room;
the landlady, a vast unwieldy good-humoured creature in boots,
without saying a word, opened her cupboard, and taking down a
bottle of gin, presented her guest with a large wine-glass full,
which he drank off, as if it had been so much cocoa-milk, and
immediately retired.

The island of Zealand is said to be very luxuriant, and abounding with picturesque scenery; its shores are lined with pretty
towns, noble chateaus, and extensive and well-wooded domains;
but upon the high road we did not observe, until our near approach
to the capital, any indication of such exuberance and beauty; although it was at this time the third of June, the gooseberries and
currants were but just formed into berries.

Upon our first post in this island, we met with, for the first
time in Denmark, a turnpike-gate, which was erected at the
end of every Danish mile. As the roads were tolerably good,
the impost was unobjectionable, which for a carriage and four
horses is six skillings Danish currency. This toll, in consequence
of a recent ordinance, is paid before the traveller sets off, to the
post-master, which saves the inconvenience of stopping. The
turnpike-gate, like all the barrier gates of the north, is simply constructed of a long pole or bar, which turns upon a pivot, fastened
in a strong post, about four feet high, placed on one side of the

road : the end of this pole is charged at the end with a preponde-
rating weight of stone, or blocks of wood, so that when the post-
master slackens the string or slight chain which attaches it hori-
zontally to a post on the other side of the road, the bar rises sufficiently high to let a carriage pass under.

Themile stones here, the first which we saw in the country, are
formed of granite in the shape of a handsome obelisk, and enumerate the miles and half miles, and bear the names of Christian
and sometimes of Fred. V. In our route we saw several storks,
who shewed no other symptoms of alarm when we approached
them, than awkwardly moving from us upon their red, tall, lean
legs, upon which the body seemed mounted, as upon stilts. The
country from Slagelse to Ringsted was very picturesque. The
most ancient church in Denmark is in this town ; it is built of
brick, with two low towers : there are some royal tombs here,
very ancient, which are principally filled with the ashes of the
descendants of Sweyn II, and are level with the pavement.
We passed many forests of fine beech and oak, feathering the
shores of several extensive and beautiful lakes. As we approached
the capital we were a little surprised to find every thing become
cheaper, and the horses and drivers leaner and shabbier.

I must not omit to state, for the honour of the female sex, that,
however we were at a loss to explain ourselves on account of our
ignorance of the Danish language, and had exhausted our stock of
gestures upon the men in vain, we always found that the women
comprehended us with one-third of our pantomimic action ; and
to the end of my days I shall gratefully and experimentally contend for the superior quickness of female comprehension.

We arrived on a Sunday at Roskild, which, according to
Holberg, was formerly a city of many parishes, and contained
within its walls twenty-seven churches, and an equal number of
convents, though now a place of very little import. We went to
the cathedral, a heavy pile of brick covered with copper, with two
spires, the most ancient part of which was erected under the auspices of Harold, the grandfather of Canute the Great, king of
England and Denmark. The inside of this building owes its grandeur to its size : the ceiling is stained with little sprigs of flowers
in a vile taste, and are wholly unenriched by those exquisite
interlacings in the roof that form the principal beauty of Gothic

architecture, the rudiments of which nature first imparted to our early forefathers; by placing before their imitative eyes the graceful intersections of a simple bower: the organ is upon an immense scale, and the tone very fine: the stops are moved by the feet of the organist. In a large octagon chapel, divided from the body of the cathedral by an iron grate, so finely wrought, that at a distance it resembles black gauze, and in a subterranean vault, repose the remains of the royal family of Denmark, in several raised stone coffins, which are covered with black velvet palls, embroidered with small crowns of gold, falling in full drapery upon the floor. It is foreign to my purpose to enumerate them all. The most superb tomb is that of Juliana Maria, whose sanguinary conduct towards the hapless Queen Matilda and the unfortunate counts Struensee and Brandt excited so much sensation some years since. As I gazed upon this gloomy depository of unrelenting jealousy and ambition, imagination raised the bleeding shades of those devoted men, consigned from the pinnacle of power and royal favour to the dungeon and the scaffold. Alas! the common tyrant, in no wide lapse of time, has closed the eyes of the ruthless destroyer and her victims.

I must not omit the tomb of that wonderful woman Margaret of Voldemar, or, as she was styled, with a derision which she well revenged, the *king in petticoats*. She flourished in the 13th century, and bore upon her brow the crowns of Denmark, Sweden, and Norway. The northern Semiramis was destined to astonish the world by her marvellous exploits, and her very entrance into it was rendered somewhat extraordinary on account of her being the legitimate daughter of her father and mother. The former becoming disgusted with her mother, confined her in a castle, and about the same time fell violently in love with one of her *dames d'honneur*, and was a suitor for her favours; the good-humoured girl affected to consent, but imparted the assignation to the unhappy queen, was instrumental in conveying her in disguise to the spot; and Margaret was the fruit of this singular intrigue.

We were much gratified by seeing in one of the chapels the rich and beautiful mausoleums of Frederick II and Christian III. They were designed and made in Italy, at an immense cost, by the order of Christian IV. The sovereigns are represented in recumbent postures, the size of life, under a stone canopy, supported by

Corinthian pillars; the basso relievos which adorn the tomb of Frederic II are exquisite pieces of sculpture. Here are also interred many distinguished heroes, who have raised the glory of their country, and live in the page of history.

The beautiful ideas of Addison came into my mind—" When " I see kings lying by those who deposed them; when I consider " rival wits placed side by side, or the holy men that divided the " world with their contests and disputes, I reflect with sorrow and " astonishment on the little competitions and debates of mankind. " When I read the several dates of the tombs, of some that died " yesterday, and some six hundred years ago, I consider that " great day when we shall all of us be cotemporaries, and make " our appearance together."

As we crossed the church-yard, to return to the inn, we were stopped by the appearance of an interesting young woman, who, with much grief in her countenance, was scattering slips of lilac and half-blown tulips and fine sand from a little basket which she held in her hand, upon a fresh grave, which, from its size, and from her looks, I conjectured to be that of her infant child. It was the custom of the country, and an affecting one it was.

We met with nothing to denote our approach to the capital till we reached Fredericksberg, one of the king's country palaces, about two English miles from Copenhagen. The appearance of much bustle, and lounging lacqueys in scarlet and silver, announced that the court was here. As we rolled down from the beautiful eminence, upon the open summit of which the palace stands, the city, crowned by its palace in ruins, the Sound, and the surrounding country, presented a delightful prospect. The road was crowded with people in their Sunday dresses and merry faces, hurrying to pass the evening in the gardens of Fredericksberg, which, with the permission of his majesty, is the favourite resort of the people. We were detained a few minutes at the custom-house, adjoining the first draw-bridge, over which and an inner one we passed to the gates of the capital, which we entered, through a long arch, forming part of the ramparts.

As we approached Lubel's hotel, to which we were recommended, we passed by the walls of the royal palace, which bore ample and afflicting testimony to the colossal size and magnificence which must have formerly distinguished it, before it fell

a victim to the flames in 1794. Upon our visiting this splendid
pile, after dinner, we found, by an inscription remaining unde-
faced, that it was raised by Christian VI, out of his own private
purse, without pinching his subjects, and cost six millions of dollars: it stands in an island, formed by a canal, and has several
gates; the principal entrance is of wrought iron, and has a noble
effect: the front has twenty-five enormous windows in a line, and
is composed of six stories, three of which are upon a large, and
the remaining three upon a small scale. This front is three
hundred and sixty-seven feet long; the sides three hundred and
eighty-nine, and the elevation one hundred and fourteen. All the
grand apartments of state were upon the fourth story; the court
is surrounded with two wings of piazza, twelve feet deep, and on
each side are stables for saddle and carriage horses, which are
arched: these have escaped the fury of the conflagration, and are
truly magnificent. The racks of that which holds forty-eight
horses are of copper, and the pillars which separate the stalls are
of brick stuccoed. In another we observed the racks and columns
were of Norwegian marble; the floor of the stalls is of stone, and
the breadth of each is six feet. The court is three hundred and
ninety feet long, and three hundred and forty in its greatest
breadth; the pilastres are of the composite order, and the columns
Ionic; there are also two lateral courts, which are surrounded
with buildings of two hundred and forty-five feet by one hundred
and six. The stable to the left is divided by the riding-house,
which is one hundred and seventy-six feet by fifty-six, and lighted
by fifteen cross-bar windows, with a gallery for the royal family
and spectators, and has altogether a very grand appearance. Here
all the branches of the royal family were formerly lodged. So
rapid was the fury of the conflagration, and such the panic which
it inspired, that but little of the treasure of its pictures, furniture,
and gorgeous decorations could be saved. Of the internal magnificence of this palace, some idea may be formed by the following description of the *ritta saal*, or knight's saloon: it was one
hundred and eighteen feet long by fifty-eight, was lighted by day
by nine windows, and at night by three lustres which contained
more than twelve hundred wax lights: on each side was a gallery
richly gilded, and supported by forty-four columns of cinnamon
wood, the bases and capitals of which were also richly gilded. An

E

artist of the name of Abilgaad was commissioned to embellish the hall with twenty-three large paintings, from subjects arising from the Danish history, at one thousand rix-dollars a-piece. The library of the king, which suffered much by the fire, contained one hundred and thirty thousand volumes, and three thousand manuscripts. The palace was too enormous for that of the capital and kingdom, and forms a striking contrast to the present residence of the royal family.

Whilst I was contemplating these stupendous remains, a splendid English vis-à-vis dashed by, drawn by a pair of noble greys, which, with a profusion of gold-lace upon the coats of the coachman and footman, attracted the notice and surprise of the good people of Copenhagen, who had never even seen their beloved Crown Prince in such finery: it was the equipage of a foreign quack doctor, who had had the good fortune to live and flourish in England in an *age of pills*.

Copenhagen is a small but very neat city ; its circumference between four and five English miles : the streets are broad and handsome ; the houses, of which there are about four thousand, exclusive of the quarter belonging to the sailors, and garrisons for three regiments, are generally of brick stuccoed to resemble stone, and some are of freestone, and in an elegant style of Italian architecture : the shops are in the basement story, and by making no prominent appearance, do not disfigure the beauty of the rest of the building. Such is the case upon every part of the Continent which I have visited. In England every tradesman's shop is the raree-show of the street, and perhaps it is in allusion to this, as much as to any other cause, that our neighbours on the other side of the channel have pronounced us to be a nation of shop-keepers. The streets are divided by canals, which afford great facility to the transport of goods, but have narrow and inconvenient foot paths : the population is estimated at eighty-two thousand. La rue de Goths is a beautiful street, and is about three quarters of an English mile long. The Kongens nye Tow, or King's place, which is also the market-place, is a noble, spacious, irregular area, adorned with many fine houses, several of which have been raised since the late fire. The only theatre in the city is here : it was not open during our stay. This building is detached, small, but handsome without, and within is elegantly decorated : in the

season, the performers play four times in the week, alternately
opera and play, which is generally in the language of the country.
On account of the vast number of persons who have free admission
to it, amongst whom are all marine and land officers, the receipts
are but very little; and the deficiency, which is supplied by the
king, generally amounts to about one hundred thousand rix
dollars per annum. Upon the whole the court is not a very
munificent patron of the drama, and the performers seldom
exceed mediocrity. In the middle of the market-place is an
equestrian statue in bronze of Christian V, but too deficient in
merit to attract the notice of a traveller. One of the large buildings in this place is the castle of Charlottenberg, part of which is
devoted to the royal academy of painting, architecture, and sculpture; it has eight professors and four masters: the day for the
annual distribution of the prizes is the 31st of March, the birth-
day of the prince, Frederic, who is the patron. Those pupils who
obtain the golden medal are sent to travel at the expense of the
crown. Such of the productions of the pupils and professors as I
saw did not excite a very high opinion of the arts in Denmark.

No respectable stranger can enter Copenhagen without speedily
becoming the object of its frank and generous hospitality. The
day after our arrival enabled us to partake of the hearty profusion
of a Danish dinner; it was given at the country house of one of the
most respectable inhabitants of the city, and appeared in the following succession: soups top and bottom, Norwegian beef boiled,
ham strongly salted, fish, pigeons, fowls, stewed spinage, and
asparagus; the meat is always cut into slices by the master of the
house, and handed round by the servants. Etiquette proscribes
the touching of any particular dish out of its regular course, although the table may be groaning under the weight of its covers;
this ceremony is occasionally a little tantalizing. Creams, confec-
tionery, and dried fruits followed: the wines were various and
excellent. Our party was composed of English, Norwegians,
Flemish, Swiss, Russians, Danish, and French. Would to heaven
that their respective nations could for ever be as cordial and joyous
as was this chequered collection of their merry natives! The
repast lasted a formidable length of time: it was two hours of
hard stuffing in a fog of hot meats. The appetite of the fair ones
present was far, I might say very far, from being puny or fastidious, but, in the homely phrase, what they eat did them good.

The Danish ladies are *enbonpoint*, and possess that frank and generous countenance, which, the moment the eye sees, the heart understands and loves; they much resemble the higher class of Wouvermann's figures, and very largely partake of that gay good humour, which is so generally the companion of a plump and portly figure. Having said so much in their favour, which they eminently deserve, I cannot help hinting that they are not so attentive to neatness of dress as their neighbours; they want such a man as Addison to rally them with his delicate satire out of a slovenly habit, which induces them, when they buy a gown, almost always to prefer a dark cotton, because *it does not want washing.* The Danish ladies would immediately feel the force of the remark, without being offended at its freedom. They speak English with its proper accent, as well as French and German fluently. The English language forms a prominent part of female education.

Upon my complimenting a Danish lady on her accurate knowledge of the English language, she said, " We are obliged to learn " that, and French and German, *in our own defence*, otherwise we " should frequently be obliged to sit mute, which you know is a " very unpleasant situation for any woman; for beyond the islands," meaning Zealand and Funen, " our language, which is a dialect " of the Teutonic, is not understood." This I found afterwards verified: upon my return to Holstein from Prussia, a Danish serjeant in drilling a recruit from the former place, was obliged to speak to him in German.

: Here, as in France, the company rise and retire with the lady of the house.⁕ In the garden we found coffee, and a droll fellow of a wandering mendicant Norwegian, who occupied, *sans ceremonie*, one of the garden seats, and upon his rustic guitar had collected the little folks of the family round him, who were dancing to some of the wildest and sweetest sounds that ever issued from the touch of simplicity.

, On our return to the city, and about a mile from it, a turfed hillock of small poplars attracted our notice: it was the national tomb of the heroes who fell in the memorable battle of Copenhagen roads, on the second of April, 1801, and stood in a meadow about two hundred yards from the road, and looked towards the Crown battery. As we approached it, we saw a small monumental obelisk, which was raised to the memory of Captain Albert

Thurah, by the Crown Prince. It appeared by the inscription, that during the heat of that sanguinary battle a signal was made from one of the block ships, that all the officers on board were killed; the Crown Prince, who behaved with distinguished judgment and composure during the whole of that terrific and anxious day, and was giving his orders on shore, exclaimed, " who will " take the command?" The gallant Thurah replied, " I will, my Prince ;" and immediately leaped into a boat, and as he was mounting the deck of the block ship, a British shot numbered him amongst the dead, which formed a ghastly pile before him, and consigned his spirit and his glory to the regions of immortality. He was a young man of great promise. It is thus that death often

Strikes the poor peasant ; he sinks in the dark,
Nor leaves e'en the wreck of a name.
He strikes the young warrior, a glorious mark!
He sinks in the blaze of his fame.

As the battle, under all its circumstances, was as awful and affecting as any in the English and Danish history, the reader will, I am sure, feel no reluctance minutely to contemplate the larger tomb which first attracted our notice: it is a pyramidal hillock, neatly turfed and planted with sapling poplars, corresponding with the number of officers who fell. At the base of the principal front are tomb-stones recording the names of each of these officers and their respective ships. A little above is an obelisk of grey northern marble, raised upon a pedestal of granite bearing this inscription :

To the memory of those who fell for their country, their grateful fellow citizens raise this monument, April 2, 1801.

And beneath, on a white marble tablet, under a wreath of laurel, oak, and cypress, bound together, is inscribed :

The wreath which the country bestows never withers over the grave of the fallen warrior.

The whole is enclosed in a square palisado. As a national monument, it is too diminutive.

The next day I visited the spot where so much blood was shed. A young Danish officer upon the Crown battery obligingly pointed out the disposition of the ships, and spoke of the battle with great impartiality. From the position of the British fleets, before the squadron under Lord Nelson bore down, and rendered his intention indubitable, the Danes were firmly of opinion that the British commander intended to proceed either to Calscrona or Revel, and made no preparation for defence; their ships were lying in ordinary; they therefore trusted solely to their block ships and batteries.

On that day the hero of the Nile surpassed those achievements, which an admiring and astonished world conceived must for ever remain without imitation, as they had been without example, in the annals of the British navy. Favoured by a fortunate shift of wind, and an extraordinary elevation of the tide, which at the time was higher than the Danes had long remembered it, he placed his unsupported squadron, and, as it is said, with an *unobserved* signal of retreat flying at the mast head of the ship of the chief in command, in a most advantageous and formidable position. The citizens of Copenhagen in a moment flew to their posts; all distinctions were lost in the love of their country. Nobles and mechanics, gentlemen and shopmen rushed together in crowds to the quays; the sick crawled out of their beds, and the very lame were led to the sea side, imploring to be taken in the boats, which were perpetually going off with crowds to the block ships. A carnage at once tremendous and novel only served to encrease their enthusiasm. What an awful moment! The invoked vengeance of the British nation, with the fury and velocity of lightning, was falling with terrible desolation upon a race of gallant people, in their very capital, whose kings were once seated upon the throne of England, and in the veins of whose magnanimous prince flowed the blood of her august family. Nature must have shuddered as she contemplated such a war of brethren: the conflict was short, but sanguinary beyond example. In the midst of the slaughter the heroic Nelson dispatched a flag of truce on shore with a note to the Crown Prince, in which he expressed a wish that a stop should be put to the further effusion of human blood, and to avert the destruction of the Danish arsenal and of the capital, which he observed that the Danes must then see were at his mercy. He once more proposed their withdrawing from the triple league, and acknowledging the supremacy of the British flag. As soon as the Prince's answer was received a cessation of hostilities took place, and Lord Nelson left his ship to go on shore. Upon his arrival at the quay he found a carriage which had been sent for him by Mr. D., a merchant of high respectability, the confusion being too great to enable the Prince to send one of the royal carriages; in the former the gallant admiral proceeded to the palace in the Octagon, through crowds of people, whose fury was rising to frenzy, and amongst whom his person was in more imminent danger than even from the cannon of the block ships; but nothing could shake the soul of such a man. Arrived at the palace in the Octagon he calmly descended from the carriage amidst the murmurs and groans of the enraged concourse, which not even the presence of the Danish officers who accompanied him could restrain. The Crown Prince received him in the hall, and conducted him up stairs, and presented him to the King, whose long-shattered state of mind had left him but very little sensibility to display upon the trying occasion. The objects of this impressive interview were soon adjusted, to the perfect satisfaction of Lord Nelson and his applauding country; that done, he assumed the gaiety and good humour of a visitor, and partook of some refreshment with the Crown Prince.

During the repast, Lord Nelson spoke in raptures of the bravery of the Danes, and particularly requested the Prince to introduce him to a very young officer, whom he described as having performed wonders during the battle, by attacking his own ship immediately under her lower guns. It proved to be the gallant young Welmoes, a stripling of seventeen; the British hero embraced him with the enthusiasm of a brother, and delicately intimated to the Prince that he ought to make him an admiral; to which the Prince very happily replied, "If, my Lord, I were to make all my brave officers admirals, I should have no captains or lieutenants in my service." This heroic youth had volunteered the command of a praam, which is a sort of raft, carrying six small cannon, and manned with twenty-four men, who pushed off from shore, and in the fury of the battle placed themselves under the stern of Lord Nelson's ship, which they most successfully attacked, in such a manner that, although they were below the reach of his stern chasers, the British marines made terrible slaughter amongst them: twenty of these gallant men fell by their bullets, but their young commander continued knee-deep in dead at his post, until the truce was announced. He has been honoured, as he most eminently deserved to be, with the grateful remembrance of his country and of his Prince, who, as a mark of his regard, presented him with a medallion commemorative of his gallantry, and has appointed him to the command of his yacht, in which he makes his annual visit to Holstein. The issue of this contest was glorious and decisive. Could it be otherwise, when its destinies were committed to Nelson?

To shew how brittle must be the bands of a confederacy of powers, whose jealousy and dislike is ever unhappily in proportion to their proximity, the Swedes very composedly contemplated the battle from their hills, and appeared to lose all sensation of their share of its mortifying results in the humiliation of a rival country. So nature pulls the strings of a little man and a great nation; the latter is only the larger puppet, and requires more strength to put it in motion.

La place Frederic, or the Octagon, containing the palaces of the royal family, and where Lord Nelson had the audience that I have just mentioned, is composed of four small palaces, all uniform, each having two wings: four very noble streets, principally inhabited by the nobility, lead to this place: the grand entrance is through a gate composed of double rows of Corinthian pillars and a rich entablature; one of the streets is terminated by the harbour, and the other by the church of Frederic, which has been long left unfinished; it has the appearance of an elegant design, and reminded me, both by its condition and style of architecture, of l'Eglise de Madelaine at Paris. In the centre of the Octagon is an equestrian statue of Frederic V, in bronze, by Saly; it was erected in 1769, by the Danish East India Company, and is said to have cost 80,000l. An Englishman cannot help remarking the slovenly appearance of the grass, which is here permitted to shoot up through the stones, and particularly within the railing of the statue: the soldiers, who are always lounging about the palaces, would remove the evil in almost the time that I have taken to comment upon it.

CHAP. IV.

THERE is something very pleasant in contemplating the most inconsiderable actions, even the little badinage of great men. I forgot in my last chapter to mention the playful good-humour which Lord Nelson displayed soon after the battle of Copenhagen roads. By the ship which conveyed his dispatches to England, he sent a note to some respectable wine-merchants to whom he was indebted for some wine, in which he sportively said, that " he trusted they would pardon his not having sooner sent a " checque for his bill, on account of his having been lately much " engaged."

In one of the wings of the burnt palace, to which the flames did not extend, the gallery of pictures and museum of curiosities are placed. In the former we found a few excellent pictures, and particularly noticed a Jesus betrayed, by Michael Angelo; a naked Venus, in a very singular posture, by Titian; a good Woman, by Leonardo de Vinci; the Holy Family, by Raphael; a dead Christ on the cross, by Rubens; adjoining to this is an unaccountable picture upon a large scale, the subject, Fallen Angels: the artist, with singular whim, has substituted butter-flies for fig-leaves.

In the cabinet of curiosities is a very ingenious invention for tranquillizing the fears of jealous husbands; a stuffed stag, said to have lived several centuries; a lion and bear. There is here also a celestial globe made by Tycho Brahe, who was sent to Copenhagen by his father in the sixteenth century to study rhetoric and philosophy; but the great eclipse of the sun on August

F

the 21st, 1562, engaged him to study astronomy. He was the in-
ventor of a new system of the world, and had some followers; but
it is said that his *learning* made him *superstitious*, and his *philosophy irritable*, to such a degree, that, in a philosophical dispute
the argument rose to such a pitch of personal violence, that he
lost his nose, which he supplied by a gold and silver one, admirably
constructed; he was also very fond of Automata, and the reputation which he obtained of a conjurer.

I was much pleased with the convivial cup of the celebrated
Margaret of Valdemar: it had ten lips, which were marked with
the respective names of those whom she honoured with her intimacy, who were the companions of her table, and were permitted
to taste of the Tuscan grape out of the same vessel. There are
here also some exquisite carvings in wood, by a Norwegian farmer,
with a common knife; some mummies badly preserved; a piece
of amber weighing more than twenty-seven pounds, found in Jutland; lustres of amber; several models of ships in amber, ivory,
shell, and mother of pearl; beautiful works of ivory; a toilet of
amber of surprising workmanship; a great lustre of the same,
with twenty-four branches, made by M. Spengler. A complete
closet filled with bits of wood, carved by the peasants of Norway,
who are extremely expert in this work; a portrait of Denner; a
bit of ivory, prettily worked by Queen Louise, mother of the present King; others of the same kind, by Pierre Legrand; the emperors Leopold, Rodolph II, &c.; Jesus Christ on the cross, carved
in wood, of so fine a workmanship that it must be seen through a
magnifying glass; it is attributed to Albert Durer; a carriage with
six horses, of an inconceivable smallness; a great jug of ivory,
with a triumph of Bacchus of a very fine workmanship, by Jacob
Hollander, a Norwegian; the descent from the cross, a superb
piece, by Magnus Berg; several figures dressed in foreign dresses,
Indian, Chinese, &c.; great vases of gold and silver; a flagon or
decanter of rock chrystal, very beautifully engraved; a horn of
gold, found in Jutland, in 1639, the inscription on which has
puzzled the learned; a bust of Brutus in bronze; many precious
antiquities of the country; a portrait of Charles XII; the skull of
archbishop Absalom, with his dress: the prelate's skull reminded
me of the ridiculous question which a lady put to one of the li-
brarians of the British museum, " Pray sir, haven't you a skull of

Oliver Cromwell here?" "No, madam," replied the man of learning and antiquity. "Dear me!" said she, "I wonder at that; for
they have a very fine one in the museum at Oxford." There are
also some curious religious utensils, which were used by the ancient natives of the north. Such is a sketch of the Danish gallery
and museum, which is worthy the notice of the traveller.

In order to have a better view of the city, upon leaving the museum, I ascended, by an external spiral stair-case, the top of the
church in Christian-haven, one of the quarters of Copenhagen;
from this eminence the view was delightful; the city, its palaces,
churches, docks, arsenals, and the little Dutch town, which lay
about two English miles off; the roads, the shores of Sweden,
and the Sound embellished with ships, lay like a map below me.
Immediately underneath us we saw a funeral procession of a
principal inhabitant, proceeding to that " dark and narrow house,
whose mark is one grey stone;" the coffin, covered with a pall,
was placed upon a bier, surmounted with a canopy, which moved
upon four little broad wheels, and was drawn by a pair of horses.
I regretted to observe that the Danes pursue the same pernicious
custom which obtains in England, of burying their dead in the
city. There are people who live in the tower of the church, to
give signals in case of fire breaking out, of which the Danes have
a great dread; for no people have suffered more from its destruc-
tive visitation. A precautionary warning to the inhabitants to take
care of their fires and candles, and a long string of blessings upon
the heads of all the royal family of Denmark, constitute the elaborate subject of the watchman's comment after he has announced
the time. Nothing can be more annoying to a fatigued stranger
than his noisy and melancholy ditty every half-hour; but the police is admirable, and the city safe at all hours of the night. This
church was the only one which was worthy of notice. The Lutheran religion seldom arrays herself in the graceful drapery of
the arts; confiding in the purity of her precepts, and the devotional spirit of her unaspiring followers, she is satisfied if her shed
but repel the storm of the heavens; nor does she seek to attract
the wanderer to her temple, by the elegant and expressive powers
of the architect, the painter, and the statuary. The Exchange is
a large ancient building of brick: within are little shops, very much
resembling Exeter-Change, in London, but more commodious

and handsome. At the entrance nearest to the burnt palace, the merchants assemble. In this quarter of the town there are some excellent pastry shops, where the English and other foreign newspapers are taken in. The beautiful appearance of the evening attracted us to Fredericksberg, the palace of which is small, and stands upon an eminence; the gardens slope from its terrace; they are confined, but tastefully arranged: the Crown Prince shares the delight they afford in common with the meanest of his subjects.

As the King resided at this time in the palace, we could not see it, and from all that I could learn we had not much occasion for regret. He passes much of his time here, which he divides between billiards, romances, and his flute; he enjoys good health, but his mind is so infirm that his royal functions seldom exceed the signing of state papers. I was much disappointed in not having the honour of being presented to the Crown Prince, who at this time was in Holstein with that able and excellent minister, count Bernstoff. The Prince is virtually the sovereign of the kingdom, as his father has for many years presented only the phantom of a king. The misfortunes of the august mother of the Prince, his virtues, and his wisdom, unite to render him very interesting to an Englishman. In person I was informed that he was short and slender, his eyes are of a light blue, his nose aquiline, his face singularly fair, and his hair almost white; his mind is very capacious, cultivated, and active: his disposition is very amiable; and in the discharge of his august duties he is indefatigable. He is an enemy to dissipation and parade, and avoids the latter upon all but necessary occasions: his virtues constitute his guard of honour, and excite distinction and respect wherever he moves: in his youth he was a prince of great promise, and every blossom has ripened into fruit. At the age of sixteen he effected a revolution in the councils, and crushed the powerful ambition of the sanguinary Juliana Maria, and consigned her intriguing and turbulent spirit to the shades and seclusion of Friedensberg, by a master-piece of discretion, eloquence, and policy.

If the Prince has any fault, it is that he does not sufficiently appreciate the genius of his country, which is more commercial than military. Impelled by a martial enthusiasm, he appears to consider the encouragement of commerce as an object less worthy of his notice than the discipline, and, perhaps, superfluous augmentation of his troops, whose energies will, in all human probability, be long confined to defensive operation; yet, in another mode this Prince has sagaciously consulted the interests of his country and the happiness of his people, by abstaining from any material participation in those conflicts, which have so long deteriorated the interests of the rest of Europe. Small in size and resources, Denmark has every thing to lose and nothing to gain. A dwarf amongst giants, had she moved in the general confusion, she would have been crushed by some powerful foe, or trodden upon by some ponderous ally. The king's daughter is married to the Prince of Augustenbourg, and is spoken of as a very beautiful and accomplished woman. The daughters of Prince Frederic, the brother of the king, and the favourite son of Juliana Maria, are also much beloved and admired.

The court days in summer are few: in winter there is a levee once a fortnight; on these days there are suppers, when strangers, upon the presumption of their having the rank of colonels, are invited. At this meeting the number of men and women is equal, and all precedence, except that of the royal family, is determined by drawing lots as at a ball in England. In the winter, when people aggregate from necessity together, the social meetings in Copenhagen are said to be very frequent and delightful, and the ministers are very polite to strangers well introduced.

The action of the 2d of April was of too short a duration to produce any other impression on the country than a temporary irritation, and the event of that day taught her the impolicy and danger of departing from a state of unequivocal neutrality; at the same time it displayed to the world what never yet was questioned, the valour and enthusiastic patriotism of the Danes. It will be considered, however, as somewhat singular, that, for two successive years, they commemorated the return of that day, as a day of victory. A whimsical Dane adopted another mode of softening the affair, by endeavouring to prove, what was his own irremoveable conviction, that Lord Nelson was of Danish extraction. They now, however, confine themselves to the glory of a gallant but unavailing resistance, and in a little lapse of time their love for the English will return to its former channels.

The conduct of England, upon this memorable occasion, reminds me of the policy of a certain fashionable schoolmaster who had the care of three pupils of distinction, a duke, a viscount, and a baronet; the boy of the highest rank, who was the oldest and the most mischievous, during the absence of the learned doctor, prevailed upon his comrades to spend an evening at a fashionable bagnio; the doctor unexpectedly returned in the interim, and upon discovering where his pupils had been, felt a reluctance in wounding the high feelings of the duke and viscount, and visited the sins of all three upon the hapless lower seat of honour of the poor little baronet.   Thus Russia and Sweden led Denmark into the northern confederacy against the supremacy of the British flag, and Lord Nelson whipped the latter for the presumption of all the parties to the said league.   Denmark has reaped the fruits of her neutrality; and, without fatiguing the reader by a long string of comparative exports and imports, nothing can be clearer than that her interests have been in a state of progressive amelioration for several years past.   The radical emancipation of her peasantry has remunerated her with a merited reward,—the love of a free people, and the happy results of unshackled enterprise.   This blessing has not only been felt, but expressed.

. A few miles from the capital, on one side of the public road, is a plain and simple monument, expressive of the condition of those who raised it: it was erected by the peasants of the late Count Bernstoff, in gratitude for their liberation:

> 'Tis liberty alone that gives the flow'r
> Of fleeting life its lustre and perfume;
> And we are weeds without it.   COWPER.

Curiosity led me one day into the principal court of judicature: it was a handsome large room, in a range of buildings, in which the governor of the city resides: the throne was in front; twelve judges presided, attired in rich costume; there were only two advocates present, who wore embroidered capes and blue silk gowns.   The laws of Denmark, with an exception to the forest laws, are simple and wholesome, and are impartially administered, although the king is despotic.   Justice does not ap-

pear, preceded by Corruption, and followed by Famine. There
is one law in Denmark which restrains the tyranny of parents
towards their children, that deserves to be particularly mentioned: No parent can, by his own act, disinherit his child: if
he thinks that his son will dishonour him, and dissipate his fortune, he cannot change the usual channel of his property, without applying to the sovereign for permission, who, in council,
cautiously considers the allegation and answer; and thus the
refusal or permission is the result of a public process. Admirable as the laws of England are, it would be well if such a law
as this, adapted to the genius of the constitution, could be introduced. Alas! in England, how often is the happiness of an
excellent child sacrificed to the unnatural caprice or pride of an
angry, foolish, mercenary parent!

The mildness of the Danish government is such, that when
the king and the subject, as is frequently the case, happen to be
engaged in litigation, respecting titles to land, the judges are
recommended, if the point be dubious, to decree in favour of the
subject. A short time before we arrived, a woman had been
found guilty of murder, and she was sentenced only to four years
of solitary confinement. The Crown Prince is unwilling to see
the sword of justice stained with human blood: he is merciful
almost to a fault;

> The quality of mercy is not strained;
> It droppeth, as the gentle rain from heav'n,
> Upon the place beneath. It is twice blessed:
> It blesseth him that gives, and him that takes.

The internal taxes are raised or reduced at the discretion of
the king, which, with the customs and tolls upon exports and imports, the duties paid by foreigners, and his own demesne lands
and confiscations, constitute the revenues of the crown. The
land tax *ad valorem* is admirably managed in Denmark, by which
the soil is charged according to its fertility, which is estimated
by the quantity of grain required to sow a certain quantity of
land. This tax is formed into classes: the peasants have no as-
signable property in the soil, like tenants in England upon long
leases; they contract with their lord to cultivate so much land, in
the manner prescribed by the ordinances respecting agriculture,

and pay their rent either in money or provision. Such is the law now, that they can experience no oppression :

> Princes and Lords may flourish or may fade,
> A breath can make them, as a breath hath made;
> But a bold Peasantry, their Country's pride,
> When once destroy'd can never be supply'd.

The hospitality of the numerous and highly respectable family of the De Conincks, the principal merchants at Copenhagen, would not suffer us to quit the capital, without visiting their beautiful seat called Dronningaard or Queen's palace. As we reserved Sunday for this little country excursion, we learned, not without some inconvenience, that the Danes are remarkably rigid in their observance of the hours of worship.   On that day, during divine service, no one is permitted to quit or enter the city but at one gate.   Immediately after we had passed the wrong drawbridge, the clock struck eleven, and the gate closed upon all erratic sinners : this unlucky event compelled us to go round the ramparts, and make a deviation of several miles.   Thoroughly impressed as I am with the necessity of preserving the sanctity of the Sabbath, I must confess I am at a loss to see the utility of barring gates, to keep religion in.   This expedient appears to me as useless as that of a burgomaster, who, upon a favourite lady flying to him in tears, to tell him that her canary-bird had escaped from its cage, ordered the drawbridges of the town to be raised, to prevent the elopement of the little fugitive.   The gates are shut in summer at twelve, and in winter at seven, at night.

Dronningaard is the first private residence in Denmark, lies about sixteen English miles from the city ; the grounds, which are very extensive, and tastefully laid out, slope down to a noble lake, twelve English miles in circumference, and is skirted with fine woods, and romantic country houses. At the end of a beautiful walk I was struck with the appearance of an elegant marble column, on a tablet affixed to which was inscribed :

> " This Monument is erected in gratitude to a mild and
>   beneficent Government, under whose auspices
>   I enjoy the blessings that surround me."

In another part of the grounds, in a spot of deep seclusion, we beheld the ruins of a hermitage, before which was the channel of a little brook, then dried up; and a little further, in a nook, an open grave and a tomb-stone.

The story of this retired spot deserves to be mentioned. Time has shed many winter snows upon the romantic beauties of Dronningaard, since one who, weary of the pomp of courts and the tumult of camps, in the prime of life, covered with honours and with fortune, sought from its hospitable owner permission to raise a sequestered cell, in which he might pass the remainder of his days in all the austerities and privation of an anchorite. This singular man had long, previous to the revolution in Holland, distinguished himself at the head of his regiment; but, in an unhappy moment, the love of aggrandizement took possession of his heart, and marrying under its influence, misery followed: and here, in a little wood of tall firs he raised this simple fabric: moss warmed it within, and the bark of the birch defended it without; a stream of rock water once ran in a bed of pebbles before the door, in which the young willow dipped its leaves; and at a little distance from a bed of wild roses the laburnum gracefully rose and suspended her yellow flowers; he selected an adjoining spot for the depository of his remains, when death

> —— like a lover's pinch,
> That hurts, but is desired,

should have terminated all his sufferings here. Every day he dug a small portion of his grave, until he had finished it: he then composed his epitaph in French, and had ■ inscribed upon a stone. The reader, I think, will be pleased with it in the English dress, which it has received from the distinguished pen of William Hayley, esq.

THE HERMIT'S EPITAPH.

Here may he rest, who, shunning scenes of strife,
Enjoy'd at Dronningaard a Hermit's life;
The faithless splendour of a court he knew,
　And all the ardour of the tented field,
Soft Passion's idler charm, not less untrue,
　And all that listless Luxury can yield.

G

He tasted, tender Love! thy chaster sweet;
Thy promis'd happiness prov'd mere deceit.
To Hymen's hallow'd fane by Reason led,
    He deem'd the path he trod, the path of bliss;
Oh! ever mourn'd mistake! from int'rest bred,
    Its dupe was plung'd in Misery's abyss.
But Friendship offer'd him, benignant pow'r!
Her cheering hand, in trouble's darkest hour.
    Beside this shaded stream, her soothing voice
    Bade the disconsolate again rejoice:
Peace in his heart revives, serenely sweet;
    The calm content, so sought for as his choice,
Quits him no more in this belov'd retreat.

In this singular solitude he passed several years, when the plans
of his life became suddenly reversed, by a letter of recall from his
prince, which contained the most flattering expressions of regard.
The wishes of his sovereign and of his country were imperative;
he flew to Holland, and, at the head of his regiment, fought and
fell. The night preceding his departure, he composed a farewel
to the enchanting scenery in whose bosom he had found repose,
which, as an affectionate remembrance of the unfortunate hermit,
is inscribed upon a tablet of marble, rai ed in a little grove not far
from the hermitage. For the following translation I am indebted
to the poetic and elegant mind of Leigh Hunt, esq.

FAREWEL OF THE HERMIT OF DRONNINGAARD.

Vain would life's pilgrim, ling'ring on his way,
Snatch the short respite of a summer's day;
Pale Sorrow, bending o'er his sad repose,
Still finds a tear in ev'ry shelt'ring rose:
Still breaks his dream, and leads th' unwilling slave
To weep, and wander to a distant grave.
E'en he, whose steps since life's ungenial morn
Have found no path unfretted with rude thorn:
From all he lov'd must turn his looks away,
Far, far from thee, fair Dronningaard, must stray,
Must leave the Eden of his fancy's dreams,
Its twilight groves and long resounding streams;
Streams, where the tears of fond regret have ran,
And back return to sorrow and to man!
O yet once more, ye groves, your sighs repeat,
And bid farewel to these reluctant feet:
Once more arise, thou soft, thou soothing wave,

In weeping murmurs, ere I seek my grave;
Ere yet a thousand social ills I share,
Consuming war, and more consuming care,
Pleasures that ill conceal their future pains,
Virtue in want, blest Liberty in chains,
Vice, proud and powerful as the winter's wind,
And all the dire deliriums of mankind.

Yet e'en this heart may hail its rest to come;
Sorrow, thy reign is ended in the tomb!
There close the eyes, that wept their fires away;
There drop the hands, that clasp'd to mourn and pray;
There sleeps the restlessness of aching hearts;
There Love, the tyrant, buries all his darts!

O grant me, heav'n, thus sweetly to repose!
'Tis thus my soul shall triumph o'er its woes;
Spring from the world, nor drop one painful tear
On all it leaves, on all it treasures here;
Save once, perhaps, when pensive moonlight gleams
O'er Dronningaard's meek shades and murm'ring streams,
The sacred grief, to dear remembrance true,
O'er her soft flow'rs may shed its gentlest dew,
May once in sounds, that soothe the suff'ring mind,
Breathe its lorn murmurs through the solemn wind;
Lament, sweet spot, thy charms must wither'd be,
And linger e'en from heav'n to sigh for thee!

The dispatch with which nature pushes on her vegetation in these cold climates is amazing. This delightful spot, which was now in full foliage, presented nothing but naked branches a fortnight before. I quitted Dronningaard with almost as much regret as did the devoted eremite.

A visit to the Crown-battery was very interesting. A young Danish officer, who was present at the battle of the second of April, pointed out the respective positions of the fleets and block ships, and described with great candour and liberality the particulars of the engagement. This formidable battery is about half an English mile from shore, is square, and the water flows into the middle of it; it is now very rapidly enlarging, and undergoing such alterations as will make it a place of great strength. It is also in contemplation to raise a fresh battery to the southward in addition to that called the lunette. The harbour is very capacious and safe. The holm, or arsenal, is not shown without the permission of the admiral. The ships in ordinary are finely arranged and make a gallant show : a gallery or narrow bridge, resting upon piles, runs on each side of the line, which is patroled day and night. The magazines, forges, and workshops are upon an admirable construction : each ship has her different magazine, containing all the materials for her rapid equipment. This depot is furnished with iron from Norway, hemp from Riga, cloth from Russia and Holland, and wood from Pomerania. The rope-walks are each a thousand feet long. As I was enjoying, one fine afternoon, a row in that part of the harbour where the arsenal is, and nothing can be more beautiful or interesting than such an excursion, I observed a man-of-war lying near the quay, of a peculiar construction : she swelled amazingly. in the upper sides, forming a considerable portion of a circle, for the purpose of enabling her to bring several of her after guns to act with her bow guns or with her stern chasers : she had a very clumsy appearance, and I was informed that the experiment had not answered the wishes of government. The number of merchant vessels we saw at the quay confirmed the account we received of the magnitude of the Danish commerce. Nature, which has broken the kingdom into islands, has instinctively made the Danes merchants and sailors : their principal foreign trade is with France, Portugal, and Italy, and the East and West Indies : their principal domestic trade is with Norway, and even with Iceland, which, to all but its patriotic and contented native, is a most deplorable country, the very outskirts of the world. The seamen are registered, and are divided into two classes : the stationary sailors, who are always in the employ of the crown ; the others are, in time of peace, permitted to enter into merchant ships, subject to recall in case of war, and have a small annual stipend. The academy of marine cadets forms one of the palaces in the Octagon : it was founded by Frederic V. Here, and at an hotel which belongs to it, sixty youths are maintained and instructed in the principles of navigation, at the expense of the crown. There are also several other young gentlemen admitted to the school, but are not maintained there. Every year several of these gallant pupils make a cruise in a brig of war, that they may. blend practice with theory. The academy of land cadets. is, pretty nearly upon the same establishment : fifty boys are main-

tained and educated for a military life by the crown, and others
are admitted to the school, but maintained at their own expense.
The former are well fed, but are never permitted to drink tea. In
the academy is a riding house, and in the adjoining stables eight
horses are kept for the use of the young pupils in the art of riding.

In the course of my rambles I visited the citadel, which is
small, and stands at the extremity of the city, and contains two
battalions. It has two gates; one towards the city, and the other
towards the country; the latter is well fortified by five bastions.
Adjoining the chapel is the dungeon in which the count Struensee
was confined; it is indeed a most dismal hole; it was here that he
lightened the weight of his chains and the horrors of imprisonment by his flute, upon which, so little apprehensive was he of
his impending fate, that his favourite air was from the *Deserteur*,
beginning with *Mourir c'est notre dernier ressort*. Upon quitting
this melancholy abode we requested the soldier who conducted us
to shew us that of his unhappy fellow-sufferer, Brandt. He accordingly led us through a gloomy stone passage; and, after un-
locking and unbarring a massy door, conducted us up a winding
stone staircase into the cell, where, to my surprise, a sun-beam,
slanting through a small grated window, presented to us the figure
of a man of respectable appearance, and of about the middle age
of life, emaciated by long confinement, and bowed down by grief.
As we approached him, a faint blush partially spread over his
sallow cheek, and a tear stood in his eye, which he endeavoured
to conceal with his hand, and with a bow of humiliation turned
from us to a little bird-cage, which he was constructing. We
apologized for our intrusion, and hastily turning towards the
door, we beheld a beautiful boy standing near it, apparently a-
bout eight years old; his look at once explained that the prisoner
was his father: the face of this little child of sorrow was the
most artless and expressive I ever beheld. As we descended, he
followed; and when at the bottom of the stairs, we asked him
why he looked so pale; the little creature replied in French, "Ah,
sir! I look so because I have just recovered from a fever. I do
not always look so: I shall soon be well; but my poor papa never
will." We put money in his hand, and begged him to take it to
his father: this he immediately returned, saying, "No, sir, indeed I must not; my father will be angry with me." All our

efforts were in vain; it was a scene of affecting mystery. The soldier took up the child and kissed it, and bidding him return to his father, closed the door. He informed us that the prisoner had been convicted of forgery, but stated that there were many strong circumstances in his favour. Oh, how I wished that that merciful prince, whose ears are ever more open to the sounds of suffering than of flattery, had heard what we heard! the looks and language of the little prattler would have pleaded for the wretched prisoner.

The little ancient palace of Rosenberg, said to be built by Inigo Jones, attracted our notice; the gardens belonging to which form the principal town-parade of the belles and beaux of Copenhagen. The statues in these gardens are not worthy of notice, although recommended to the notice of travellers by many of the Copenhagers. In the street adjoining are the barracks for the foot guards, and a covered hall for military exercise, of four hundred feet long. This Gothic edifice is principally remarkable for containing the room in which the King holds his annual bed of justice, and for the jewel office: the former is a long low room, the whole length of the building. Before the throne, upon the floor, stand three lions of massy silver, in different attitudes, as large as life, and excite a fine idea of barbarous grandeur: the walls are surrounded with large pieces of ancient tapestry, somewhat the worse for age, representing the exploits of the most military of the Danish monarchs in their wars with the Swedes. In a little room adjoining the hall are several services of plate, vases, wine-glasses, and goblets, in chrystal, which were presented to Frederic IV, by the Venetian States; the collection is very valuable, and tastefully arranged. In another small apartment we saw the saddle of Christian IV, covered with pearls, said to be worth 30,000*l.* which he once used upon a magnificent gala-day in Copenhagen. In the cabinet of jewels are the coronation chairs, crowns, and various valuable and curious assortments of jewelry; but I was most gratified by a beautiful service of Danish porcelain, which was made in the new manufactory of china, on which was exquisitely painted the Flora Danica, or the indigenous botanical productions of Denmark and Norway. We found it difficult to get a peep at this place, on account, as we were told, of the grand marshal of the court always having the custody of the key. An old officer, of the rank of colonel, shewed the curiosities, and through the hands of an attendant received a ducat for his trouble.

From the palace I proceeded to the observatory, a noble round tower, one hundred and twenty feet high, in which a spiral road of brick nearly winds to the top; so that thus far any one might ascend or descend on horseback with perfect ease and safety: at the top is the observatory of the celebrated Tycho Brahe. The instruments are good, and in excellent condition; amongst the telescopes there is one that is twelve Danish feet long, and magnifies eight hundred times, made by Alh of Copenhagen. From this tower a young Dane precipitated himself, a short time before we visited it, and was dashed to pieces: at the school to which he belonged, the master had passed over his merits, as he too rashly thought, to compliment a boy of higher rank, but his inferior in learning. The wounded sensibility of the former drove him to frenzy, and caused the melancholy catastrophe above related. Nor far from the observatory is the university library; it contains about four thousand volumes; they are chiefly upon theology and jurisprudence. There are also about two thousand manuscripts: amongst the most rare of the latter is a bible in Runic characters. This library has an annual revenue of eight hundred crowns for the sole purpose of purchasing books, and is open to the public. The school of surgery is a small, neat and handsome modern building: under this roof a singular instance of acute sensibility happened a few years since, which is still much talked of: As Kruger, a celebrated anatomical lecturer, was addressing his pupils, he received a letter announcing the death of a very dear friend at Paris; he was observed to be much agitated, and exclaimed, " I have received intelligence which I shall never long survive; I cannot recover the shock." His scholars, who very much loved him, pressed round, and bore him to his home in their arms, where he expired a few hours after. The hospital for secret lying-in is a handsome edifice: here pregnant women, who have reasons for seeking concealment, are received, upon paying a small stipend; they enter at night in masks, and are never seen but by those who are necessary to their comfort, and their names are never required. This is a noble institution, and is said 'to have produced a very visible diminution in the crime of infanticide.

At the *tables-d'hote* at Copenhagen, a stranger is at first struck with the appearance of noblemen with stars glittering upon their breast, being seated at the same table with the rest of the company. This seldom occurs but in the summer, when the heads of noble families, who pass that season of the year at their chateaus, come occasionally to town, where their houses are generally shut up till the winter. It was at one of these places that I met with an extraordinary instance of the ignorance in which a native of one country may remain of the manners of another. A Danish gentleman, as he was picking his teeth with his *fork*, a *délicate* custom, very prevalent upon the continent amongst all classes, observed that he had heard the English women were very pretty, but he was confident that he never could love them : upon being pressed for his reason, he replied, because he understood they were never seen without a pipe in their mouths ! We told him that it was very true they had frequently *pipes* in their mouths, and very *sweet* ones too, but that they never smoked ; nay, so much did they abhor it, that they regarded the man with disgust who indulged himself in the habit.

At Copenhagen I had an opportunity of observing that a Turk in a Lutheran country can get as gloriously drunk as a Christian. At a *table d'hote* which I frequented, we were occasionally amused by a little fat follower of Mahomet, who had just arrived, with some appearance of consequence, but with a suspicious application to the Danish government : the mussulman very soon forgot or defied the sumptuary provisions of the Alcoran, and became enamoured with some excellent port wine and English bottled porter; his libations, which were pretty copious, were generally followed by dancing and kicking his turban round the room ; at length, he was suddenly told to look out for other quarters. A little facetious waiter was asked whether he had removed him, to prevent his further augmenting the anger of the prophet ? " I know no-" thing about his prophet" said he; " all that I know is, that he " has got no more money."

After having perused the description which travellers have given of the grounds and house of count Bernstoff, I was somewhat disappointed upon visiting them: the former are certainly finely wooded, and command a beautiful view of the Sound, but they are not laid out with much taste; the latter is by no means splendid. I was more gratified with the King's park, which is extensive and highly picturesque, as I was with the grounds and gardens of Prince Frederic, the King's brother: this spot is very delightful; and, on acount of the motley crowds which flock to it, is in miniature (a very small one) at once the Versailles and Greenwich-park of Denmark.

The laws of Denmark prevent the gratifications of shooting: a young Dane, who had been in England, observed to me one day, with a most serious countenance, that nothing could exceed the impertinence of the hawks, who, availing themselves of the laws, flew into the room and killed his canary birds.

A gloomy curiosity conducted us to the Rasp-house, where capital offenders are confined for life: the male convicts, some of whom were ironed, rasp and saw Brasil wood and rein-deer's horns; the latter is used in soup. The females spin. The prisoners are separately confined: the house of correction is on the right: here offenders of both sexes are enclosed in the same room, many of them young and healthy, but, strange to relate! I only saw one little child in the apartment: they all looked neat and clean, and are made by their labour to contribute towards their support. It has often surprised me that the latter arrangement has not been adopted in the principal prisons of England; surely it is a subject well worthy the notice of the statesman. We have hundreds of miserable wretches shut up in confinement after conviction, who, with the exception of picking oakum in some of the correctional houses, and that too in a very desultory and unprofitable manner, do nothing but render their depravity more desperate. Justice demands that their services, if possible, should atone for their crimes; policy that they should help to maintain themselves; and humanity, that their health should be promoted by their labour.

The Admiralty-hospital, the Citizen's-hospital, the Orphan's-house, and the hospital of Frederic, are all very humane foundations, and well maintained; there is nothing in them worthy of elaborate description. To an Englishman such establishments, and every other institution by which misfortune can be relieved,

misery alleviated, and infirmity recovered, are proudly familiar to
his eye: they constitute the principal beauty of every town and
city in his country. Although the manufactories of the north are
much inferior to those of the south, I must not omit to mention
the gratification which we derived from visiting the manufactory
of china, which is very beautiful, and, although in its infancy, is
thought to rival those of Saxony, Berlin, and Vienna. This manufactory furnished the beautiful service which we saw in the palace of Rosenberg: it is under the care of directors, who very
liberally and politely shew the whole of this very curious and elegant establishment to strangers.

I did not leave Copenhagen without visiting the Dutch town in
the isle of Amak, about two English miles from the capital, which
is inhabited by about four thousand people, descendants of a colony
from East Friesland, who were invited to reside here, with certain
privileges, by one of the ancient kings of Denmark, for the purpose of supplying the city with milk, cheese, butter, and vegetables; the neatness and luxuriance of their little gardens cannot
be surpassed: they dress in the Dutch style, and are governed by
their own laws. The road from this village to the city is constantly
crowded with these indefatigable people, who, by their bustle and
activity, give it the appearance of a great ant-hill. In Denmark
no other money is to be seen than the money of the country, the
currency of which is penally protected: I must except, however,
Dutch ducats, which pass all over Europe, and are very seldom
below par. There is here a *plentiful lack* of gold and silver coin,
and abundance of copper.

Having seen most of the *lions* of Copenhagen, we prepared to
bid adieu to our friends, and shape our course towards Sweden:
as a necessary preliminary we exchanged our Danish money for
Swedish *small* notes: the exchange was about three per cent. in
our favour; by this precaution we obviated the difficulty of procuring change for *large* Swedish notes in the country, and the inconvenience (and not a small one it is) of carrying its coin. We
also procured a servant who spoke Swedish, which was very necessary, and purchased ropes and cross-bars to enable us to con-
struct a new harness and tackling in Sweden, according to the custom of travelling there. When a man is about to set out on a long
journey, it is a fortunate thing for him if some little pleasant or

ridiculous event occur to set him off in good humour: nothing therefore could happen more opportunely than the following circumstance: Just before our departure we had occasion to go to a leather breeches maker, to which we were conducted by our *laquais de place*: our gentleman, who, by the by, was an Italian, and the coolest of his countrymen, with the greatest *sang froid* addressed himself very familiarly to the Baron B———, the Bavarian minister, who was in the shop when we entered, and at last begged to have the honour of introducing him to us. We bowed to each other with a smile of astonishment at the intrepid assurance of our mutual friend. We took the road to Elsineur, attended by several of our Copenhagen friends, who begged to accompany us as far as Fredericksberg, where it was agreed that we should dine and part. Every thing in Denmark is very dear, pretty nearly as much so as in England.

CHAP. V.

FREDERICKSBERG—STORKS—FASTIDIOUS MARES—FOREST LAWN—PE-
NALTIES OF TRAVELLING—PRINCE WILLIAM OF GLOUCESTER—
CONTINENTAL EQUIPAGES—HAMLETS—ORCHARD—CRONBERG CAS-
TLE—SOME AFFECTING SCENES WHICH PASSED THERE—THE FARE-
WEL KISS—THE GALLANTRY OF CAPTAIN MACBRIDE—THE LIT-
TLE COURT OF ZELL—THE DEATH OF THE QUEEN MATILDA.

THE road from Copenhagen to Fredericksberg, distant about
sixteen English miles, is very beautiful, and presents a luxuriant
display of lakes, woods, corn-fields, and forests of beech, oak,
and fir. Before we reached that town, we passed through a forest of wild horses, some of which we saw; they had a noble,
rough appearance, and presented a fine study for such a pencil
as Gilpin's. Whilst our dinner was preparing we visited the
palace, a heavy and most incongruous massy pile of building, in
which black marble contends with red brick, and the simple graces
of the Grecian order with all the minute fretted perplexities of
the Gothic; the whole is covered with copper, and was built by
Christian IV: it stands in a lake, and seems to be fit only for the
residence of frogs, and, I believe, with the exception of two old
housekeepers, it has no other inmates. The Sal de Chevalier is
a very long room, crowded with paintings, badly arranged, and
perishing with damp and mildew: some of them seemed to deserve a better fate. The pillars which support the cornice of
the fire-place in this room were once crowned with silver capitals, which the Swedes carried off in one of their irruptions. In
the chapel we saw the throne upon which the kings of Denmark
were formerly crowned; the roof is most superbly gilt and decorated, and the walls are covered with the arms of the knights of
the first order. As we passed through one of the old galleries,
over a moat, a gust of wind shook the crazy casement, and the
great clock heavily struck its hour: it was altogether a place well
suited for a second edition of the exploits of Sir Bertrand, or
would form an appropriate academy for the spectre-loving pupils
of the German school.

In the gloomy grounds of this palace we again saw our old friend the stork. This subject of his Danish Majesty generally quits his territories in October, and returns in Spring ; and what is singular, he always returns to his own nest.

From this place we walked to the royal stud, about half a mile distant (the road to which was exquisitely picturesque), where the king has two thousand fine horses, each of which is disfigured, by being marked with a large letter on one side of the haunch, and the year of his birth on the other. There is here a beautiful and very rare breed of milk-white horses ; they always herd together, and the mares will not permit the stallions of any other breed to approach them. I have been informed that there is a similar breed in the island of Ceylon. There is as much good nature as policy in the permission which his Danish Majesty grants to all the farmers, to have their mares covered by his finest stallions gratuitously : hence the fine breed of horses in Denmark, the keep of which, happily for that noble animal, is the only cheap thing in the kingdom.

This part of the country is said to abound more in game than any other, but although the forest-laws prevail with all their rigour in Denmark Proper, except that the punishment of death is commuted into perpetual imprisonment, yet there is but little game, and but little increase in the breed of deer. It is a just retribution for the severity of the prohibition. After a glass of excellent Burgundy, which, as it was the signal of departure, seemed to lose half its flavour, we pressed our excellent friends by the hands, and proceeded on the road to Elsineur.

It is one of the penalties of travelling, and a painful one it is, to meet with here and there a being, who delights, attaches, and is gone for ever. It was even so with one from whom I parted on this very spot, in all human probability never more to meet on this side the grave. He was a youth full of genius, accomplished, diffident, gentle, brave, and generous : he came from the region of mountains and cataracts, from the Swisserland of the north, where the winter snow is seen undisturbed to settle on the naked breast of the hardy and happy peasant. I must again borrow the language of my adored Shakespeare, to paint my noble young Norwegian :

> " His head unmellow'd, but his judgment ripe :
> And, in a word (for far behind his worth
> Come all the praises that I now bestow),
> He was complete in feature and in mind,
> With all good grace to grace a gentleman."

My memory will long dwell with delight upon the name of Knudtzon.

Time would not admit of our seeing Fredericvaark, which is near this place. The cannon-foundry and manufactories were established by general Claussen, who, by his skill and perseverance, has triumphed over the most formidable difficulties of local situation: the whole is at present under the superintendence of our ingenious countryman, Mr. English. It is said that this establishment can completely equip a fifty-gun ship in two months; in all her guns, powder, and stores.

The country houses, many of which we passed, are generally built of wood, painted red or light yellow: they seldom exceed two stories, frequently containing only a suite of ground floor apartments, and are far more comfortable within, than handsome without. Sometimes they are built of brick, when the frame and timbers are visible, and have a very unpleasant appearance. The gardens are in general formally laid out, and the garden door is remarkable for being formed of a frame covered with fine wire netting, through which the grounds behind appear as through a muslin veil, and the garden railing is almost invariably heavy and tasteless.

Through a forest of fine beech, the sun shining gloriously, and making the trunk of many a tree look like a pillar of gold, and illuminating the casement of many a romantic little cottage, we reached the palace of Fredensborg, or the Mansion of Peace: it stands in a valley, and was the retreat of the remorseless Juliana Maria, after the young Crown Prince had taken possession of the reins of government, which, having stained with blood, she vainly endeavoured to retain. Here in solitude she resigned her breath. No doubt her last moments were agonized by the compunctious visitings of conscience, for the wrongs which she had heaped upon the unfortunate Matilda, and her savage sacrifice of Struensee and Brandt. The grass was growing in the court, and upon the steps. The building is a large square front, surmounted with a dome, and extensive crescent wings; the whole is of brick, stuccoed white. The window-shutters were closed, and the glass in several places broken; all looked dreary and desolate: after thundering at the door with a stick, we at length gained admittance. The apartments were handsome, and contained several good Flemish paintings. The domestic shewed us, with great exultation, the hall in which the Crown Prince entertained Prince William of Gloucester with a grand dinner about two years before. The Danes always mentioned this Prince with expressions of regard and admiration, that shewed how favourable were the impressions created by his amiable deportment and engaging manners during his visit to Denmark. The gardens and woods are very beautiful, but neglected, and gently slope down to the extensive lake of Esserom. As we roved along, the birds, with plaintive melodies, hailed the moist approach of evening, and our time just admitted of our visiting, which we did with real satisfaction, a vast number of statues, which are circularly ranged in an open space surrounded by shrubs, representing the various costumes of the Norwegian peasantry: some of them appeared to be admirably chiselled.

Upon returning to the carriage, the images of what I had just seen produced the following lines:

FREDENSBORG.

THE DESERTED PALACE OF THE LATE QUEEN DOWAGER JULIANA MARIA.

Blest are the steps of Virtue's queen!
Where'er she moves fresh roses bloom,
And when she droops, kind Nature pours
Her genuine tears in gentle show'rs,
That love to dew the willow green
That over-canopies her tomb.

But ah! no willing mourner here
Attends to tell the tale of woe:
Why is yon statue prostrate thrown?
Why has the grass green'd o'er the stone?
Why 'gainst the spider'd casement drear
So sullen seems the wind to blow?

How mournful was the lonely bird,
Within yon dark neglected grove!
Say, was it fancy? From its throat
Issu'd a strange and cheerless note;
'Twas not so sad as grief I heard,
Nor yet so wildly sweet as love.

In the deep gloom of yonder dell,
Ambition's blood-stain'd victims sighed:
While time beholds, without a tear,
Fell Desolation hovering near,
Whose angry blushes seem to tell,
Here Juliana shudd'ring died.

As we descended to Elsineur, the town, the Sound, enlivened
by shipping at anchor and under sail, and the shores of Sweden,
presented an enchanting prospect, which the brilliancy of the sky
at this season of the year, in these northern climates, enabled me
to contemplate till midnight. The next morning, as I was quitting my hotel to take another ramble, the governor of Copenhagen,
Prince W., and his Princess and suite, who had been spending
the preceding day at Elsineur, were setting off for the capital:
they were all crammed into a shabby coach, drawn by six horses
in rope harness. It is astonishing how little a handsome travelling
equipage is understood upon the Continent. The town, which is
principally built of brick, is large, and has a very respectable
appearance.

The gardens of Marie Lyst, or Maria's Delight, which are
within half an English mile of Elsineur, cannot fail to prove
very interesting to every admirer of our immortal Shakespeare.
I here trod upon the very spot, where, with all the uncertainty
of antiquity, tradition asserts that the father of Hamlet was
murdered: that affecting drama is doubly dear to me. Its beauties are above all eulogium; and I well remember, the desire of
seeing a ghost occasioned its being the first I ever beheld. As I
stood under the shade of a spreading beech, the " Majesty of
buried Denmark" seemed to say to the afflicted prince:

——————————— Sleeping within my orchard,
My custom always in the afternoon,
Upon my secure hour thine uncle stole,
With juice of cursed hebenon in a vial,

And in the porches of mine ears did pour
The leperous distilment————————
Thus was I, sleeping, by a brother's hand
Of life, of crown, of queen, at once dispatch'd.
Cut off, e'en in the blossoms of my sin,
Unhousel'd, unappointed, unaneal'd,
No reckoning made, but sent to my account,
With all my imperfections on my head.

A more beautiful spot for such a frightful conference could not have been selected. The walks from this celebrated scene, to the tower which overhangs the cliff, and from whence there is a fine view of Cronberg Castle, are enchanting. There is a little chateau near Hamlet's Orchard belonging to the Crown Prince, who permits one of his chamberlains, called a kammerherr (a nobleman) to reside here: the symbol of his distinction is a singular one; a golden key, fastened by a blue riband to the back part of the body of his coat.

The spires of the fortress of Cronberg, which appeared immediately below me, and the battlements upon which the hapless Matilda was permitted to walk during her confinement in that castle, excited an irresistible wish to lay before my reader a few of the most affecting circumstances, which passed under its gloomy roof during her captivity.

It is well known what neglect and suffering the Queen, in the bloom of youth and beauty, endured, from the fatal imbecility of the King's mind, and the hatred and jealousy of Sophia Magdalen, the grandmother, and Juliana Maria, the step-mother, of his Majesty; and that the anger of the latter was encreased by Matilda's producing a prince, an event which annihilated the hopes that Juliana cherished of seeing the elevation of her favourite son, Prince Frederic, to the throne. The Queen, about this period, 1769, was saved from ruin, only by attaching to her confidence the count Struensee, who, sagacious, penetrating, bold, enterprising, and handsome, without the pretensions of birth, had ascended to an unlimited power over the will of the sovereign, had obtained the reins of government, and had far advanced with almost unexampled celerity and unshaken firmness in reforming the mighty abuses which encumbered and distorted the finance, the laws, the administration of justice, the police, the marine,

I

the army, and the exchequer, and in short every department of government. Struensee restored the Queen to the bosom of her sovereign, and, with the assistance of count Brandt, the friend of Struensee, environed the King, and made him inaccessible to every other person. His Majesty's great delight at this period arose from the society of a negro boy, and a little girl about ten years of age, who used to amuse him by breaking the windows of the palace, soiling and tearing the furniture, and throwing dung and turf at the statues in the garden. Struensee experienced the usual fate of reformers, the abhorrence of those whom he corrected, and the suspicions or indifference of the people whom he served. He dislodged a nest of hornets. Juliana, with the keen unwearied vigilance of the tyger-cat, watched her victims from the gloomy shades of Fredensborg; where herself and her party, consisting of counts Ranzau, Köller, and others, fixed on the 17th of January, 1772, to close the career of their hated rivals: their savage resolve was facilitated by the last fatal and infatuated measures of Struensee, who beheld too late the phrenzy of precipitate systems of reform: he prevailed upon the King to issue an edict empowering every creditor to arrest his debtor without reference to birth or rank; the nobility flew to their estates in all directions, with revenge in their hearts; he terrified and grievously offended the mild and rigid citizens of Copenhagen, by assimilating its police to that of Paris, and by disbanding the royal foot-guards, composed of Norwegians, for the purpose of drafting them into other regiments. His days, his hours, were now numbered: on the night of the 16th of January, a magnificent *bal paré* was given at the great palace, since, as I have related, burned. The young Queen never looked more lovely: she was the very soul of this scene of festive grandeur:

> Grace was in every step, heaven in her eye.

It was the collected brilliancy of the expiring flame. At three o'clock a dead silence reigned throughout the palace: the conspirators, with several guards, passed the bridge over the canal, and surrounded the avenues. Juliana, Prince Frederic, and Ranzau, went to the door of the King's apartment, which at first the fidelity of a page in waiting refused to unlock; they terrified the

monarch by their representations of an impending plot, and thrust
into his hands, for signature, the orders for seizing the Queen,
Struensee, and Brandt. Upon seeing the name of Matilda upon
the order, love and reason for a moment took possession of the
King's mind, and he threw the paper from him, but, upon being
ardently pressed, he signed it, put his head upon his pillow,
pulled the bed-cloaths over him, and in a short time forgot what
he had done. Köller proceeded to Struensee's room, and being a
powerful man, seized the latter by the throat, and with some
assistance sent him and Brandt in a close carriage, strongly guarded, to the citadel. Ranzau and colonel Eickstädt opened the door
of the Queen's chamber, and awoke her from profound sleep to
unexpected horror. These savage intruders are said, upon her
resisting, to have struck her. The indecency and indignity of the
scene can scarcely be imagined. After the Queen had hurried .
on her cloaths, she was forced into a carriage, attended by a squadron of dragoons, and sent off to the fortress of Cronberg. Upon her
arrival, she was supported to her bed-chamber, a cold, damp, stone
room. Upon observing the bed, she exclaimed, " Take me away !
" take me away ! rest is not for the miserable ; there is no rest for
" me." After some violent convulsions of nature, tears came to
her relief : " Thank God," said the wretched Queen, " for this
" blessing ! my enemies cannot rob me of it." Upon hearing the
voice of her infant, the Princess Louisa, who had been sent after
her in another carriage, she pressed her to her bosom, kissed her
with the most impassioned affection, and bathed her with tears.
" Ah ! art thou here ?" said she, " poor unfortunate innocent ; this
" is indeed some balm to thy wretched mother." In the capital
a scene of terror, tumult, and forced festivity followed : at twelve
o'clock the next day, Juliana and her son paraded the King in his
state coach, arrayed in his regalia, through the principal streets,
but only here and there a solitary shout of joy was heard. For
three days the imprisoned Queen refused to take any food, and

" Three times she crossed the shade of sleepless night."

It is said that the King never once enquired for her, and now became the sole property of the infamous Juliana, who guarded her
treasure with the eye of a basilisk. The court of Great Britain

made a mild but firm communication upon the subject of the personal safety of the Queen. Nine commissioners were appointed to examine the prisoners : the following were the principal charges against Struensee:

1. A horrid design against the life of his sacred Majesty.

2. An attempt to oblige the King to resign the crown.

3. A criminal connection with the Queen.

4. The improper manner in which he had educated the Prince Royal.

5. The great power and decisive influence he had acquired in the government of the state.

6. The manner in which he used this power and influence in the administration of affairs.

Amongst the charges preferred against the count Brandt was the following ridiculous one :

" While the King was playing in his *usual manner* with count " Brandt, the count bit his Majesty's finger."

Four commissioners proceeded to examine the Queen, who, with the wretched Constance, might have exclaimed

————— Here I and Sorrow sit.
Here is my throne: let kings come bow to it.

Her answers were pointed, luminous, and dignified : she denied most solemnly any criminal intercourse with Struensee. S——, a counsellor of state, abruptly informed the Queen, that Struensee had already signed a confession in the highest degree disgraceful to the honour and dignity of her Majesty. " Impossible!" exclaimed the astonished Queen, "Struensee never could make such " a confession : and if he did, I here call heaven to witness, that " what he said was false." The artful S—— played off a masterpiece of subtilty, which would have done honour to a demon : " Well then," said he, " as your Majesty has protested against " the truth of his confession, he deserves to die for having so trai- " torously defiled the sacred character of the Queen of Denmark." This remark struck the wretched Princess senseless in her chair. After a terrible conflict between honour and humanity, pale and trembling, in a faultering voice she said, " And if I confess what " Struensee has said to be true, may he hope for mercy ?" which

words she pronounced with the most affecting voice, and with all
the captivations of youth, beauty, and majesty, in distress : S——
nodded, as if to assure her of Struensee's safety upon those terms,
and immediately drew up her confession to that effect, and presented it to her to sign ; upon this, her frame became agitated with
the most violent emotions; she took up the pen and began to
write her name, and proceeded as far as Carol—, when, observing
the malicious joy which sparkled in the eyes of S———, she became convinced that the whole was a base stratagem, and, throw-
ing away the pen, exclaimed, " I am deceived, Struensee never
" accused me. I know him too well ; he never could have been
" guilty of so great a crime." She endeavoured to rise, but her
strength failed her ; she sunk down, fainted, and fell back into her
chair. In this state, the barbarous and audacious S——— put the
pen between her fingers, which he held and guided, and before
the unfortunate Princess could recover, the letters —ina Matilda
were added. The commissioners immediately departed, and left
her alone: upon her recovering and finding them gone, she conjectured the full horror of her situation.

To afford some colouring to the mock trial which followed, the
advocate Uhldal was appointed her defender : his speech on be-
half of the Queen was in the highest degree able, pathetic, and
convincing. Uhldal discharged such duties as in a few years afterwards devolved upon the eloquent Malsherbes, and with equal
effect: the illustrious clients of both were prejudged : it was the
show of justice, not to investigate, but to give a spurious *eclat* to
their fate. How opposite was this tribunal to that which Sheridan,
in a blaze of eloquence, apostrophized upon the trial of Warren
Hastings, esq.! " From such a base caricature of justice," exclaimed the orator, " I turn my eyes with horror. I turn them
" here to this dignified and high tribunal, where the Majesty of real
" Justice sits enthroned. Here I perceive her in her proper robes
" of truth and mercy, chaste and simple, accessible and patient,
" awful without severity, inquisitive without meanness ; her love-
" liest attribute appears in stooping to raise the oppressed, and to
" bind up the wounds of the afflicted."

The grand tribunal divorced the Queen, and separated her for
ever from the King, and proposed to blemish the birth of the
Princess Louisa, by their decree, and reduce the little innocent

to that orphanage " which springs not from the grave, that falls
" not from the hand of Providence, or the stroke of death;" but
the cruel design was never executed. Uhldal also exerted all the
powers of his eloquence for the two unfortunate counts. Humanity
revolts at their sentence, which the unhappy King, it is said, signed
with thoughtless gaiety. They had been confined from the seventeenth of January, and, on the twenty-eighth of March, at eleven
o'clock, were drawn out to execution in two separate carriages, in
a field near the east gate of the town : Brandt ascended the scaffold first, and displayed the most undaunted intrepidity. After his
sentence was read, and his coat of arms torn, he calmly prayed a
few minutes, and then spoke with great mildness to the people.
Upon the executioner endeavouring to assist him in taking off
his pelisse, he said, " Stand off ! do not presume to touch me!
he then stretched out his hand, which, without shrinking from
the blow, was struck off, and almost at the same moment his
head was severed from his body.   Struensee, during this bloody
scene, stood at the bottom of the scaffold in trembling agony,
and became so faint when his friend's blood gushed through
the boards, and trickled down the steps, that he was obliged to
be supported as he ascended them : here his courage wholly
forsook him ; he several times drew back his hand, which was
dreadfully maimed before it was cut off, and at length he was
obliged to be held down before the executioner could perform his
last office. Copenhagen was unpeopled on the day of this savage
sacrifice ; but, although the feelings of the vast crowd which
surrounded the scaffold had been artfully wrought upon by Juliana
and her partizans, they beheld the scene of butchery with horror,
and retired to their homes in sullen silence. Nothing but the
spirited conduct of our then ambassador, Sir Robert Keith, prevented the Queen from being immolated at the same time.

On the 27th of May, a squadron of two British frigates and
a cutter, under the command of the gallant captain Macbride,
cast anchor off Helsingfors, and on the 30th every thing was
finally arranged for the removal of the Queen : upon the barge
being announced, she clasped her infant daughter to her breast,
and shed upon her a shower of tears. The Queen then sunk into
an apparent stupor ; upon recovering, she prepared to tear herself
away, but the voice, the smiles, and endearing motions of the

babe chained her to the spot; at last, summoning up all her resolution, she once more took it to her arms, and, in all the ardour and agony of distracted love, imprinted upon its lips the farewel kiss, and returning it to the attendant, exclaimed, " Away ! away ! I now possess nothing here," and was supported to the barge in a state of agony which baffles description. Upon the Queen approaching the frigate, the squadron saluted her as the sister of his Britannic Majesty, and when she came on board, captain Macbride hoisted the Danish colours, and insisted upon the fortress of Cronberg saluting her as Queen of Denmark, which salute was returned with two guns less. The squadron then set sail for Stade, in the Hanoverian dominions, but, owing to contrary winds, was detained within sight of the castle the whole day, and in the early part of the following morning its spires were still faintly visible, and, until they completely faded in the mist of distance, the Queen sat upon the deck, her eyes rivetted upon them, and her hands clasped in silent agony. Shall we follow the wretched Matilda a little farther? The path is solitary, very short, and at the end of it is her tomb. Upon her landing at Stade she proceeded to a little remote hunting-seat, upon the borders of the Elbe, where she remained a few months, until the castle of Zell, destined for her future residence, was prepared for her: she removed to it in the autumn. Here her little court was remarked for its elegance and accomplishments, for its bounty to the peasantry, and the cheerful serenity which reigned throughout. The Queen spent much of her time alone; and, having obtained the portraits of her children from Denmark, she placed them in a retired apartment, and frequently addressed them in the most affecting manner, as if present.

So passed away the time of this beautiful and accomplished exile, until the eleventh of May, 1775, when a rapid inflammatory fever put a period to her afflictions in the twenty-fourth year of her age. Her coffin is next to that of the dukes of Zell. Farewel poor Queen!

" Ah! while we sigh we sink, and are what we deplore."

CHAP. VI.

THE traveller will do right to obtain letters of introduction to
Mr. Fenwick, our consul at Elsineur : they will be the means of
making him acquainted with an amiable and highly respectable
family, whose manners, information, and hospitality, must afford
gratification. In the evening we procured a boat, embarked ourselves and baggage, and, by the assistance of a gentle breeze,
that just curled the water, we crossed the Sound, about four
English miles in breadth, and in three quarters of an hour found
ourselves in Sweden. We passed close by Cronberg Castle, which
stands upon a peninsular point the nearest to Sweden. I was a-
gain forcibly struck with the abbey-like appearance of this building : it now forms the residence of the governor of Elsineur. It
mounts three hundred and sixty-five pieces of cannon, and its
subterranean apartments will hold more than a regiment of men.
Fame, at one period, assigned to it the character of the impregnable and impassable fortress. On the celebrated second of April,
admirals Parker and Nelson passed it with perfect security, and
disdained to return a shot. Two British seventy-fours judiciously
moored, and well served, would, in a short time, blow all its
boasted bastions and intrenchments at the moon. No visitor,
without special permission from the governor (seldom granted),
is allowed to put his foot upon the drawbridge : why all this caution is used, I know not; perhaps to keep up the mystery of
invincibility. For my part, I am so well assured that the policy
of power is unostentatiously to shew itself, that, could I have discharged a paper bullet from my little boat into this redoubted
castle, I would have enclosed in it this sentence: " Where there
is concealment there is apprehension." This place was open to
every one, until the wand of Fatima was broken on the second of

April. The Crown-battery is a place of real force, and even Englishmen are permitted to see it without the least difficulty.

We disembarked under the steep and rocky shores of Helsin-borg, a small town upon a long pier, where the carriage was landed with considerable risk and difficulty ; and I warn those who travel with one, to take good care that they cross the Sound in calm weather, as it is obliged to be lifted out of the boat by mere manual strength. On landing, a Swedish hussar, a fine-looking fellow, in blue loose trowsers and jacket, with his two side-locks plaited, and fastened at the end by little weights of lead, demanded very civilly our passports ; and, whilst he went to the commander with them, we paid our robust boatmen in Danish money :

			Dollars	Marks	Skillings
For the boat	-	-	3	0	0
Carriage	-	-	2	0	0
Drink Money	-	-	0	3	0

We now settled all our accounts with Denmark, and proceeded to a very neat little inn, not far from the shore, where we found comfortable accommodations, which I suppose are improved by the neighbourhood of Ramlos, where the nobility of this province assemble every season to drink the waters. Having refreshed ourselves with some excellent coffee, we hastened to the duties of the evening, which proved a very busy one, for we intended to start direct for Stockholm at five o'clock in the morning, and our impatience cost our *pride* nothing less than figuring away a few days afterwards in the Stockholm Gazette, as a couple of couriers just landed. The reader who never means to make a nearer approach to Sweden than from his fireside to his library, may as well pass over the following dull but necessary detail of money matters :

SWEDISH MONEY.

SILVER.

12 Runstycks make 1 skilling.
48 Skillings — 1 silver dollar or Banco dollar.
1 Silver dollar is worth at par five shillings English.

PAPER.

The notes of Government are in Plotes, Ricksgalds, and Banco dollars.

K

A *flote* is equal to 16 skillings, or one third of a silver dollar, or 1*s*. 8*d*. English. This small paper is very useful to travellers.

A *Ricksgalds dollar* carries an agio of 50 per cent.; so that one silver dollar is equal to one and a half of a Ricksgalds dollar.

A *Banco dollar* is worth at par 5*s*. English, the same as the silver dollar.

N. B. Banco money is both coin and paper.

To the Swedish collector of the customs we paid

			Drs.	Marks.	Sks.
For tax and wharfage	-	-	2	12	0
Porterage	-	-	1	12	0

We paid also a little sum to the custom-house officer for a slight search.

Whilst we were settling these little matters, a young fellow, from whose face the picture of honesty might have been penciled, with the additional recommendation of a military hat, cockade and feather, such as might belong to the rank of a serjeant, made a low bow, and an application, which will be more clearly understood when the reader is informed that in Sweden, the traveller who is not willing to wait an hour and a half for his horses at the end of a post, will take special care to dispatch, some hours before he sets off, an avant courier, called a *vorbode*, who will proceed to the end of the journey for a mere trifle per mile Swedish, which is equal to six miles and three quarters English, and will order horses to be ready at the proper post-houses, at the hours which are mentioned in his instructions.

The peasants are obliged by law to furnish the adjoining post-houses with a certain number of horses, according to the value of their farms, and are under the control of the post-master. The horses are obliged to remain twenty-four hours at the post-house: their owners are paid for their time and trouble, if a traveller arrives; if not, they lose both. This regulation must be oppressive to the peasant, and injurious to agriculture, and calls loudly for amelioration. The price of posting is twelve skillings, or eight pence English, for a horse, per Swedish mile. When the post-house happens to be in a town, the price is doubled. The object of our visitor was to state that he was going to Feltza (a great

part of the way to Stockholm), and if we would pay for the hire of
a little cart and horse he would act as our vorbode, and carry some
of the luggage: to these terms we soon acceded, and he retired to
rest, in order to-start at two o'clock in the morning, which he did
in a little carriage, somewhat of the size and shape of that which
in London I have seen drawn by a large mastiff, and filled with
dogs' meat. Our servant, who had been in Sweden before, and
knew its characteristic honesty, entrusted him with his trunk, to
which we added another. Our next care was to prepare our rope
harness, as our tackling was to be entirely of a new construction,
and to lay in provision for the journey, the most valuable part of
which was some ribs of roasted mutton, cooked after our own
fashion; but lo! and behold! when we rose in the morning, our
basket in which it had been most carefully deposited, had been
rifled by some vile dog, and only a mangled and indented wreck
remained. The unprovided traveller may vainly expect to find
any thing which he can eat on the road; even eggs in this part of
the country are a rarity.

As I had it in contemplation to spend the winter at Venice or
Rome, I was obliged with regret to proceed direct to Stockholm,
instead of visiting Carlscrona, the celebrated Swedish arsenal, the
town of which we understood was much improved since its revival
after the dreadful conflagration of 1790, and that the new docks,
hewn out of rocks of granite, as far as they are advanced, are marvellous monuments of labour and enterprise. For the same reason also I was obliged to relinquish the gratification of seeing
Gotheborg, the second city of Sweden, and the stupendous falls
and works of Trolhætta. In these routes I am informed that provisions and accommodations are better. A lucky discovery made
by our good-humoured host in his pantry, supplied the melan-
cholly emptiness of our basket, with an admirable piece of cold
stewed beef, and thus provided we commenced our journey. Our
servant drove us, attended by two peasants, to whom the horses
belonged; one of them was seated on the box, and the other stood
behind the carriage, yet with such a weight our four little horses
conveyed us with the most surprising velocity. The animals
looked as if Cinderella's protective Genius had waved her wand
over them, and had raised them from mice to the rank of tiny
horses: they started in full gallop, and scarcely ever slackened

their pace, until they had reached the end of their post. The
peasants drive very skilfully, and it is not unusual to see a blooming damsel assume the reins. The roads, which are of rock, thinly
covered with gravel and earth, are said to be, and I believe with
truth, the finest in the world. We accomplished several stages
at the rate of thirteen and even fourteen English miles an hour.
At the end of each stage the traveller is presented with a book
called a dagbok, to enter his name, his age, whence he came,
whither he is going, the number of horses, and whether he is
satisfied with his postilion.

The spring here is scarcely perceived; and although it was the
seventeenth of June, the morning air was very cold and nipping.
Our road lay through Scone or Scania, said to be one of the finest
provinces of Sweden.   The nightingale has seldom been known
to extend her northern visit beyond this province, and even here
she but feebly pours " her amorous descant." Farther northward,
only magpies, woodpeckers, crows, and birds of the rock, are to
found. We passed through forests of beech and fir; many of the
latter were blasted, and had a very picturesque appearance. The
first stage was sixteen English miles, during which the only animated creatures we saw were a group of dancing goats, and a boy
with a flageolet, going to the fair. Between Astrop and Lynngby
is one of the most convenient ferries on which I ever floated : we
drove upon it without any difficulty, and were immediately conveyed to the other side. At the first post-house where we stopped my astonishment was not a little excited, by the peasants,
whimsically enough, as I then thought, asking us to tell them
where their beloved king was.

The first day we dined at Orke Ginga under the porch of a
little cottage : the scenery about us was very desolate and dreary.
As we skirted some of the lakes, which abound in Sweden, we saw
the peasant women, half-knee deep in water, washing their linen :
they looked hardy and happy. The architect must ever be governed by nature in the size, shape, and materials of his building.
Sweden is one continued rock of granite, covered with fir : hence
the cottages, which are only one story high, and many of the superior houses, are constructed of wood, the planks of which are let
into each other in a layer of moss, and the outside is painted of a
red colour; the roof is formed with the bark of the birch, and

covered with turf, which generally presents a bed of grass sufficiently high for the scythe of the mower. The floors of the
rooms are strewed with the slips of young fir, which give them the
appearance of litter and disorder, and the smell is far from being
pleasant. Nothing can be more dreary than winding through the
forests, which every now and then present to the weary eye little
patches of cleared ground, where firs had been felled by fire, the
stumps of which, to a considerable height, were left in the ground,
and, at a distance, resembled so many large stones. Inexhaustible
abundance of wood induces the peasant to think it labour lost to
root them up, and they remain to augment the general dreariness
of the scenery.

The population in both the provinces of Scania and Smaland is
very thinly diffused : except in the very few towns between Flensborg and Stockholm, the abode of man but rarely refreshes the
eye of the weary traveller. At dawn of day, and all day long, he
moves in a forest, and at night he sleeps in one. The only birds
we saw were woodpeckers. The peasantry are poorly housed and
clad ; yet, amidst such discouraging appearances, their cheeks
boast the bloom of health and the smile of content. Their cloaths
and stockings are generally of light cloth; their hats raised in the
crown, pointed at top, with a large broad rim, and round their
waist they frequently wear a leathern girdle, to which are fastened
two knives in a leather case. The country in these provinces appears to be very sterile; only small portions of its rocky surface
were covered with a sprinkling of vegetable mould.

One day, wearied by the eternal repetition of firs, we were, without the least preparation, suddenly enlivened by the sounds of a
military band, and an abrupt opening in the forest displayed, as
by enchantment, an encampment of a fine regiment of the Lind-
koping, or, as it is pronounced, Lindchipping infantry : their uniform, which is national, is blue faced with yellow. The instantaneous transition from the silence and gloom of woods to the
gaiety and bustle of the camp was very pleasing.

At the next post from this sprightly spot, whilst we were changing horses, our servant was again addressed by a respectable peasant, who, with a serious face, asked him, as he was a foreigner,
to be good enough to tell him in what part of the world his beloved king was. Heavens! thought I, how strange it is that these

virtuous people, who are so much attached to their sovereign, should not know where he is ; and how happy must that prince be who is enquired after with so much affection and solicitude !

We dined at Johnkopping, or, as the Swedes call it, Johnchippig: it is a well-built town of wooden houses, situated on the extremity of the lake Wettern, which is about one hundred English miles long. At dinner, here, and every where in Sweden, we found that the bread and cheese had in them an immense number of caraway seeds, by which they were not improved.

· In our road to Grenna we passed by the base of vast impending rocks, and commanding a fine view of this lake, upon which we saw an island about twelve miles long. The Weller lake, which lies further to the north-west, has, I am informed, two hundred trading vessels upon its bosom, many of which are ships of considerable tonnage, and its shores are so wide that ships are frequently out of sight of them.

I mentioned that sometimes the grass grew very high upon the houses ; a singular instance of this occurred just before we reached Nordkoping, or Nordchipping. We saw a sheep grazing upon the side of a smith's house, which was low ; an adjoining pigstye had afforded the poor animal an easy ascent, and he appeared to enjoy himself as comfortably as if he had been in a rich well-watered meadow.

Nordkoping is in East Gothland, is a large and handsome town, and ranks third to the capital ; but the appearance of so many houses covered with high grass excites an impression of poverty and wretchedness which their interior immediately dispels. The principal beauty of this place is produced by the waters of the river Motala, which, at that part, where the principal manufactories are, descends in broken masses with uncommon violence, and presents the appearance of a fine cascade. The town has a high mercantile character : its principal manufactories consist of brass, cloth, paper, and guns. We made a curious mistake here. · On the evening of our arrival, after tea, as we strolled in the streets, we were surprised to find them so silent and apparently deserted ; for we only saw very few persons who were slowly moving homewards : at length eleven distinct strokes of the church clock satisfied us that sleep had hushed the population of the town. At this time the light was equal to that of a fine day in London, which, united to our ignorance of the time, and to our having just drank tea when we ought to have supped, produced our error. We were pressed the next day to spend it with a very respectable inhabitant; but were obliged to decline his civilities, alledging that our horses were ordered. As the little compliment which he paid us is cha-racteristic of the hospitable urbanity of the well-bred people of this country, I must be permitted to state that our amiable friend re-plied—" It is the first time that a Swede ever doubted an English-" man; but I must attend you to the inn, to see if your reason be " a sincere one, that I may reclaim you if it is not; and if it is, " that I may see the last of you."

As we ascended the hills which surround Nordkoping, the scenery below was highly picturesque and beautiful, and is said to resemble that of Swisserland, consisting of vast rocks, lakes, forests of fir, and scattered hamlets. This was by far the finest prospect which I beheld in Sweden. It is singular that Sweden should abound with lakes and rivers, whilst Denmark, an adjoining coun-try, should be so destitute of both. Whilst our horses were changing at the next post, I walked forward, and was much en-chanted with the romantic scenery which surrounded a neat little peasant's cottage. Out flew my sketch-book and my pencil, but the latter would do nothing but write verses.

A SWEDISH COTTAGE.

Here, far from all the pomp ambition seeks,
　　Much sought, but only whilst untasted prais'd,
Content and Innocence, with rosy cheeks,
　　Enjoy the simple shed their hands have rais'd.

On a grey rock it stands, whose fretted base
　　The distant cat'ract's murm'ring waters lave;
Whilst, o'er its grassy roof, with varying grace,
　　The slender branches of the white birch wave.

Behind, the forest fir is heard to sigh,
　　On which the pensive ear delights to dwell;
And, as the gazing stranger passes by,
　　The grazing goat looks up and rings his bell.

Oh! in my native land, ere life's decline,
May such a spot, so wild, so sweet, be mine!

Fortunate would it be for the peasantry, as well as the traveller, if I could present this cottage as a representation of all the cottages in Sweden. In the interior of these abodes of simplicity, a stranger is struck with the pastoral appearance of lines of large round cakes of bread, made of rye and oats, as broad as a common plate, and about the thickness of a finger, with a hole in the middle, through which a string or stick is passed, and suspended from the ceilings: this bread is very hard, but sweet. The peasants bake only once, at most twice, in the year: in times of scarcity they add the bark of the birch well pounded, the hard consistency of which requires the jaws of a stone-eater to penetrate. The family presents a perpetual scene of industry in weaving coarse cloths, spinning thread, or carding flax. They drink a poor wretched beer; but, in most of their post-houses, a traveller is sure to find excellent coffee and sugar. Amongst the peasantry we saw several Swedish women with black crape veils: in the winter they afford protection to the eye against the glare of the snow; and, in the summer, against the fierce and sparkling reflection of the sun upon the rocks. We were surprised to find that almost the only currency of the country was paper. I never saw, although I understood the coin had been much improved, but one bit of silver, from our entering until we quitted Sweden.

Upon our arrival at Feltja, the last post to the capital, our *vorbode* took leave of us, and expressed very affectionately his regret that he could not proceed with our luggage farther. We were much pleased with his civility on the road; for he halted every evening at the same inn with us, and started three or four hours before us every morning, to have our horses ready at the different posts; and indeed I never saw a more frank, honest-looking fellow.

We entered the suburbs of Stockholm over a long floating bridge under a gate, and, at the custom-house which adjoins it, we underwent a rigorous examination, which we could neither mitigate by money nor persuasion: it was the delay only that we dreaded. The search, however, introduced us to a very interesting secret. Just as I had finished, in my careless way, sitting upon one of the trunks which had been strapped, a little eulogium in my memorandum-book upon the simple fidelity of our young Swede, we discovered the cause of his having so tenderly regretted that he could proceed no farther with us than

Feltja. His *vorbodeship* had, during his custody of our trunks, picked their locks, and made free with a great coat, nankeen breeches, some shirts and handkerchiefs; but what our poor servant, who partook of the loss, regretted most, although I never witnessed greater philosophy in grief, was a golden locket, given to him by some cherry-lipp'd princess or another, to prevent the usual effects of time and distance on roving lovers. Some wanderers, like Voltaire's traveller, who, observing that the host of the first inn he entered had carotty locks, made a memorandum that all the men of that country were red-haired, would, from this unexpected development, have protested against the honesty of all Sweden. Heavens! what a fool should I have been, had I permitted the felonious treachery of this fellow to make me think unworthily of a race of men through ages so justly renowned for their valour and their virtue: perhaps Sweden never enrolled this man amongst her children. The forbidden fruit too was placed close to his lips, and all suspicion and vigilance withdrawn; and forlorn indeed would be the condition of society, if property had no other protection than an appeal to the virtues of mankind. Our misfortune, however, was a feather, compared to that which befel an English merchant on this very spot a few days before, who was proceeding to Petersburg; and, as it may operate as a serviceable caution, I shall mention it. In his packages were some English bonnets, gloves, and shoes, presents to some beloved sisters: the rude talons of the law pounced upon the whole collection, and condemned their unfortunate bearer to the penalty of £130. Having replaced our goods and chattels, we proceeded, passing through a suburbal part of more than an English mile long, terribly paved with large unwieldy and unequal stones, and entered the city, which promised us great gratification. We drove to the *Hotel Francais*, so called perchance, because not a soul in the house could speak a word of French. Like Bottom's idea, in the Midsummer Night's Dream, " I will get Peter Quince to write a ballad of this " dream: it shall be called *Bottom's Dream*, because it hath *no* " *bottom*." After groping up a dark winding stone staircase, we were, with much difficulty, shewn into a comfortable suite of apartments. It is surprising that the hotels in Stockholm are so few and so bad.

L

CHAP. VII.

NATIONAL WELCOME—BRIEF DESCRIPTION OF STOCKHOLM—A GREAT
GENIUS IN DECLINE—PAINTING—SHORT SKETCH OF GUSTAVUS III
—FEMALE STRATAGEM—THE PALACE—STATE BED—THE OPERA-
HOUSE—ASSASSINATION—FORGIVENESS—A HINT NOT INTENDED TO
OFFEND.

IN the morning our slumbers were gently dispelled by music,
which " came o'er our ears like the sweet south." According to
the custom of the country, several musicians, I believe belonging
to the military band, serenaded us at our chamber door, with some
exquisite soft national airs, which induced us to rise. After breakfast we ascended an eminence of rock called Mount Moses, in the
south suburb, from whence we beheld in a bird's eye view this
singular and beautiful city, which appears to be a little larger than
Bristol, is situated in 59 deg. 20 min. of northern latitude, and
stands upon a small portion of two peninsulas and seven islands
of grey granite, washed by a branch of the Baltic, the lake Mæler
and the streams that flow from it. The palace, a large quadrangular building, uniting elegance to grandeur, rises from the centre
of the city, which it commands in all directions. It will be more
particularly described afterwards. The merchants' houses, which
are in the south suburb, run parallel with the spacious quay, and
front the ships which are moored close to it, are lofty, and in a
graceful style of Italian architecture. Most of the buildings, rising
amphitheatrically one above another, are either stone or brick stuccoed, of a white or light yellow colour, and the roofs are covered
with dark or light brown tiles, and presents with the surrounding
scenery of scattered half-covered rock, thin forests of fir, the lake,
and the windings of the Baltic, a most romantic and enchanting
prospect. The streets are very badly paved.

The reputation of Sergell the statuary speedily attracted us to
his house, where we beheld his beautiful Cupid and Psyche, which
he has determined shall not be sold, until that event shall have happened which stops and sanctifies the works of genius. These
figures display the finest conceptions of feeling, grace, and ele-

gance, and heartily did I rejoice to find it in that country, which I trust will never permit it to be removed. In a temporary building, we had also the gratification of seeing the colossal pedestrian statue of the late Gustavus III, in bronze, which had just been cast, and was then polishing: it is a present from the citizens of Stockholm, and will cost when finished, 40,000l. and is intended to commemorate the marine victory, obtained by that illustrious prince over the Russians, in 1790. The King, with a mild but intrepid countenance, which I was informed is a most faithful likeness of him, is represented holding a rudder in one hand, and extending an olive branch with the other: he is attired in the very graceful costume which he introduced, resembling that of the old Spanish, and the feet are sandalled. It is a noble work of art, and may, in all human probability, be considered as the last effort of its distinguished author: a pedestal of one solid block of porphyry is already raised near the palace, to receive it upon the quay, which in that part is formed into a crescent.

Sergell, so long and so justly celebrated, is rapidly descending into the vale of years, and although honoured and enriched, a morbid melancholy, such as might arise from neglect and poverty, disrobes his graceful occupation of her attractions, and renders him disgusted with himself and with the world. It has been said, and very justly, that only extreme mental wretchedness can make a man indifferent to the applauses of his fellow-creatures: such is the forlorn case of the great but hapless Sergell; the friends of his youth have no charm for him, the admiration of his countrymen and of foreigners no exhilaration. Visible only to his workmen, and that reluctantly, the illustrious artist is sinking into the melancholy misanthrope; but when his hand shall no longer display its skill, taste will worship, and wealth will covet, the marble which it has touched, and time will enrol his name amongst the most favoured sons of Genius.

In painting, the two Martins, who are brothers, may be considered as reflecting considerable honour upon their country; one of them, I believe the youngest, has painted and engraved a series of views of Stockholm with great fidelity and beauty.

In the academy of sculpture and painting, raised by Adolphus Frederick, are some fine casts, said to be the first impressions of the only moulds ever permitted to be taken from the antiques at

Rome: they were given to Charles XI, by Louis XIV. There
are also some casts from the bas-reliefs of Trajan's column. The
children of tradesmen are gratuitously taught to draw in this institution, that their minds may be furnished with impressions of
taste in those trades which are susceptible of them. All the
pupils furnish their own crayons and paper: out of the funds of
the academy, a certain number are sent into foreign countries to
improve themselves. The funds, unaided, would be inadequate
to the object, but the munificence of public spirited individuals,
which throughout Sweden is very great, has hitherto supplied
the deficiency.

The academy of sciences was founded in 1739, and consists of
one hundred members and foreign associates. Their researches,
reputed to possess considerable learning and ability, are published
every three months in the Swedish language. The cabinet of
natural history is enriched with several rare collections, particularly with subjects which occurred in one of captain Cook's
circumnavigations, deposited in the academy by Mr. Sparmann.

Most of the living artists of Sweden owe their elevation and
consequent fame to the protective hand of the late king, Gustavus
III, a prince, who, to the energies and capacities of an illustrious
warrior, united all the refined elegances of the most accomplished
gentleman: his active spirit knew no repose; at one time the
world beheld him amidst the most formidable difficulties and
dangers, leading his fleets to glory in the boisterous billows of the
Baltic; at another time it marked him amidst the ruins of Italy,
collecting with a sagacious eye, and profuse hand, the rich materials for ameliorating the taste and genius of his own country.
What Frederic the Great was to Berlin, Gustavus the Third was
to Stockholm: almost every object which embellishes this beautiful city arose from his patronage, frequently from his own designs, and will be durable monuments of that capacious and
graceful mind, which, had not death arrested, would, in the profusion of its munificence, have impoverished the country which
it adorned. This prince derived what hereditary talent he possessed from his mother Ulrica, who, by a capacious and highly
cultivated mind, displayed that she was worthy of being the sister
of Frederic the Great. Her marriage with Adolphus Frederic
was the fruit of her own unassisted address, which, as it has

some novelty, I shall relate : The court and senate of Sweden
sent an ambassador *incognito* to Berlin, to watch and report upon
the characters and dispositions of Frederic's two unmarried sisters, Ulrica and Amelia, the former of whom had the reputation
of being very haughty, crafty, satirical and capricious ; and the
Swedish court had already pretty nearly determined in favour of
Amelia, who was remarkable for the attraction of her person and
the sweetness of her mind. The mission of the ambassador was
soon buzzed abroad, and Amelia was overwhelmed with misery;
on account of her insuperable objection to renounce the tenets of
Calvin for those of Luther : in this state of wretchedness she
implored the assistance of her sister's counsels to prevent an
union so repugnant to her happiness. The wary Ulrica advised
her to assume the most insolent and repulsive deportment to every
one, in the presence of the Swedish ambassador, which advice
she followed, whilst Ulrica put on all those amiable qualities which
her sister had provisionally laid aside : every one, ignorant of the
cause, was astonished at the change ; the ambassador informed
his court, that fame had completely mistaken the two sisters, and
had actually reversed their reciprocal good and bad qualities.
Ulrica was consequently preferred, and mounted the throne of
Sweden, to the no little mortification of Amelia, who too late
discovered the stratagem of her sister and her adviser.

A traveller will find much gratification in occasionally dining
at the merchants' club, to which strangers are introduced by subscribers ; here we found the dinners excellent, and served up in
a handsome style at a very moderate expense ; the apartments
are elegant, consisting of a noble dinner-room, an anti-room, a
billiard-room, and a reading-room where the foreign papers are
taken in. The view from the rooms over the Mæler, upon the
rocky cliffs, crowned with straggling parts of the suburbs, is
very beautiful. There is another club superior to this in style
and expense, but as the rooms were under repair, its meetings
were suspended. One afternoon, as I was quitting the merchants'
club to go to the church of Ridderholm, the quay in that quarter
presented an uncommonly crowded appearance of gaiety and vivacity ; the little canal which runs under the bridge leading to
the church was covered with boats filled with garlands and small
poles wreathed with flowers ; the old and the young, the lame

and the vigorous, pressed eagerly forward to purchase these rural
decorations, destined to honour the festival of St. John, which
was to take place the following day.

The national religion of Sweden is Lutheran, but without jealousy it is pleased with seeing every man worship his God in his
own way.

The palace is well worthy of notice: it is built of brick stuccoed,
and stained of a light yellow, the four sides of which are visible to
the different quarters of the city.   This very elegant edifice was
begun by Charles XI and finished by Gustavus III: it is composed
of four stories, three large and one small; in the front are twenty-three noble windows; ten Doric columns support a like number of Ionic cariatides, surmounted by ten Corinthian pilasters;
the roof is Italian.   At either end of the grand entrance, which
faces the north suburbs, is a bronze lion; the basement story is of
granite, and the arch of the doors towards the quay are composed
of rude masses of that rock; on this side there are parterres over
two projecting galleries, and a garden; the chapel is very rich,
and opposite to it is the hall for the meeting of the Estates, where
the seats are amphitheatrically arranged; those of the nobles on
the right of the throne, and those of the clergy, the bourgeois,
and peasants on the left; there is a gallery round it, and the
whole has a grand effect.   As only the senators and their ladies
have the privilege of entering the grand court in their carriage on
court days, those who are not possessed of this rank are as much
exposed in bad weather as the English ladies of fashion are when
they pay their respects to their Majesties at St. James's, where
many a fair one, enveloped in a mighty hoop, is frequently obliged
to tack according to the wind.   Not many years since, an erect
stately duchess dowager, in endeavouring to reach her carriage,
right in the wind's eye, was completely blown down.

I consider myself fortunate in seeing the King's museum immediately after the opening of several packages containing five
hundred valuable paintings and antique statues from Italy, where
they had been purchased about eleven years since, by Gustavus
III, but owing to the French revolution and the wars which it
engendered, were prevented from reaching the place of their des-
tination before: they lay in great confusion, and some of them
were much damaged.   Among the antique statues were those of

Cicero and Caracalla, wonderfully fine. The state-rooms are on the third story, to which there is a most tedious ascent, under arcades of porphyry. Prince Charles's apartments, which are the first, are superb: his little drawing-room is well worthy of notice, the seats of which are in the form of a divan: at their back is a vast magnificent horizontal mirror, the frame of which is of yellow and purple-coloured glass, and was presented by the reigning Emperor of Russia. The Queen's apartments are elegant, but the windows are old fashioned, heavy, very large, high from the floor, and look into a quadrangular court; however, if they command no fine scenes in the summer, they are warmer in the winter, a better thing of the two in such a climate. There are several pretty little rooms, called cozing or chit-chat rooms; nothing could be more neat, snug, and comfortable, or better adapted for the enjoyments of unrestrained conversation. The King's apartments are very handsome, some of the rooms are adorned with beautiful Gobeline tapestry from Paris.

The chamber most interesting to us was that in which Gustavus III expired. We saw the bed on which he lay, from the time that he was brought wounded to the palace from the masquerade at the opera-house, until he breathed his last. In this room it was that the dying prince personally examined his murderer Ankerstroem, when he confessed his guilt, and was immediately ordered to retire. The general circumstances of this melancholy catastrophe are well known; perhaps it may not be as generally so, that Ankerstroem preserved such resolute coolness at the time of the perpetration of the deed, that, in order to make sure of his mark, as the King, who was dressed in a loose domino, and without a mask, was reclining, a little oppressed by the heat, against one of the side scenes, Ankerstroem placed his hands upon the back of the Sovereign, who, upon feeling him, turned shortly round, when the regicide fired. The King, who thought that he was a victim to French machinations, as he fell, exclaimed, " My assassin is a " Frenchman!" the consolation of the illustrious duke d'Enghein was denied him. The hero, the friend, and the idol of Sweden, perished by the hands of a Swede. As soon as this outrage was known, the most eminent surgeons flew to his relief. The first words which the King uttered, were to request that they would give him their candid opinion, observing, with great serenity, that

if he had only a few hours to live, he would employ them in
arranging the affairs of the state, and those of his family; and
that, in such an extremity, it would be unavailing to augment his
pains, and consume his time, in dressing his wound. The surgeon
having examined it, assured his Majesty that it was not danger-
ous; in consequence of this opinion he permitted it to be dressed,
and was conveyed to the palace. The next day an interesting
and affecting scene took place; the countess Fersen, the count
Brahé, and the baron de Geer, who had absented themselves for
a long period from court, were the first to enquire after the health
of the King, who requested them to enter the room where he was,
and received them with the most touching goodness, expressing
the cordial delight which he felt in seeing them thus forget their
animosities, in these memorable words: " My wound is not with-
" out a blessing, since it restores to me my friends." He lan-
guished in great torment for eighteen days. It is generally supposed that the malignant spirit of politics had no influence in this
horrible outrage, but that he fell the victim of private revenge and
fanatical disappointment. Several young men, who thought themselves aggrieved by the neglect of their prince, were concerned in
this conspiracy; but it was his dying request, which was observed,
that only Ankerstroem should suffer death. Upon the tomb of
this brave, eloquent, and magnanimous prince, should be engraved
the beautiful and beneficent sentence that appears in the new form
of government with which he presented the Swedes at the time of
the memorable revolution. " I regard it as the greatest honour
to be the first citizen amongst a free people." It has been asserted, and I believe with truth, that his sensibility towards the female
sex was far from being lively: he seldom cohabited with his
Queen. Strange to tell, gifted with acute feelings, and a warm
and brilliant imagination, this accomplished prince, of a race of
beautiful women, displayed an example of almost monkish continence. But, that love had not wholly renounced his heart, we
may infer from an anecdote of a little picture, which adorns one
of the apartments of the palace: it is a portrait of a lovely young
woman, of whom the King became enamoured during his tour in
Italy. Upon hearing of her death, he is said to have shed tears,
and displayed all the impassioned indications of an afflicted lover.
The royal library is very valuable, containing twenty thousand

volumes, and four hundred manuscripts. Amongst the collection are some precious books, particularly one called the *Codex Aureus*, from the great number of gilt letters which it contains. There are also two enormous latin MSS.; the vellum leaves of which are made of asses' skins, and are of an amazing size.

The Prince Royal, or heir apparent, a child between six and seven years of age, inhabited a part of this palace, which, instead of presenting the gay bustle of a court, bore all the appearance of neglect and desertion. The mysterious questions of the rustic were explained. The people of Sweden had not been gladdened with the presence of their young Sovereign and his beautiful Queen, to whom they are devotedly and deservedly attached, for a long space of time, during which the court had been removed to the territory of the Prince of Baden, the father of the Queen of Sweden. The effect of such an absence was felt and deplored every where. No doubt the virtuous suggestions of his own heart will speedily restore the King to his people, and another traveller will have the gratification which was denied me, of seeing him in the bosom of his country, where a Prince always appears to the most advantage. The King is said to possess a very amiable mind, and to regard the memory of his illustrious father with enthusiastic adoration; I contemplated a powerful proof of it in an obelisk of one solid block of porphyry, forty feet high; which is at once a monument of his taste and piety. I should not be doing justice to the King, were I not to mention the abhorrence which he, in common with his subjects, has manifested at the cold-blooded outrage committed against the person of the devoted duke d'Enghein.

The opera-house, built by Gustavus III, is an elegant square building: upon the architrave is inscribed, " *Patris Musis.*" The front is adorned with Corinthian columns and pilasters: the interior, which is small, and can not contain above nine hundred persons, is in the form of a broken ellipsis ; and, even by day-light (for there was no performance during our stay), appeared to be superbly decorated. The dresses and decorations of the performers, which solely belong to the crown, we were informed, are of great value ; and in these respects the Swedish opera is said to surpass every other in Europe. The royal seats are in the pit. Swedish plays are performed here, many of which were composed by the accomplished Gustavus III, whose taste in that species of

M

composition excited the literary jealousy of old Frederic the Great.
It was an admirable policy, worthy of such a genius as Gustavus,
to attach a nation to its own language, by making it that of the
stage; the surest, because the most flattering mode of raising it to
its utmost polish. The first Swedish opera ever performed was
Thetis and Peleus : the favourite national piece is Gustavus Vasa.
Upon the death of Gustavus III, the opera lost much of its attraction. When it is considered that, in his time, a ballet occupied
ninety personages of the light fantastic toe, and put into activity
no less than eighty fancy-dress makers, it was necessary that the
pruning knife should be used, to curtail these luxuriant suckers of
the state, the graceful, but too costly, growth of a princely and munificent mind. In this building there are some very handsome
apartments for the King's private parties. I had much to regret
that no plays were performed here during my stay.

The female, who shewed me the building, was much affected
when she pointed to the spot where Ankerstroem committed the
bloody deed. Alas! how inscrutable are the ways of Heaven!
When the illustrious victim raised this beautiful fabric from the
ground, he little thought of the part which he was to perform in
the sanguinary scene of the seventeenth of March, 1792, and that
mimic sorrow was to yield to genuine woe. This structure, and
the opposite palace of the Princess Sophia Albertina, the King's
aunt, which is uniform with the former, form the sides of a handsome square, called *la Place du Nord*, and is adorned in the centre
with a fine equestrian statue, in bronze, of Gustavus Adolphus,
who, excepting his head, which is crowned with laurel, is in
complete armour, and in his right hand is an inclined truncheon :
the horse has much animation, and the rider great elegance. This
colossal statue was cast from the designs of Archeveque, a very
distinguished French statuary, who dying before it was finished,
left its completion to the masterly hand of Sergell : it was erected
in 1790. The latter has introduced the figures of History pointing to an inscription on the pedestal, and of the chancellor Oxenstiern. The pedestal, which is of granite, is decorated by medallions of the principal favourite generals of Gustavus Adolphus,
viz. Torstenson, Baner, James de la Gardie, Horn, and Saxe Weimar; all by Sergell. The unbounded friendship and confidence
which existed between this great Prince and the upright Oxen-

stiern, form the theme of historic delight; and the gentle counter-
action of their mutual, and rather opposite, characters, rendered
each the idol and the benefactor of his country. It is said that
Gustavus having, upon·some affair of state, observed to Oxenstiern, that he was cold and phlegmatic, and that he checked him
in his career, the chancellor replied: " Sire, indeed I own that I
" am cold; but unless I had occasionally tempered and moderated
" your heat, you would have been burnt up long ago." Gustavus
Adolphus never engaged in any battle, without first praying at the
head of his troops; after which he used to thunder out, in a strong
and energetic manner, a German hymn, in which he was joined
by his whole army: the effect of thirty or forty thousand people
thus singing together was wonderful and terrible. He used to say,
that a man made a better soldier in proportion to his being a better
christian, and there was no person so happy as those who died in
the performance of their duty. Of the death of this great hero, it
was said, " that he died with his sword in his hand, the word of
" command in his mouth, and with victory in his imagination."
Only the complimentary part of the following witty epigram, which
was made upon the equestrian statue of Louis XIII, which formerly stood in the *Place des Victoires* in Paris, with the four cardinal virtues standing round it, would apply to that of Gustavus
Adolphus:

> O le beau monument! O le beau pédestal!
> Les Vertues sont à pied, et le Vice à cheval.
>
> Oh! noble statue, noble pedestal!
> Vice proudly rides, the Virtues are on foot.

In front of this statue, to the south, the eye with pleasure contem-
plates an elegant stone bridge not quite finished, crossing a rapid
stream of the Mæler, at the end of which the palace displays a
majestic and highly graceful back scene: this spot presents the
finest architecture in the city.

The traveller will be gratified, by noticing the beautiful colonnade of solid porphyry which forms the entrance to the grand
staircase of the Princess Sophia Albertina's palace. A tasteful
observer must regret that these exquisite columns are so much
concealed. The streets of the Queen and of the Regency, in

the north quarter, are by far the most handsome, and form the residence of fashion.   The spire and church of Ridderholm, rising from the centre of the principal island, add to the romantic beauties of the surrounding scenery.   The interior of this edifice, which is large and heavy, is only worthy of notice, on account of its containing the ashes of such illustrious personages as Gustavus Adolphus and his equal in bravery, but neither in prudence nor justice, Charles XII, who carried the system of daring to pretty nearly its utmost extent, and, in his end, verified the words of the great dramatist:

> " Glory is like a circle in the water
> Which never ceaseth to enlarge itself,
> Till, by broad spreading, it disperse to nought."

The tomb of the latter is very simple and characteristic: it is of black marble, upon which are thrown a lion's skin and club, in bright yellow bronze.   In another part of the building are the ashes of a general much more entitled to the admiration of posterity, the illustrious John Baner, who was deservedly the favourite of the great Gustavus Adolphus, and who, after a series of splendid victories, expired on the tenth of May, 1641.

CHAP. VIII.

A VISIT IN THE COUNTRY—OBSERVATORY—DINNER AND FASHIONS
—BLOOMING GIRLS OF DELECARLIA—DROTTINGHOLM—QUEEN
CHRISTINA'S CUNNING—WARDROBE OF CHARLES XII—BEAUTY—
CONCEALMENT AND PRUDERY—NATIONAL IMPORTANCE OF A BRI-
TISH ADVOCATE—CONTRASTED JUSTICE—HAGA—CAUSE OF THE
FRIENDSHIP OF GUSTAVUS III FOR SIR SIDNEY SMITH—A SINGU-
LAR ANECDOTE—A REVIEW—IRON MINES—LINNEUS.

AN invitation into the country enabled us to contemplate a little
of the rural character of the Swedes. In our way we passed by
the observatory, which stands upon an inconsiderable eminence in
the north suburbs: its horizon is too circumscribed on account
of the rocks which surround it; and as the artificial heat of stoves
would cloud the glasses in the winter nights, which are the best
for observation, it is of very little utility. Our ride to our friends
was occasionally very beautiful, but the funereal heads of our
old acquaintances the firs were ever and anon presenting themselves, and shedding melancholy upon us. The chateau to which
we were invited was of wood, small, but very tastefully fitted
up: the grounds, which were very extensive, were delightfully
laid out, and on one side rippled the waters of the Mæler,
embellished by vessels of various sizes gliding upon its tranquil
bosom. A short time before dinner was announced, a table was
set out with bread, cheese, butter, and liqueurs: all these good
things in this hospitable region are considered as mere prepara-
tives for the meal which is to follow; amongst the superior orders
this custom is universal. Our dinner was in the following order:
pickled fish, meats, soups, fish, pastry, ice, and dried fruits;
preserved gooseberries formed the sauce of the mutton, and the
fish floated in a new element of honey; by the by, it rather sur-
prises a stranger to meet with so little sea-fish in a country which
is washed by so many seas. The herring fishery, which has
hitherto been of so much importance to Sweden, has nearly
disappeared. To return to our dinner: each dish was carved

and handed round, as in Denmark; a regulation truly delightful to one who abhors carving and carves badly.

The spirit of French fashion, but a little disciplined, reigns in Sweden, and gives a lightness and elegance to dress: the table, and the furniture, and even their manners, partake considerably of its gaiety, except that as soon as our amiable and elegant hostess arose, upon our rising at the same time, we stood solemnly gazing upon each other for half a minute, and then exchanged profound bows and curtsies; these being dispatched, each gentleman tripped off with a lady under his arm, to coffee in the drawing-room. Nothing else like formality occurred in the course of the day.

Just as we were quitting this spot of cordial hospitality, we were stopped by the appearance of two fine female peasants from the distant province of Delecarlia: their sisterhood partake very much of the erratic spirit and character of our Welch girls: they had travelled all the way on foot, to offer themselves as haymakers; their food on the road was black bread and water, and their travelling wardrobe a solitary chemise, which, as cleanliness demanded, they washed in the passing brook, and dried on their healthy and hardy frame, which, however, was elegantly shaped; the glow of Hebe was upon their dimpled cheeks, not a little heightened by the sun, " which had made a golden set upon them;" their eyes were blue, large, sweet, and expressive; their dress was singular, composed of a jacket and short petticoat of various colours; and they were mounted upon wooden shoes with prodigious high heels, shod with iron. There was an air of neatness, innocence, delicacy and good humour about them, which would have made even a bilious spectator happy to look upon them. Unextinguishable loyalty, great strength of body, content, and sweetness of temper, beauty of face, and symmetry of person, are said to be the characteristics of the Delecarlian mountaineers, a race rendered for ever celebrated in the history of one of the greatest men that ever adorned the historic page of Sweden, Gustavus Vasa. It is thus he describes them, after he has discovered himself to them in the mines, in the beautiful language of the bard, whose dramatic genius has conspired to render his hero immortal:

—————— here last I came,
And shut me from the sun, whose hateful beams
Serv'd but to shew the ruins of my country.
When here, my friends, 'twas here at length I found
What I had left to look for: gallant spirits,
In the rough form of untaught peasantry.
Yes, I will take these rustic sons of Liberty
In the first warmth and hurry of their souls;
And should the tyrant then attempt our heights,
He comes upon his fate.

Led on by Gustavus Vasa, they restored liberty to their country,
and expelled the bloody tyrant, miscalled *Christian*. These, too,
were the peasants who, having heard in the midst of their mines
and forests that their sovereign Charles XII was a prisoner in
Turkey, dispatched a deputation to the Regency at Stockholm,
and offered to go, at their own expense, to the number of twenty
thousand men, to deliver their royal master out of the hands of
his enemies. Their sovereigns have ever found them the incor-
ruptible and enthusiastic supporters of the throne. Surrounded
with treason and peril, their king has found them faithful amongst
the faithless, and never sought their succour in vain. In consequence of the terrible defection which appeared in the Swedish
army in the campaign of the year 1788 against the Russians,
when, owing to the machinations of the Swedish traitor Spreng-
porten, who was in the pay of the Empress Catharine, the Swedish
officers, although confident of victory, refused to march, because
Gustavus III had commenced the war without consulting the
Estates, the King was compelled to retire to Stockholm, where
the insolence and intrigues of the nobility threatened the reduc-
tion of his regal rights to the mere phantom of sovereignty.
Menaced with revolt and assassination, this great prince, attended by a single domestic, in secrecy reached the mountains of
Delecarlia, the *immoveable seat of Swedish loyalty*, where, with
all that bold, affecting, and irresistible eloquence, for which he
was so justly famed, upon the very rock on which, in elder times,
their idol Gustavus Vasa had addressed them, he invoked them
to rally round the throne, and preserve their sovereign from the
cabals of treason. At the sound of his voice they formed themselves into battalions, with electric celerity, and encreasing as

they advanced, proceeded under the command of Baron Armfelt
to Drottingholm; where they overawed the factious. At this very
period, an unexpected disaster made fresh demands upon the
inexhaustible resources of Gustavus's mind, which encreased with
his emergencies. The Prince of Hesse, at the head of twelve
thousand men, marched from Norway to Gottenberg, at the
gates of which, at a late hour, the King, having surmounted
great difficulties in his way through Wermlandia, presented himself, and the next morning surprised the Danish herald, by informing him in person from the ramparts, that sooner than sur-
fender the place, the garrison should be buried under its ruins,
and accordingly ordered the bridge over the river Gothael to be
burnt. It is well known, that the wise and active mediation of
Mr. Elliott, our then minister at Copenhagen, prevailed upon
the Prince of Hesse to retire. To return to the Delecarlians:
the dress of the men is always of a grey or black coarse cloth,
and, on account of the many services which they have rendered
to government, and their proved patriotism, they enjoy the flattering and gracious privilege of taking the King's hand wherever
they meet him: the pressure must ever be delightful to both parties. From the mountains of health and liberty, Gustavus III
selected the wet nurse of the present King, that, with her milk,
he might imbibe vigour and the love of his country. This woman was the wife of a Delecarlian peasant, lineally descended
from the brave and honest Andrew Preston, who preserved Gustavus Vasa from the murderers who were sent in pursuit of him
by Christian. The houses of the Delecarlian peasants are as
simple as their owners are virtuous: they have but one hole in
the roof, exposed to the south, which answers the double purpose
of a window and a clock: their meals are regulated by the sun's
rays upon a chest, placed beneath this hole on one side; or upon
the stove, with which all the Swedish houses are warmed, standing on the other.

We were much gratified with the palace of Drottingholm: a
pleasant drive of about ten miles brought us to the island on which
it stands in the lake Mæler; the road to it lay through rocks covered
with firs, and over two large floating bridges; the building is large
but light, and is of brick stuccoed white; the hall and staircase
are in bad taste; their ornaments are white upon a dark brown

ground, resembling sugar plums upon gingerbread. The state rooms are very rich and elegant, and an Englishman is much gratified to find in the library a very large and choice collection of English authors. There is a beautiful picture here of a weeping Ariadne, by Wertmuller, a Swedish artist, who, unfortunately for his country, has for ever left it, and settled in America.

Whenever I reflect upon a neglected artist of merit, a delightful little anecdote, which is related of Francis I, always occurs to me: that sovereign having received a picture of St. Michael from the hand of Raphael d'Urbino, which he much coveted, he renumerated Raphael far beyond what his modesty conceived he ought to receive: the generous artist, however, made him a present of a Holy Family, painted by himself, which the courteous monarch received, saying, that persons famous in the arts partake of the immortality of princes, and are upon a footing with them.

In this palace there is the head of a Persian Sybil, in mosaic, exquisitely beautiful, and two costly and elegant presents from the late Empress Catharine II, of tables of lapis lazuli and Siberian agate. There are also some exquisite statues in alabaster and marble, and Etruscan vases, purchased in Italy by Gustavus III, during his southern tour. The Etruscan vases are very beautiful; but in tone of colour, classical richness, elegance and variety of shape, not equal to those which I had previously seen in England at Gillwell Lodge, the seat of William Chinnery, esq. who unquestionably has the finest private collection of this kind in England, perhaps in Europe.

There is here a portrait of that eccentric personage Queen Christina, who abdicated the throne of Sweden in 1660, and left to her successor, Charles X, the costly discovery that, amidst all her whimsical caprices, she had taken good care to clear most of the palaces of their rarest furniture previous to her retiring to Rome: picking out even the jewels of the crown before she resigned it. So completely had she secured every thing that was valuable, that Charles X. was obliged to borrow several necessary utensils for his coronation. This loss, for I suppose it must not be called a depredation, has been amply restored by the taste and munificence of Gustavus III. In the state sleeping-chamber, the royal banner of light blue and silver was fixed at the foot of the bed, and had a a very chivalrous appearance. In the garden there is a theatre,

N

which is large and handsome; but since the death of Gustavus III, who was much attached to this place, and made it the seat of his brilliant festivities, it has been little used. In the gardens there is a range of small houses in the Chinese taste, but neither the former nor the latter are worthy of much notice.

After our return from Drottingholm we gained admission, but with much difficulty, to the arsenal. This depot of military triumphs is a brick-building, consisting of a ground floor, with lofty windows down to the ground, stands at the end of the King's gardens, the only mall of Stockholm, and has all the appearance of a large green-house. The artillery, which is planted before it, has the ridiculous effect of being placed there to defend the most precious of exotic trees within from all external enemies, who either move in air or pace the earth. The contents, alas! are such fruits " as the tree of war bears," and well deserve the attention of the traveller and antiquary. Here is an immense collection of trophies and standards taken from the enemies of Sweden, and a long line of stuffed kings, in the actual armour which they wore, mounted upon wooden horses, painted to resemble, and as large as life, chronologically arranged. I was particularly struck with the clothes of Charles XII, which he wore when he was killed at the siege of Frederickshall, and very proudly put them on, viz. a long shabby blue frock of common cloth, with large flaps and brass buttons, a little greasy low cocked hat, a handsome pair of gloves, fit to have touched the delicate hands of the countess of Koningsmark, a pair of stiff high-heeled military boots, perhaps it was one of those which he threatened to send to the senate at Stockholm, to which they were to apply for orders until his return, when they were impatient at his absence during his mad freaks in Turkey. As it is natural to think that great souls generally inhabit large bodies, my surprise was excited by finding that when I had completely buttoned the frock of this mighty madman upon my greyhound figure, my lungs gave sensible tokens of an unusual pressure from without. I must be indulged in giving the following extract from an account of this marvellous madcap, which was given by a person who had seen him, and who thus speaks of him: " His coat " is plain cloth, with ordinary brass buttons, the skirts pinned up " behind and before, which shews his Majesty's old leather waist- " coat and breeches, which they tell me are sometimes so greasy

" that they may be fried. But when I saw him they were almost
" new; for he had been a gallant a little before, and had been to
" see King Augustus's Queen upon her return from Leipsic, and,
" to be fine, he put on those new leather breeches, spoke not above
" three words to her, but talked to a foolish dwarf she had, about
" a quarter of an hour; and then left her. His hair is light brown,
" very greasy, and very short, *never combed but with his fingers.*
" At dinner he eats a piece of bread and butter, which he spreads
" with his thumbs."

Think of all this as applied to " the most powerful among the
" kings that worship Jesus; redresser of wrongs and injuries,
" and protector of right in the ports and republics of south and
" north; *shining in majesty,* love of honour and glory, and of our
" sublime Porte—Charles, King of Sweden, whose enterprises
" may God crown with success!"

The said blood-besprinkled gloves, and bullet-pierced hat have
furnished abundant and fatiguing sources of vague and violent
disputation: pages, nay volumes, have been written to ascertain
whether the death of Charles was fair or foul: a fact to be found
only in the records of Heaven, and of small import to be known
here. Let the blow have been given from whatever hand it may,
Sweden had good reason to bless it, and happy are those who live
in times which furnish but little of such materials for the page of
history, as Charles supplied:

Though Charles was said to possess a great coldness of character, the following anecdote will shew that he was susceptible of
flattery: Whilst the batteries of the citadel of Frederickshall were
firing heavily at the enemy's trenches, a young woman who was
looking at the King from an adjoining house, dropped her ring
into the street: Charles observing her said, " Madam, do the guns
" of this place always make such an uproar?" " Only when we
" have such illustrious visitors as your majesty," replied the girl.
The King was much pleased, and ordered one of his soldiers to
return the ring. This extraordinary being must have sometimes
excited the smiles, as he often did the tears, of mankind. After the
Turks, irritated by his refusal to depart, were obliged to burn his
house over his head, and by main force send him to Bender,
Charles XII, a fugitive, attended only by a few wretched followers,
ruined, and his coffers completely exhausted, wrote to his envoy

at the court of Louis XIV, to send him the exact ceremonials of that brilliant and magnificent court, that he might immediately adopt them.

Hurried away by kings, palaces, and statues, I have to my shame (my cheek reddens whilst I write) staid thus long in Stockholm ere I noticed those, without whom a crown is unenviable, the most magnificent abode cheerless, and of whom the most graceful images of art are but imperfect imitations. The Swedish ladies are in general remarkably well shaped, *enbonpoint*, and have a fair transparent delicacy of complexion, yet, though the favourites of bountiful nature, strange to relate, they are more disposed to conceal than display those charms, which in other countries, with every possible assistance, the fair possessor presents to the enraptured eye to the best advantage. A long gloomy black cloak covers the beautiful Swede when she walks, confounding all the distinctions of symmetry and deformity ; and even her pretty feet, which are as neat and as well turned as those of a fine Frenchwoman, are seldom seen without the aid of a favouring breeze. Even the sultry summer has no influence in withdrawing this melancholy drapery, but I am informed that it is less worn now than formerly : often have I wished that the silk-worm had refused his contribution towards this tantalizing concealment : occasionally the streets of Stockholm displayed some bewitching seceders from the abominable habit. This custom arises from the sumptuary laws, which forbid the use of coloured silks.

The Swedish ladies are generally highly accomplished, and speak with fluency English, French, and German, and their tenderness and sensibility by no means partake of the severity of their northern latitude ; yet they exhibit two striking characteristics of whimsical prudery : In passing the streets a Swedish lady never looks behind her, nor does she ever welcome the approach or cheer the departure of a visitor by permitting him to touch the cherry of her lips ; the ardent admirer of beauty must be content to see that

> ———— Welcome ever smiles,
> And farewel goes out sighing.

This chilling custom is somewhat singular, when it is considered that the salutation of kissing, even between man and man, hateful as it is to an untravelled Englishman, prevails almost in every part of the continent.

I was very desirous of attending the courts of justice, or as they are called the *kamners-retter*, of which there are four in Stockholm; but I found they were all close, and only the judges and parties and necessary officers permitted to enter. What a contrast to the unreserved openness with which the laws in England are administered! By unfolding the gates of justice, and displaying her in all her awful majesty, her ordinances become widely promulgated, and the respect paid to her decrees augmented by the reverence which is excited by her presence; her seat is not only the depository of the law, but of all descriptions of learning, and is a school of eloquence in which the language of the country receives its highest polish. Of what national importance the powers of an illustrious advocate may become, let those say, who have witnessed the brilliant genius, exalted persuasion, and profound knowledge of an Erskine, and can trace their consequences to a country which knows how to appreciate them. The laws of Sweden are considered to be simple, mild, clear, and just; and, since the labours of Gustavus III, to render them so, have been impartially administered. In civil causes each party pays his own costs, (this must frequently be unjust; but whilst Sweden, however, may learn something from the manner in which the laws are dispensed in England, she presents to our admiration a spirit which we should do well to imitate: the prosecutor sustains no share whatever of the expenses of prosecuting a criminal.

In England there is a highly important society, first established by the celebrated Sir John Fielding, the objects of which are actively and ably conducted by its solicitor and secretary, S. S. Hunt, esq. for prosecuting felons. These objects are to prevent the impunity which too frequently follows depredation, from the heavy *extra* expenses which often attend the discovery, apprehension, and trial, of delinquents, by raising a yearly subscription fund to indemnify the suffering individual who prosecutes in the name of the Crown. How a foreigner who takes a keen and close peep at us, must be surprised to observe an institution, which, whilst it exhibits the patriotic spirit of individuals, reflects with not a little justified severity, upon the absence of a legislative provision, which is of so much consequence to the country. It may be said, that there are a certain description of these expenses which a judge in his discretion may allow *upon application.* The natural pride of a respectable British subject, to whom such expenses may prove an object, ought not, in the performance of a great public duty, in which the repose of the nation is concerned, and the King in consequence the avowed and recorded prosecutor, to be put to the blush by asking for it in *forma pauperis.* This most just indemnity ought to form a part of the law of the land. By another admirable provision Sweden is enabled to ascertain the state of her population every third year, and which is effected by the periodical returns from the clergymen and magistrates, of the births, deaths, marriages, and the number of inhabitants that are living in their several districts; a measure highly worthy of adoption in England.

The laws of Sweden, the most novel to an Englishman, are those by which primogeniture is disrobed of those exclusive rights which attach to it in other countries; all the male children of a nobleman are equally noble, but, to prevent the confusion of numbers, the eldest only, upon the decease of the father, represents the family at the Diet, and all inheritances are equally divided, but created property is subject to the will of the father.

The punishments in Sweden are beheading, hanging, whipping, and imprisonment: the three former are inflicted in the market-place; the instrument of flagellation is a rod of tough birch twigs. There is a horrid custom in Sweden, as odious as our hanging malefactors in chains, of exposing the naked bodies of delinquents who have suffered death, extended by their limbs to trees, until they rot. Two or three of these shocking objects occur in terrorem upon the road from Gotheberg to Stockholm, on account of its being a greater thoroughfare, and more robberies have been committed there. The criminal laws of Sweden may be considered as mild, and the punishment of death is rarely inflicted.

I was rather disappointed upon seeing the House of Nobles; it contains the hall and room which are reserved for that branch of the Diet, and which, as it is now convened at the will of the sovereign, may be considered as a mere phantom of power. If the authority of the states were any thing better than nominal, the country gentlemen would have some cause to complain, as they are wholly excluded from any legislative participation, this shadowy representation being confined, and it was even so when the Diet was in its plenitude of power, and held the Sovereign dependent, to the nobles, clergy, citizens, and peasants. The exterior of the building is simple but handsome. In the square before the House of Nobles is the pedestrian statue of Gustavus Vasa, by Meyer, erected by the nobles at a great expense, but in my humble opinion unworthy of the immortal man whose memory it is intended to perpetuate.

A delightful morning attracted me to Haga, which is at the short distance of a mile and a half English from the north gate of the city. As this little palace and gardens were built and disposed after the design of the graceful Gustavus III, with the assistance of Masrelior, and were the favourite retreat of the former, my gratification was certain. The approach to the villa is through a winding walk of luxuriant shrubs, the most flourishing and beautiful of any that I saw in the north : at a small distance there is a line of picturesque rocks, crowned with firs ; and at the bottom of a rich meadow, by the side of the Mœler, presenting a noble sheet of water, surrounded with forests of fir, stands the chateau, built of wood, and painted to resemble stone, containing a small front of three stories, and two long gallery wings. The grounds and ornamental buildings reminded me of the *Petit Trianon* of the unfortunate Queen of France at Versailles. The rooms are small, but elegantly fitted up. Gustavus spent much of his time here ; it is said that this spot was particularly endeared to him, on account of his having secretly consulted with his friends, in the recesses of the rocks, which constitute one of the great beauties of the scenery, upon the revolution of 1772. This circumstance induced him, when he travelled, to assume the title of count Haga. Adjoining, upon an eminence, is the foundation of a vast palace, which Gustavus III commenced in the year 1791, but which has never advanced since his death. The undertaking was too vast and expensive for the country, and is very judiciously laid aside by the reigning sovereign.

In the library I was gratified by seeing several drawings and architectural designs of its accomplished founder, which displayed much taste and genius. The friendship and confidence with which this prince honoured the heroic Sir Sidney Smith is well known ; the King first conceived an attachment for him from the resemblance which he thought, and which he frequently was heard to observe, existed between the face of the hero of Acre and Charles XII.

As Sir Sidney is one of my favourite heroes, I will run the hazard of being blamed for deviating from my narrative a little, and for detaining the reader an extra moment, to relate a singular prepossession he felt, when a youth, of his fame, and the theatre of his future glory, which has just occurred to my memory. Being sent, some years since, on shore upon the Irish coast with a brother officer, who is now holding a deservedly high situation in the service, to look for some deserters from their ship, after a long, fatiguing, and fruitless pursuit, they halted at a little inn to refresh themselves; having dined, Sir Sidney on a sudden became silent, and seemed lost in meditation: " My dirk for your thoughts," exclaimed his friend, gently tapping him on the shoulder; " what " project, Sidney, has got possession of you now ?" " My good " fellow," replied the young warrior, his expressive countenance brightening as he spoke, " you will no doubt suppose me a little " disordered in my mind, but I have been thinking that, before " twelve years shall have rolled over my head, I shall make the " British arms triumphant in Holy Land." We need not knock at the cabinet door of St. Cloud to know how splendidly this prediction was verified.

In the afternoon, after our return from Haga, we went on the Baltic to the park, situate on the east side of the city, three English miles distant, to see a review and sham fight of about four thousand troops, encamped there. The park is a place of great resort in fine weather, like our Hyde-park. Our water excursion was delightful. The manœuvres commenced at five o'clock in the evening, upon the arrival of the Prince Royal, a little sickly child about six years old, who on this occasion represented his father. He passed the line in an open carriage drawn by six horses, attended by some military officers and two pages of his household, followed by an escort of body guards. After the pages, who wore a Spanish costume, consisting of a jacket of stone-coloured cloth, with slashed sleeves and a short robe, had seated their little charge upon a rock, jutting out of a rising ground, the regiments were put in motion, and displayed a strong, martial, and well-disciplined body of men. When the bloodless battle was concluded, the regiments passed in open order before the Prince, who with great docility

held his little hat in his hand during the ceremony, then remount-
ed his carriage and returned to his nursery. The costume of the
two pages was the only relic, I met with, of the fantastic change
which Gustavus III produced in the dress of his subjects; the difficulty and danger of which, it is said, was artfully suggested by
Catherine II, when he visited her at Petersburgh, in order to induce his pride and spirit more ardently to attempt the change by
which she secretly hoped that he would disgust the Swedes, and
thereby induce them to attempt the restoration of the fallen privileges of the states, overturned by the celebrated revolution,
which he effected by his fortitude, consummate address, and eloquence. It was one of the distinguishing marks of the policy of
the modern Semiramis of the north, to embroil her royal neighbours in perpetual conflict with each other, or with their own subjects. The Swedes were too loyal, too good tempered, and too
wise to quarrel with their Prince, and such a Prince as Gustavus
III, about the cut of a coat; but they reluctantly adopted a fashion
which had no similitude in the north, and assimilated them in
appearance with a people who bear no analogy to them but in national honour, the subjects of his Castilian Majesty. Before we
left the camp, we presented a fine little peasant boy, who was
playing near us, with some fruit; his mother sent him to thank
us, which he did by kissing our hands: a token of gratitude all
over the north.

The military force of Sweden is divided into regular or garrison
regiments, and *national militia:* only the latter will require some
explanation. The levies for this establishment are made from
the lands belonging to the crown, the holders of which contribute
not only to the support of the troops, but of the clergy and civil
officers. The estates are called Hemans, and divided into rottes;
each rotte is charged in a settled proportion; the most valuable
with the support of cavalry, the others with that of infantry. The
men, thus selected from the very heart of the peasantry, are almost always healthy, stout, and well-proportioned. In war and
in peace, the crown land-holders are compellable gratuitously to
transport these levies and their baggage to their respective regiments, and to allot a cottage and barn, a small portion of ground,
and to cultivate it during the absence of the soldier upon the ser-

O

vice of government, for the support of his family, and also to supply him with a coarse suit of cloaths, two pair of shoes, and a small
yearly stipend. In peace, where the districts adjoin, the soldiers
assemble by companies every Sunday after divine worship, to be
exercised by their officers and serjeants. Before and after harvest,
the regiment is drawn out and encamped in its district for three
weeks. In every third or fourth year, encampments of several
regiments together are formed in some province, which is generally the centre of many districts; and, during the rest of their
time, these *martial husbandmen*, who are enrolled for life, are permitted to work as labourers for the landholder, at the usual price
of labour. Such is a brief abstract of the manner in which this
great constitutional force, " this cheap defence of nations," is or-
ganized.

Upon our return from the review, we were much gratified with
seeing the gun-boats from the Admiralty Isle manœuvre. These
vessels are used upon the lake Mæler, amongst the rocks, and on
the coast of Finland; but are incapable of weathering high seas or
strong winds: some of them are of forty-four oars, and carry twenty-four pounders in their bow.

Although it was the twenty-eighth of June, it was so chilly,
that I began to give credit to a remark that the north has two
winters, a *white and a green one*. We now prepared to make a
little excursion to Upsala, and the mines of Danmora, distant
about eighty-five English miles: for this expedition we hired a
little light phæton for one plote and sixteen skillings per day:
this vehicle required only two horses, and was well adapted to
the cross roads. The prevailing carriage, used by the respectable part of the inhabitants, is a gig, with a small seat behind
for a servant, who at a distance appears to be holding by the
queue of his master, and has altogether a very whimsical effect.

The traveller, whose time is not limited, would do well to visit
the founderies of Sahlahutta, the silver mines of Sahlberg and of
Herstenbotten; Afvestad, where the copper is refined; Norberg,
remarkable for its very curious mineral productions; Fahlun, the
capital of the heroic Delecarlians, the famous silver mines of
Kopparberg, the cataracts of Elfscarleby, Mr. Grill's anchor-

forge at Suderfors; at all which places, as well as at Danmora, the natural treasure and phenomena of Sweden are displayed in the most interesting and sublime manner. To secure admission to most of these places, it will be adviseable to procure letters of introduction to the proprietors or inspectors. Pressed, as I have before stated myself to have been for time, my election fell upon the mines of Danmora, and a visit to Upsala.

The country through which we passed, with our accustomed celerity, was rather rich and picturesque, and in many parts a-bounded with corn-fields; but as we approached Upsala, and afterwards Danmora, the scenery became bleak and dreary. The first evening we slept at Upsala, and very early the next morning proceeded to Danmora, where we arrived in time to hear the blowing of the rock, which commences every day at twelve o'clock precisely. As we were looking down the principal mouth of the mine, which presented a vast and frightful gulf, closing in impenetrable darkness, our ears were assailed by the deep-toned thunder of the explosion below, which rolled through the vast and gloomy caverns of this profound abyss, in sounds the most awful and sublime: frequently large masses of rock are thrown out by the violence of the discharge. In these mighty excavations, the hand of man has toiled for three centuries. These mines produce a vast quantity of ore of a superior quality, much used in the British steel manufactories. Feeling an invincible disinclination to descend the principal pit in a bucket, we reached the bottom of another abyss, about four hundred feet deep, by crazy ladders placed almost perpendicularly, a mode which was attended with much trouble and considerable peril: we found the bottom covered with indissoluble ice. Our curiosity was speedily satisfied, and we gladly regained the summit. Mark the force of habit! Two elderly miners stepped from the firm earth upon the rim of a bucket, which hung over this dizzy depth, and, holding the cord, descended; one singing, and the other taking snuff. The hydraulic machinery by which the mines are kept dry, move a chain of six thousand feet, which, after drawing the water from the mine, forces it through an aqueduct of five thousand feet: this mine is called the Peru of Sweden. From the mines we proceeded to Mr. Tanner's forges at Osterby, about one English mile off, where one thousand persons are employed:

———Bath'd in the laborious drop
Of painful industry.———

The ore, as it comes from the mine, is piled upon layers of fir,
and partially melted: it is then pounded by vast hammers moved
by water, afterwards liquefied in a furnace of charcoal, whence
it runs into a long mould of sand, where, as soon as it hardens,
it is drawn out and laid in piles in the open air.   These enormous
rough pieces are again melted, and beaten into bars for exportation.

See, pale and hollow-eyed, in his blue shirt,
Before the scorching furnace, reeking stands
The weary smith! a thundering water-wheel
Alternately uplifts his cumbrous pair
Of roaring bellows———

The town of Osterby is small, but neat, and principally inhabited by persons who have concerns with the mines.   At the
inn, which is very pretty and romantic, we fared sumptuously
upon strumlins and a cock of the woods, that had been preserved
in butter; and, after a hearty repast, returned to Upsala.   This
town, which is an archiepiscopal see, and one of the most ancient
Christian establishments in Sweden, stands in a vast plain, in
which the general character of barrenness is occasionally relieved
by some few corn-fields and partial spots of meadow.   Some of
the private dwellings and the colleges are handsome, and are
generally stuccoed and stained of a yellow colour; but the majority of houses are composed of wood, painted red, and have
behind them little gardens filled with apple and other fruit trees.
The river Sala, which communicates with the Mæler, divides the
town.   I never saw the grass so high and so green upon the roofs
of the houses as here.

Upon looking from my bed-room window at the inn, I could
not distinguish several of them from the green hill on whose summit the ancient palace stands.   Upon entering the court gate of
this edifice, which is of brick, and has at one angle a large round
tower, with a copper cupola, a number of baggage carriages were
preparing to follow the Duke of Sudermania (the King's uncle,

and, during his minority, the Regent of Sweden), who had left
the apartments which he has here, the day before, to join his regiment.

This prince possesses considerable talents : unfortunately there
is at present a coolness between his Royal Highness and his august nephew. Part of the palace only remains, the rest having
been consumed by fire. From the height upon which it stands,
the scite of the ancient tower of Upsala, formerly the capital of
Sweden, and the residence of the high priest of Oden, are dis-
cernible. Our time would not admit of our seeing the celebrated
Morasteen, or stone of Mora, on which the ancient sovereigns
of Sweden were crowned ; the last in 1512 : it is preserved, with
other curious stones, in a shed, about seven miles from Upsala.
Under a heap of rubbish, which formerly composed a part of the
palace, we were informed are the remains of some state dungeons, in one of which the following affecting scene occurred :

In the year 1567, Eric IV, the most bloody tyrant ever seated
upon the throne of Sweden, seized upon the illustrious family of
the Stures, who were the objects of his jealousy, and, in a moment of anger, descended the dungeon in which count Sture was
confined, and stabbed him in the arm : the young captive fell upon
his knees, implored his clemency, and drawing the dagger from
the wound, kissed it, and presented it to his enraged and remorseless sovereign, who caused him to be immediately dispatched. It
would form a fine subject for the pencil.

The cathedral is a prodigious unwieldy pile of brick, with two
square towers at the west end, in the gothic style, which have
been recently decorated with a doric architrave, and surmounted
by two cupolas of copper, supported by doric pillars of iron. In
contemplating such a heterogeneous mixture of architecture, in
a spot dedicated to the sciences, I could scarcely give credit to
the evidence of my eyes ; but the worst wine is always drank in
the vineyard. The present cathedral is erected upon the scite of
the ancient one, which was burnt down about one hundred and
fifty years since. The interior is handsome, and is adorned with
a magnificent organ, which was playing when we entered, and
poured forth some of the most powerful tones I ever heard. As
I was looking upon the ground, I found that I was standing

upon the slab that covered the ashes of the immortal Linneus
and his son, as appeared by the following simple and very inadequate inscription :

Ossa

CAROLI A LINNE

equitis aurati

marito optimo

filio unico

CAROLO A LINNE

patris successori

et

sibi

SARA ELIZABETA MORÆA.

The affectionate reverence of the pupils of this distinguished ex-
pounder of nature, and the powers of his celebrated friend, Sergell,
have endeavoured to supply the humility of the preceding tribute,
by raising, in a little recess, a monument of Swedish porphyry,
supporting a large medallion of the head of the illustrious natu-
ralist, which is said to be an admirable likeness of him ; under it
is the following plain inscription :

CAROLO A LINNE

Botanicorum

principi

Amici et discipuli,

1798.

Although this monument is more worthy of him, yet it is far below
what a traveller would have expected to find in the northern seat
of learning, and in the place which gave Linneus birth. His spirit
still seems to pervade and consecrate this celebrated spot. The
traveller hears every remark enriched with the name of Linneus.
" There," said a Swede, with a smile of national pride and an eye
of delight, " is the house in which he lived, and there the garden

" and bower in which he studied ; over these fields he used to fly,
" when the sun refreshed them with his earliest beam, attended
" by a numerous body of affectionate students, to explore the
" beauties, and unfold, with the eye of a subordinate Providence,
" the secrets of nature ; there, if in their rambles any one dis-
" covered a curious plant or insect, the sound of a French-horn
" collected the herborizing party, who assembled round their
" chief, to listen to the wisdom that fell from his tongue."

In a private chapel in this cathedral is the tomb of the glorious
Gustavus Vasa, whose effigy is placed between that of his two
wives, Catherine and Margaret ; and in another, that of the Stures,
whom I have before mentioned ; the Latin inscription upon this
monument thus affectingly concludes : " All that was noble and
" magnanimous could not soften the iron heart of their sovereign !
" Reader, if thou art not as unfeeling, lament the undeserved fate
" of such virtue." In one of the recesses we saw a small recumbent statue of John III, which experienced a similar fate ; the ship
that was conveying it to Sweden from Italy, where it was made, sunk
near Dantzig, and the statue remained under water for one hundred and fifty years, when it was fished up, and presented by the
burghers of Dantzig to Eric, and was deposited in the old cathedral. Here repose also the remains of the celebrated chancellor Oxenstiern. It is surprising that neither this great man,
nor Christian IV of Denmark, the two great ornaments and bene-
factors of their countries, have any monuments raised to their
memories.

The reader may be pleased with the following account of the
chancellor, from the pen of the eccentric Christina, queen of Sweden, who was placed, during her minority, under the guardianship
of Oxenstiern. " This extraordinary man had amassed a great
" deal of learning, having been a hard student in his youth: he
" read even in the midst of his important occupations. He had a
" great knowledge of the affairs and of the interests of mankind :
" he knew the forte and the foible of all the states of Europe: he
" was master of great talents, a consummate prudence, a vast ca-
" pacity, and a noble soul: he was indefatigable: he possessed a
" most incredible assiduity and application to business ; he made
" it his pleasure and his only occupation : he was as sober as any

" person could be, in a country and in an age when that virtue was
" unknown. He was a sound sleeper, and used to say, that nothing
" had either prevented his sleeping, or awakened him out of his
" sleep, during the whole course of his life, except the death of
" my father Gustavus, and the loss of the battle of Nordingue.
" He has often told me that, when he went to bed, he put off his
" cares with his cloaths, and let them both go to rest till the next
" morning. In other respects, he was ambitious but honest, incor-
" ruptible, and a little too slow and phlegmatic."

As we proceeded to the College of Botany and its gardens, it
was singular to see the professors of philosophy *booted*. Every
thing in Sweden is performed in boots: as soon as a child can walk
he is booted; perhaps the cheapness of leather may be the cause
of this. The college was erected under the auspices of the late
king, with his accustomed taste and magnificence. Monsieur
Aftzelius, professor of chemistry, and who presides over the cabinet of mineralogies, attended us with great politeness. This gentleman has lately returned to Sweden from a very interesting and
perilous investigation of the natural history of the interior of Af-
rica, and has enriched the department over which he ably presides,
with several rare and precious objects, which he brought from
that country. His mineral collection is much esteemed, but I confess my inability to describe it.

Amongst other matters, the conversation turned upon the authenticity of many of Mungo Parke's marvellous stories; upon
which the Professor assured us, that he believed his relation to be
perfectly true, and declared, that in that distant and unfrequented
region he had himself met with many extraordinary objects and
occurrences, which it required great courage to relate. I have,
since my return to England, seen some beautiful drawings made
upon the spot, descriptive of the manners, and particularly of the
rural economy of the interior Africans, by a highly ingenious and
enterprising artist, Samuel Daniell, esq. which fully confirm the
observation of the learned Professor, and might, from their con-
curring and convincing testimony, abate the force of his apprehensions. Upon the subject of abolishing the slave-trade, the
Professor made a remark, which, flowing from local knowledge
and long intercourse, strongly impressed my mind: he deprecated

any other than a gradual abolition, for which the minds of the negroes should be prepared; and declared, in a very emphatic manner, his perfect conviction that a *violent emancipation* would only shock and endanger this great cause of humanity.

Although unacquainted with botany, I was much gratified by seeing one of the rooms, in which there were some beautiful and flourishing date and plane trees, bedded in fine mould, and several rare plants from the South Sea islands, growing against a green treillage that ran on all sides of the apartment, which was formed into walks, and had a very agreeable effect.

Amongst the curiosities in this room, I did not fail to pay my respects to a venerable parrot, which we were assured had exceeded his hundreth year: he displayed the marks of great antiquity, part of his plumage was entirely gone, and there was a very visible appearance of feebleness both in his eyes and in his beak; but he is still likely to see several years more roll over his tufted head. The warmth of the room affords the temperature of native climate to the plants; it was gratifying to see art thus supporting nature in a bleak and hostile climate.

The hot-house, which is just finished, is a magnificent hall, supported by doric pillars, and which, when finished, will be warmed by fourteen stoves and nine flues, concealed in the columns. There were no plants here at this time. The room for the museum is also not yet completed; the design is excellent. The lecture-room is very capacious and handsome, and opens into that part of the garden which is finished and ready for the students, under a portico of pestum columns. The plants in this garden are arranged agreeable to the plan and classification of Linneus, and afford, no doubt, a rich mental banquet for the erudite herbalist. The library of the university is not now thought deserving of the high reputation which was once affixed to it: it is divided into three apartments, the first is dedicated to belles-lettres, history, and natural history; the second is miscellaneous, and was presented to the university by the late King; and the third is confined to theology, jurisprudence, and medicine. This library has been augmented at various times by the literary collections of those countries which have bowed to the Swedish sword. The librarian, who had lived some years with Sir Joseph Banks in that capacity, shewed us a very

P

precious manuscript of a Gothic translation of the four gospels, supposed to have been made in the fourth century, upon vellum, richly illuminated with large silver and some golden letters, which have been made by the brush: the former are faded, but the latter are in excellent preservation. This book formed a part of the literary pillage of Prague, in 1648, and was sent to Christina by count Konigsmark; from that princess it was pilfered by a Dutchman, upon whose death it was purchased for 250l. by some good patriotic Swede, and presented to the university.

We were shewn some curiosities, which, in justice to the university of Upsala, I must acknowledge that even those who displayed them were ashamed of, and were better calculated to augment the cabinet of some little, capricious, spoiled princess, who was just capable of running alone, than that of a grave and learned body, viz. the slippers of the Virgin Mary, Judas's purse, &c.

In a small room in the library we saw a large chest, about the size of a bureau bedstead, double locked and sealed, containing the manuscripts of the late King, which he directed should not be opened till fifty years after his decease. Conjecture and expectation frequently hover over this case, which will, no doubt, one day unfold to Sweden much interesting memoir, and literary treasure. Here we were shewn some Icelandic manuscripts, said to be upwards of eight hundred years old, and several Lapland tracts. How wonderful, that literature should have lived, and even smiled, in regions which the sun rarely warms!

In one of the mineralogical collections, separate from that of M. Afzelius, we were much gratified by seeing some transparent agates containing flies, elastic sand-stones, incombustible purses of asbestos, a mineral found in the iron mines of Danmora, some beautiful chrystals and many other rarities, which were displayed and explained with the greatest perspicuity and urbanity. The students amount to about one thousand, lodge, and board themselves according to their finances and inclinations in the town: in general they wear a black gown without sleeves.

By an unaccountable mistake we omitted to bring with us some letters of introduction to the university, which were offered to us at Stockholm; but upon a professor, who happened to be in the cathedral at the same time with ourselves, observing that we were

Englishmen, &c. in the politest manner, enabled us to see what was most worthy of our attention. Our emission, and professor Afzelius's imperfect knowledge of the English language, produced a momentary embarrassment: How dare you," said he, making a low bow, " come home without letters of introduction?" What he meant is obvious, from the politeness with which he received us. The professor will not be angry, I am sure; and the following whimsical error will completely keep him in countenance; it was related by the brave and venerable Prince de Ligne, whom I had the pleasure of meeting at Mr. Jackson's, our ambassador at Berlin, of an Englishman who had been introduced to him, and who was vehemently anxious to make himself master of the French language. It was the custom with this gentleman, for the purpose of restraining as much as possible the blunders which he was perpetually committing, always in conversation to speak each sentence in English first, and then to translate it into French. One day he called upon the Prince, who is a very active man, although far advanced in years, and finding him on his couch, and wishing to rally him on the occasion, thus began : " My prince, *Mon prince*— " I am glad to see you, *je suis charmé de vous voir*—On your " couch, *dans votre accouchement*—that is, instead of ' on your so- " pha,' ' in your lying in."

The revenues of this university, the first in the north of Europe, are rather narrow; fortunate would it be for this learned institution if it were more the fashion to commit the sons of gentlemen and noblemen to its care ; nothing but such patronage is wanting to expand its energies; genius and learning having made this spot their favourite residence. The attentions that we received there, and which our own forgetfulness rendered *accidental*, have left a lasting impression upon my mind of the respect which is paid to Englishmen.

It is by quitting it that we are able best to appreciate the value of our country ; every Englishman who leaves it from honourable motives, becomes a subordinate representative of it, and ought to revolt at tarnishing a name which is every where honoured.

The population of Sweden, including Finland, is rapidly encreasing; it is at present ascertained to exceed three millions. The revenues of Sweden arise from the poll-tax, about one shil-

ling and three-pence each person, with certain exceptions; royal
demesnes, windows, horses, equipages, supernumerary servants,
watches, tobacco, snuff, duties on exports and imports and distilled
spirits, on mines and forges, part of the great tythes, deductions
from salaries, pensions and places, and monopoly of saltpetre.
The herring fishery is said to be much on the decline. We found
every thing, except cloth, very cheap in Sweden.

CHAP. IX.

POOR POST-HORSES——LANGUAGE——MERRY CRIMINAL——PRISONS——
PSALM-SINGING WATCHMAN——WASHERWOMEN——FRENCH COMEDY——
PASSPORTS——INDECORUM OF A LITTLE DOG——SET SAIL FOR SWEDISH
FINLAND——BEGGING ON A NEW ELEMENT——ISLANDS UPON ISLANDS
——A MASSACRE——THE ARTS——ABO——FLIES——FORESTS ON FIRE——RUSSIA
——FREDERICKSHAM——RUSSIAN COINS.

THE Swedish peasantry are certainly not so merciful to their
horses as their neighbours the Danes : but provident and generous
Nature, who, foreseeing the cruelty of man towards the poor ass,
armed his sides with the toughest hide, made his temper patient,
and taught him to feed contentedly upon the thistle, seems to have
fortified the Swedish post-horse against hardships and neglect. I
have frequently seen this poor animal, after he has brought us to
the end of a long station, left to stand in the road, refreshed only
now and then by some little bits of hard bread, broken from a circle which the driver generally wears slung over his shoulders.
During this excursion, as well as on our first progress through
the country, my ear was frequently delighted by the strong resemblance between, and even identity of the Swedish and English languages, as in the following words: god dag, good day ; farvel, fare-
well; efter, after; go, go; vel, well; hott, hat; long, long; eta, eat;
fisk, fish; peppar, pepper; salt, salt; vinn, wine; liten, little; tvo,
two; go out, go out; streum, river; rod, red, &c. &c.

The Swedish language, which is derived from the Gothic, has
two different pronunciations ; one in which every letter in a word
is heard just as it is written, such as it is used in the various
branches of oratory ; the other, established by custom for common
use, has many abbreviations, and, in many instances, I was informed by an intelligent Swede, deviates from the rules of gram-
mar. The language is very sonorous: it places, as does the
Danish, the article at the end of the nouns, as in the most ancient
languages, contrary to the English and German, as *the man* der
man; Swedish, *mannen*.

Some of the national songs are said to be very sweet, and to breathe the true spirit of poetry. Amongst their modern poets, they speak with great rapture of Dalin; and amongst their ancient, of Stiernhielm, who flourished in the reign of Gustavus Adolphus, and, wonderful to relate, was the greatest *mathematician* and *poet* of his age. Perhaps it was the life of that singular man that suggested that whimsical satyrical poem, " the Loves of the Tri-" angles."

The higher orders of the Swedes are highly cultivated, well-informed, and accomplished. In consequence of every parish having a public school, almost every peasant can read, and many of the sons of the peasants are sent from these schools to the colleges at Upsala.

As I was strolling through the streets of Stockholm, just after our return from Upsala, I met with an occurrence which clearly established that an innate sentiment of submission to the laws will better ensure the safe custody of their violator than guards and jailers; and it is admitted that the Swedes are more under the influence of such an impulse than any other people. Turning a corner, I was overtaken by a raw flaxen-headed countryman, who, as it afterwards proved, had never been in the city before, driving, in a little country cart, a very robust merry looking fellow, whose hands were fastened by a large clumsy pair of handcuffs, and one leg chained to some little slips of wood which composed part of the body of the vehicle. Both driver and culprit had, it appeared, indulged themselves with a few snaps on the road, and were neither of them very sober nor sorrowful. The prisoner, who, from his superior size and strength, might, I am satisfied, have easily knocked down the rustic with the iron round his hands, if he had been so disposed, and effected his escape with little or no difficulty, sat at his ease, amusing himself with now and then pinching his conductor, which was always followed by a joke, and a mutual hearty laugh. In this way they jogged on through the city, the thief shewing his driver the road to the jail, as merrily as if he had been going to the house of festivity. I saw several prisoners passed from one town to another, under similar circumstances of apparent insecurity. They all appeared to be too unconcerned, if not cheerful, to be secured by the trammels of conscience, which is said to be sometimes capable of holding a ruffian by a hair.

Upon visiting the principal prison, the rooms appeared to me to be too small and close, were much too crowded with prisoners, and the healthy and the sick were confined together. The prisoners were not compelled to work, as in Copenhagen, to which circumstance, and the preceding causes, their sallow looks may be attributable: they are permitted to take the air only for a short time in the court-yard twice in the day. I was shocked to see a bar of iron, as long and as thick as a great kitchen poker, rivetted to each man's leg, and which, to enable him to move, he was obliged to preserve in a horizontal position, by a cord fastened to the end of it, and suspended from his waist. To load a prisoner with irons of any other weight or shape than what are necessary for security, is a reflection upon the justice, humanity, and policy of the government that permits it. The women were confined in a separate division of the building: they were not ironed, but their cells were too close and crowded; and they were also permitted to live in indolence. I must confess, when I reflected upon the enlightened benevolence of the Swedish nation, I was surprised to see how little this place appeared to have shared in its solicitude, and most cordially do I hope that the time is not distant, when these miserable wretches will be rendered more comfortable, and less burthensome to the state.

The watchmen of Stockholm, like their brethren of Copenhagen, cry the hour most lustily, and sing anthems almost all night, to the no little annoyance of foreigners who have been accustomed to confine their devotions to the day. These important personages of the night perambulate the town with a curious weapon like a pitch-fork, each side of the fork having a spring barb, used in securing a thief by the leg. The use of it requires some skill and practice, and constitutes no inconsiderable part of the valuable art and mystery of thief-catching.

Before I quit this charming city, I cannot help paying a compliment to a deserving and meritorious part of its female inhabitants, I mean the washerwomen, which I am sure all lovers of clean linen will re-echo. It is refreshing to see them enter one's room with the greatest *propreté*, with their baskets filled with linen as white as the driven snows of Lapland, and lay it out upon the table with that look and movement of conscious, but decent pride, which every creature feels who has reason to be in good humour with her own works: their bills are surprisingly moderate.   Perhaps, when the merits of these ladies are more widely known, luxury, delighting in whatever is foreign, may seek their aid, and the winds of heaven may waft into Swedish harbours vessels freighted with *foul linen* from English shores.

We found the French comedy tolerably well attended: the interior of the theatre is small, and of an oblong shape, meanly decorated, and badly lighted: the royal box is in the centre of the front, the whole of which it occupies. The performers were respectable, and receive very liberal encouragement from the public: the scenery was tolerable. The embellishments of this theatre suffer from the prodigal bounty which has been lavished upon the opera.

As the time fixed for our departure was rapidly advancing, to enable us to pass through Russia, we were obliged to furnish ourselves with a passport from the governor of Stockholm, for which we paid eight rix-dollars and a half, and another passport from the Russian minister, resident at the Swedish court, which cost two rix-dollars; and as it is attended with the least trouble and expense to cross the gulf of Bothnia to Abo, by proceeding from Stockholm up the Baltic, we hired half a packet, the other half being engaged for fifteen rix-dollars. The distance from Stockholm to Abo is about three hundred and fifteen English miles. The vessels, which are hired upon these occasions, are single-masted, and resemble a shallop with a raised deck, and a pink or sharp stern, which is much lower than the fore part, and is frequently under water: they cannot live long in rough weather.

On the day of our departure we dined with one of the most amiable and hospitable men in Stockholm. Few respectable Englishmen can pass through this capital, without knowing and consequently esteeming him; I allude to M. Winnerquist the banker. From his house I once more ran up to the church of St. Catherine, at the top of Mount Moses, to take my last farewel of this enchanting city, which, warmed by a brilliant suntint, lay beautifully expanded below me.

Having laid in our provisions,—and let me recommend the travel-ler to secure a good quantity of bread, for none can be procured till he reaches Abo,—we proceeded to the quay, where our vessel lay in front of the palace: here, whilst I was waiting on shore the ope-ration of hoisting the mainsail, a little trait of national character oc-curred, which did not fail to set me off in good humour. The walls of the casement story of the royal castle, and of the garden on this side, are of granite, vast, enormously thick and long, and cannot be taken by sap. A tradesman passed with a little dog trudging after him: the animal, it is to be presumed, had not had experience enough to know that, in the north, the very stones which form the royal pile are held even penally sacred against defilement of every sort, for irre-sistibly impelled, he raised one of his hinder feet against this said royal wall; a sentinel, who had a little whip in his hand, I suppose for this special purpose, sent this four-footed disloyal violator of deco-rum howling, with many a backward look of reproach, after his mas-ter, whom he vehemently scolded, for not having taken care to pre-vent such disrespectful behaviour towards the seat of majesty.

At five o'clock in the evening of the sixth of July, with very little wind, we slowly withdrew from Stockholm. Before night we were completely becalmed; our captain rowed us up to a rock, and throw-ing out a gang-board, tied the vessel to a fir tree for the night. Here we landed, and ascended the rocks, which, sparingly clothed with gray moss, rose from the water's edge in the most grand, romantic, and picturesque disorder. Before us the rich crimson suffusion of the sun, just sunk behind a dark undulating line of fir-forests, gave at once tranquillity and tone to the lake-appearance of this arm of the Baltic, which was enlivened by the white-lagging sails of a few boats, that on the opposite side softly and slowly creeped through the deep shadows of the shores, crowned with the woods of Liston-cottage; whilst in the south, the tower of St. Catherine's, mounted upon her airy summit, the houses, the palace, and the spires, seemed composed of light cloud and mist. The silence of this delicious repose of na-ture was only faintly broken by the dashing of the oar, and the carol of the distant boatmen; in the language of the divine Milton:

> " Now came still evening on, and twilight gray
> Had in her sober livery all things clad:

Q

Silence accompanied ; for beast and bird,
They to their grassy couch, these to their nests,
Were slunk——————————————————
——————————now glowed the firmament
With living saphirs."

Seated upon a rock, we for a long time contemplated this exquisite
scene, till at length the calls of sleep induced us to descend into our
cabin, where our accommodations were very comfortable. With the
sun, which was an early riser, we unmoored, and advanced but very
slowly; as we proceeded, misery in a new shape presented itself.
From a wretched hovel, upon one of the islands which began to appear in clusters, hanging over the edge of the water, and ready to
drop into it, an old man in rags, and nearly blind, put off in a little
crazy boat, and rowing towards us, implored our charity in the most
touching manner, and seemed very grateful for the trifle we gave
him.

In the evening, having made but little way, the master again
moored the vessel to another island for the night ; as I found was
the custom, on account of the danger and difficulty of the navigation.
This island was indeed a most enchanting scene ; upon its romantic
summit of gray rock we found a little cottage, embowered in trees of
fir, ash, and elder, that might well be called "*the peasant's nest.*" A
fisherman, his aged mother, his wife and his children, formed the
population of this beautiful spot. A little field of grass, in which a
cow was grazing, another of corn, a garden, and the waters of the
Baltic, which again resembled a lake, supplied them with all their
wants, and all their riches. Here it seemed as if the heart could no
longer ache, as if ambition might wish to be what he beheld, and
that love might ponder on the past without a pang. The inside of
the cottage was neat and cheerful; the good old lady, with the
children in their shirts playing round her, sat knitting by the light
of a sprightly fire, and under locks of snow presented a face at peace
with all the world. Upon hearing that we wished to have some supper, the fisherman, with a countenance of health and gaiety, descended into a little creek, where his boats were moored, for some perch,
confined in a wicker-well in the water, whilst his young wife,
who had a pair of very sweet expressive eyes, laid the cloth in a

detached room facing the cottage. Whilst supper was preparing I rambled over this little paradise. Night came on, and all the beauties of the preceding evening, with some variety of new forms, returned; the same bright bespangled Heaven! the same serenity; the same silence! yielding only to the unceasing rippling of a little stream of rock water, to which, as it gushed from a bed of long moss, and as our fair hostess presented her pitcher, thriftily fenced with wicker, might be applied the beautiful inscription of Bosquillon, on the fountain in the street of Notre Dame des Victoires in Paris:

> " La nymphe qui donne de cette eau
>   Au plus creux de rocher se cache :
> Suivez un exemple si beau ;
>   Donnez sans vouloir qu'on le sache."

Or thus in English :

> " Prompt to relieve, tho' *viewless* wrapp'd in stone,
> The nymph of waters pours her generous stream :
> Go, gentle reader, do as she has done ;
> See while you bless, but *blessing be unseen*."

J. C.

It was just such a spot as the poetical spirit of Cowper would have coveted: his eye would have penetrated, and his pen could alone have painted every beauty.

On the third day of this voyage of islands, we touched at another, and procured a noble pike, fresh from the net, and some eggs. Our skipper very ingeniously kindled a fire and cooked it in his little canoe, which was towing astern, by placing upon the bottom of it a large stone, upon which he set fire to some chips and pieces of fir, and suspended over it, from an oar laid across the sides of the boat, an iron pot containing the fish; our eggs formed the sauce, and with a broken saucer for a plate, we made an excellent Robinson Crusoe repast.

One morning, as I was looking over the deck from the stern, I beheld an operation somewhat ridiculous; but as it originated in rude notions of cleanliness, and moreover is one of the domestic customs of the country, I shall relate it. Our skipper was lying at the feet of a good-natured brawny girl, who was a passenger; his head was on her lap, just as Goliah some time since rested his in that of Delilah; but the fingers of our fair companion were more kindly employed than were those of the woman of the valley of Sorek: the skipper had no comb, perhaps never heard of such a thing, and this kind-hearted creature was sedulously consigning with a humane, because an instantaneous destruction of sensation in every vital part by an equal and forcible pressure, every restless disturber of his peace in that region, which most assuredly must be, though doctors may dispute the point, the seat of reason; the cabin-boy succeeded his master, and in return, with the keen eye and nimble finger of a monkey, gratefully repaid the obligation upon the head of his benefactress. In Italy, these engaging *little offices of kindness* constitute the principal delights of courtship.

The islands, after we had passed Aland, and as we approached the gulf, ceased to present any picturesque object; they appeared but a little above the water, and were scantily covered with slender weak firs, whose naked branches were whitened over with hoary moss, and at length, from their number and similarity, became very tedious, and as dull as the melancholy forests through which our road lay on shore.

In the midst of the heavy *ennui* inseparable from such a situation, by good fortune, upon rummaging my portmanteau, I found a catalogue of the year's exhibition; with this precious prize in my hand, I jumped into the little canoe astern, and defied the gloom of the rocks and firs; with fresh vigour my memory revisited that splendid gallery of the British arts. The genius of West, of Westall, and of Smirke, in history; of the Daniells, and of Turner, in landscape; and Lawrence, in portrait painting, again filled my mind with the proudest sensations of delight. During these meditations I had prevailed upon the president and council to confine the admission of portraits to a certain number, that the public eye might no longer be confused and disgusted by a *mob of faces*, in which nature had done nothing for the originals, or the painter but little for nature. With a thrifty use of my treasure, it lasted till the tenth, when, as I was gazing in my mind's eye, with silent rapture, upon the bust of the lovely lady Ribblesdale, by Bacon, the fairy fabric of my reveries was in a moment destroyed by a cry of " there is Abo, there is Abo."

About two English miles before we reached the town, we entered
a very narrow channel, not above forty feet wide, which was marked out by piles, not wide enough to admit of large vessels, which
are obliged to moor a little before the entrance of it.   On the left
we passed by the castle, built of brick stuccoed: it is very ancient,
and has a very picturesque appearance, and was once the prison of
the bloody Eric IV, but is now a garrison.   A little further on the
same side is the house of the gallant admiral Steddynk, who in the
last reign displayed distinguished skill and bravery in several engagements with the Russians, and who has the command of the
gun-boats, which are ranged in a long line of boat-houses near his
residence.   It is a matter worthy of observation, particularly at this
period, that the gun-boats used in the naval conflicts between Russia
and Sweden with so much effect, originally suggested to France the
idea of using them against this country.   In the seven years war
they were recommended to the Duc de Choiseul, the minister of
Louis XV, by captain Kergvagelin, of the Swedish navy, and in the
late revolution by captain Muskein, who was also a lieutenant in the
same service: this small craft is capable of acting in the Baltic,
where no tides ever interfere with manœuvres; but it has excited
astonishment, not only in Sweden but in every other part of the continent which I visited, (and I mention it with more shame than reluctance, because with the millions of England, I believed at the
time in the romantic practicability of the long, very long threatened, invasion), that any reflecting Englishman could believe in the
possibility of a flotilla of gun-boats crossing such an expanse of water
as divides the Isle of Wight from Boulogne, subject to the tides,
currents, and winds, which are with more or less certainty felt there,
omitting the proud and confident reflections which our gallant cruisers and channel fleet naturally suggest.   We well know, that in
the year 1791 Muskein, without having much dread from the natural difficulties before enumerated, on account of the shortness of the
distance, attacked that dot in the channel, the island of St. Marcou,
with fifty of his redoubted gun-boats; that the battery of the little
wave-girt fortress blew her rash and presuming enemies to atoms;
and that their commander with difficulty escaped only to be disgrac-
ed by the directory.   In mere patriotic ardour and enthusiasm, independent of tides, currents, winds, cruisers, and fleets, the French,

if they reflect at all, will regard St. Marcou as a miniature of a greater island.

Beyond the boat-houses is the custom-house, from whence an officer came on board, and proceeded up the river with us to the town, which, with the cathedral, now presented the appearance of a large and populous city. We soon reached the quay, and very gladly landed in the capital of Swedish Finland.

In our inn yard I beheld the first indication of our being in the neighbourhood of Russia, in a clumsy kibitka, the ordinary carriage of that country, and which was here exposed for sale. It is a small cart, very much resembling a cradle, round at the bottom, about five feet long, and in which two persons can sit or lie, the latter is the usual posture, and who are protected from the weather by a semicircular tilt, open in front, made of broad laths interwoven, and covered with birch or beech bark ; it has no iron in it, but is fastened to the body of the carriage without springs, by wooden pins and ropes: the driver sits upon the front of it, close to the horses' tails. At dinner we had some delicious wild strawberries, the first fruit that we had tasted for the year.

Abo is situated upon a point of land where the gulfs of Finland and Bothnia unite, is a large town, and carries on a tolerable commerce. Many of the houses are handsome : they are mostly built of wood, but some are of brick stuccoed, and the inhabitants are said to exceed ten thousand. The fir of Finland is superior to that of any other part of Sweden, and particularly preferred for building : great quantities of it are annually sent from Abo to Stockholm. The cathedral is a very ancient massy pile of brick, displaying no attractions to the eye ; and the gloom of the interior is augmented by a barbarous representation of drapery in blue, upon a lead-coloured ground : it contains the tombs of many illustrious families. Christina, who with all her levities was a learned woman, and the munificent friend of learning, endowed an university here, which has a library containing ten thousand indifferent volumes : the former is not in a flourishing condition, and the latter worthy of little notice. We ascended the craggy rocks impending over one side of the town, which, with the windings of the Aura, and occasional glimpses of the gulf of Finland, shining through the openings of those dark forests that cover its shores on this side, presented a somewhat interesting but sombre prospect.

In the course of my northern excursion, it was generally my fate, when we passed a night in a town, to have a ball or a public coffee-room for my chamber, which, on account of their size, are generally the most comfortless apartments that a man can attempt to close his eyes in. At Abo, my bed was made up in an appendage to the ball-room, and had much of Finnish decoration to recommend it. The walls were laboriously painted in glowing colours, with flaming swords, fiddles, and flutes, and seraphim's heads, which were saved from the voracious and expanded beaks of griffins, by the tender in-terposition of baskets of flowers, and over the whole there was a pretty sprinkling of sphinxes and the royal arms of Sweden. Here we provided ourselves with a stock of provisions for our journey, and early the morning after our arrival bade adieu to Abo. The regu-lation of the post and the coin are the same here as in the other parts of Sweden.

As we proceeded the face of the country began to undulate; we observed that the houses were constructed of fir trees rudely squared by the axe, and laid, with a little moss between, upon each other, the ends of which, instead of being cut off, are generally left projecting beyond the sides of the building, and have a most savage and sloven-ly appearance. The roof is also of fir, sometimes stained red; the windows are frequently cut with the axe after the sides of the houses are raised. Such of these as were well finished had a good appear-ance, and are very warm and comfortable within. Our servant, who was well acquainted with the Swedish language, began to find him-self, every mile we advanced, more and more puzzled. The *patois* of this province is a barbarous and unintelligible mixture of Swedish and Russ. The summer, now the eleventh of July, *burst* upon us with *fiery fury*, with no other precursors than grass and green leaves. On a sudden the flies, which experience a longer date of existence in the north than in the milder regions of Europe, on account of the stoves used in the former, awoke from the torpor in which they had remained, between the discontinuance of artificial warmth and the decisive arrival of the hot weather, and annoyed us beyond imagina-tion. They are the musquitoes and plague of the north. No one, but those who have suffered, could believe them capable of producing so much torment.

One night we put up at Mjolbollsted, a solitary post-house, in the midst of a gloomy forest of fir, which lay upon the borders of an arm

of the gulf of Finland.   The post-master ushered us into a little hole
in a wooden shed, opposite to the post-house, the latter being occupied by his family.   We had the consolation of finding that we had
the place to ourselves, from which we could never have expected to
emerge, if, notwithstanding the treachery of our vorbode some time
before, we had not formed an high opinion of Swedish morality.   The
windows which looked into the depth of the forest, were as immoveable as the building; this was somewhat satisfactory.   It is always a
pleasant thing to strengthen favourable impressions with judicious
precautions.   The sides of the room were completely encrusted with
flies, who at this moment were recruiting themselves for the mischief of the next day; and mice and tarrakans, or beetles, shared the
possession of the floor.   In two corners of this dolorous hole stood
two cribs, each furnished with a bed of straw, a bronze-coloured
blanket well charged with fleas, and a greasy coverlid.   Cribs are the
usual bedsteads in the north.   Here we endeavoured to invoke that
sweet power which

> " ——————————— seldom visits sorrow ; when it doth,
> " It is a comforter."

Alas! our wretched taper, and the bustle of bringing in our luggage,
had excited an alarm amongst our tormentors, who besieged us in
battalions.   These busy many-eyed marauders, with their gossamer
wing and incessant hum, opposed the approach of sleep, and fairly
kept her aloof for two long dreary hours.   Weary, yet incapable of
repose, something was to be done.   I resolved upon revenge, and accordingly made an irritable effort to surprise three of my enemies,
who in a row were audaciously washing their little slender black
hands upon one of mine; I gained nothing by my rage but (such is
the association of ideas) the recollection of an admirable representation, which I once saw in a private room, of an ideot attempting to
do the same thing, and the wild delight which he displayed in succeeding, by a gentleman who, closely and chastely copying nature,
the only model capable of making any actor great, may be ranked
amongst the first comedians of his time, I mean Mr. Matthews.
The impression of that surprising display of imitative power so
completely occupied me, that, in spite of my opponents, I succeeded
in closing my eye-lids, and never opened them until the full day

broke in great glory. Upon rising I found some brother travellers, who arrived after we had retired to rest, had slept on the earth under their carriage, and were in the act of shaking themselves and setting off for Abo. I must confess, agreeable as solitude frequently is to me, I was glad to retire from this species of it. As the sultry sun was flaming in the meridian, we passed a large portion of a forest on fire. This circumstance was not the effect of accident nor of a natural cause, which in these regions is frequently followed by the most direful consequences, and to which I shall have occasion to allude hereafter. By some smart touches of the whip we saved our servant, horses and carriage from being a little toasted on one side. What we saw arose from the farmers clearing the ground, who confine the flames to the proper boundary by making an interval of felled trees. In the evening we passed by, at some distance, another forest which was in the same predicament, and had a very sublime and novel effect.

The country about Borgo, a garrison town most miserably paved, and where our passports were demanded, is undulating and fertile, but the cottages in that part of Swedish Finland are very miserable, and the peasantry wretchedly clothed. The men, the women, and the children, had no other covering than ragged shirts; although the sun was too intense to induce any one to pity them on account of their exposure to the weather, yet their appearance was that of extreme penury. The roads were still excellent, and enabled us to proceed with our accustomed velocity. The time did not admit of our attempting to see the celebrated Swedish fortress of Sveaborg, which occupies seven islands in the gulf of Finland, and is capable of protecting the fleets of Sweden against the Russians. The batteries, basons, and docks, are of hewn granite, and said to be stupendous. I was reconciled afterwards to my not having attempted to see this place, as I found some English travellers, of great respectability, were about this time refused permission to view it, and that too with some degree of rudeness.

About three miles from Louisa, another garrison town, we reached the frontier of Sweden, and in a custom and guard house beheld the last remains of that country. A Swedish soldier raised the cross bar, such as I described in Denmark; we passed over a bridge which crosses a branch of the river Kymen, and divides Sweden from Russia. The *exclusive right* of *painting* this little bridge had very nearly

R

inflamed these rival nations to the renewal of all those horrors which
have so long and so prodigally wasted the blood and treasure of both
countries. It has been contended, that aggregate bodies of men are
governed by other rules of conduct than those which ordinarily influence mere individuals: for my part I regard a nation only as a
man magnified, constantly displaying all the anger, inveteracy,
caprice, and petulance of the solitary being. This marvellous dispute,
after a stormy discussion, with the sword half-drawn, was settled in
the following manner, viz. Sweden was to use what sized brush and
what colours she preferred, upon one half of the bridge, and on the
other Russia the like materials in the way that best suited her fancy;
but it is useless to talk about a few piles and planks; they were the
ostensible, but the *real* cause of the difference was, and ever will be,
the *vicinity* of the countries, for, unhappily! nations are more disposed to mutual attachment, if they cannot see each other.

Russia has exercised the privilege of her brush with a vengeance,
not only upon her half of this said bridge, but upon all her public
buildings, which she has distinguished by a *magpye colour*. This
predilection is said to have arisen from the result of the late unfortunate emperor's reflections upon mankind, whom he arranged under
two classes, the good and the bad, thinking no doubt with the Spanish proverb, that heaven will be filled with those who have done good
actions, and hell with those who intended to do them, and accordingly he ordered the fronts of all public railings, offices, &c. to be
striped with white and black. Sancho Pança, a man of no little wit
and sagacity, thought life susceptible of being represented by an in-
termediate colour; upon returning from an important commission,
he was asked by his master, whether he should mark the day with a
black or a white stone. " Faith, sir," replied his trusty servant, " if
" you will be ruled by me, with neither, but with *good brown ochre*,"
the colour best suited to describe it. I heard another reason assigned for this magpye appearance when I reached the capital.

A new race of beings, in green uniform, stout, whiskered, and sun-
browned, raised the bar of the barrier on the other side of the
bridge, stopped the carriage, and conducted us to the guard-house, a
square wooden building, with a projecting roof, resting upon little
pillars of wood, under the shade of which several soldiers were sleeping. This building was of course embellished after the fashion of
the bridge, and had a most frightful appearance : we were ushered
into a small shabby room, in the windows were some flower pots, and

upon an old table the poems of Ossian in French, open, and by their
side a vast snuff-box and most filthy handkerchief; presently a little
old Russian major entered, in a white linen dressing-gown, and in
French demanded our passports, with which he was satisfied, and
immediately made out our order for post-horses, without which no
one can travel in Russia, called a *poduragina;* upon presenting the
paper to us, he demanded six rubles and forty copecs, which he informed us constituted a part of the revenues of his imperial majesty; we told him that we had no Russian money whatever, but offered
to pay him in Swedish rix dollar notes: " If you have any of them,"
said he, " I must seize them," and went into another room; but he
uttered this without severity: perhaps the consideration that he was
speaking to a couple of Englishmen softened his tone and look. In
a moment we found ourselves like two ill-starred mice, who unexpectedly find themselves within the basilisk beam of a cat's eye.

Our station from the last post-house in Sweden, extended to the
seventh verst post in Russian Finland, and we never entertained an
idea that any law so pregnant with inconvenience existed in Russia,
for making Swedish money found within its barrier forfeitable, more
especially as there is no bank upon the confines of either country.
The major presently returned with a pile of notes, exclaiming,
" See what a quantity I seized a few days since from a Danish gen-
" tleman !" We endeavoured to give a turn to the conversation, in
which his urbanity assisted, and at length we paid him in Dutch
ducats, one proof at least of the safety and convenience of this valuable coin. Before we parted, we observed that he entered our names
in a register as arrivals on the second of July: at first we were surprised, for, according to my journal, it was the fourteenth; but a
moment's recollection informed us that we were in a country in
which the Julian calendar, with the old style, obtains, before which
our calculation always precedes, by an advanced march of twelve
days. Both old and new style are superior to the poetical absurdity
of the French calendar, which must be at perpetual variance with
the immutable law of climates and geography: for instance, when a
merchant is melting away under the fiery sun of the French West
India islands, his correspondence will be dated Nivose, or the month
of snow.

After making our bows to the little major, and secretly wishing,
for his civility, in the language of his favourite author, that he might
be " the stolen sigh of the soul " of some fair Finn girl, and that

" her fine blue eyes might roll to him in secret," but not for ever, a
circumstance, by the by, which age, form, and feature, had rendered not very likely to happen, we were most vexatiously detained
on the opposite side of the way by the custom-house officers, who,
under a broiling sun, ransacked every article of our luggage; even
the private recesses of the writing-desk were not sacred. The scrupulous fidelity with which they performed their duty, was, on this
occasion, as, alas! on many others of more importance, the reason of
our leaving virtue to be its own reward ; for, provoked with the trouble they caused us, we gave them nothing but black looks, and a few
private *inverted blessings*.

We now began to reckon our stations by versts : a verst is about
three quarters of an English mile, and is marked upon a post, painted like the bridge, somewhat resembling, only that the verst post is
square and much taller, a barber's pole. The rapidity of our travelling, and the frequent appearance of these memorials of our velocity, were the only cheering circumstances that we met with. Upon
the road we saw several peasants bare-headed, cropped, fair, with
shorn beards, and booted. We met with little or no delay for horses:
the peasant, to whom they belonged, attended us to take them back.
After passing through a country the most wretched and rocky imaginable, a country formerly wrested by the Russians from the Swedes,
in which the gloomy sterility of nature was only once relieved by the
waterfalls which attracted our notice at Hagfors, and a large camp of
several Russian regiments, who had a very fine appearance, we
reached, at eleven o'clock at night, the drawbridge of Fredericksham, the gates of which had been some time closed. After repeatedly knocking, a little beardless officer presented himself, and very
politely requested to have our passports and post-order, with which
he disappeared. Here we waited in suspense for three quarters of an
hour: all owing to the provoking integrity and detention of the custom-house officer at the barrier. At length we heard some massy
bolts move, the gates unfolded, and we entered the town through a
long arch under the ramparts, and anxiously looked out for an hotel :
it was then as light as the day, but as silent as the tomb. At length we
halted before a house, which our little officer, as well as we could understand him, informed us was the only inn in the town. Here we
found no person moving: after trying at the door for some time in
vain, I peeped into the front room, and beheld a spectacle *à la mode
de Russe*, to me completely novel ; it was a collection of nine or ten

men and women all lying, with their cloaths on, promiscuously upon the floor, like pigs, heads and tails together. An officer passing by informed us that this was a private house, and that the inn, in Russ called a kabac, was the next door; but that it was locked up and empty, the host having gone to enjoy the breezes of the sea-side for a few days. This circumstance plainly demonstrated one of two things; either that this part of Russia is not much frequented by travellers, or, as I frequently experienced, that an inn-keeper, however poor, is very indifferent whether he affords them any accommodation.

We had been travelling all day under a fervid sun, were covered with dust, and parched with thirst; our Abo ham was glowing to the bone, our last bottle of claret was as warm as milk from the cow, and our poor exhausted horses were licking the walls of an adjoining building to cool their tongues. In this dilemma I beheld an elegant young officer, uncovered, in a dark bottle-green uniform (the legionary colour of Russia), and an elderly gentleman, upon whose breast two resplendent stars shone, coming towards us: these stars were two propitious constellations. The principal personage addressed us in a very kind and conciliatory manner in French. Upon our explaining our situation, he said, " I am very sorry this " fellow is out of the way, but it shall make no difference. When " Englishmen enter Russia it is to experience hospitality, not in- " convenience; trust to me, I will immediately provide for you:" he bowed, gave directions to an officer who followed at a distance, and passed on. This amiable man proved to be the count Meriandoff, the governor of Russian Finland, who, fortunately for us, had arrived about an hour before from Wibourg. An officer soon afterwards came to us, and conducted us to a very handsome house belonging to a Russian gentleman of fortune. Our kind host, who spoke a little English, introduced us into a spacious drawing-room, where we went to rest upon two delightful beds which were mounted upon chairs. Our poor servant, after the manner of the Russians, ranked no higher in our host's estimation than a faithful mastiff, and was left to make a bed of our great coats on the floor of the entry, and to sleep *comme il plait à Dieu*.

The next day we had a peep at the town, which is small but handsome: from the square in which the guard-house stands, a building of brick stuccoed, and painted green and white, almost every street may be seen, It was here, in the year 1783, that Catherine II and

Gustavus III had an interview. Upon this occasion, to impress the
Swedish monarch with the magnificence of the Russian empire, and
to render their intercourse less restrained, a temporary wooden palace was erected, containing a grand suite of rooms, and a theatre,
by the order of the empress. The town appeared to be filled with
military. The Russians of consequence generally despise a pedestrian. I was uncommonly struck with seeing officers going to the
camp, and even the parade in the town, upon a droska, or, as they
are called in Russ, a drojeka, an open carriage, mounted upon
springs, and four little wheels, formed for holding two persons, who
sit sideways, with their backs towards each other, upon a stuffed
seat, frequently made of satin ; the driver wore a long beard (which
we now began to see upon every rustic face), a large coarse brown
coat, fastened round the middle by a red sash, was booted, and sat in
front, close to the horses' heels, whose pace was, as is usual in Russia, a full trot.

We here exchanged our Swedish money at Mr. Broom's, and
found the exchange against us. After having been so long strangers
to the sight of any coin, we were surprised by seeing his Russian
clerk, habited in a long blue coat, fastened round the middle by a
sash, enter the room, perspiring under the weight of a coarse bag
of five-copec pieces, a monstrous coin, fit for some infantine repub-
lic, that might wish to excite a distaste for riches amongst her virtuous citizens, worth about three-pence English. It may be as well
to run over the coin of the country now:

COPPER.

One-fourth of a copec, called a polushka, very few in circulation.
One-half of a copec, called a denishka.
One copec.
Two copecs.
Five copecs.
Ten copecs.

SILVER.

Five silver copec piece, rare.
Ten ditto.
Fifteen ditto.
Twenty ditto.
One-fourth of a ruble, worth twenty-five copecs.
One-half of a ruble, worth fifty copecs.
A ruble, worth one hundred copecs.

The agio between silver and bank notes is now about twenty-five per cent.

GOLD.

A half imperial, worth five rubles.

An imperial, worth ten rubles.

NOTES.

The bills are for five, ten, twenty-five, fifty, and one hundred rubles.

The Russians calculate always by rubles. A ruble is now worth about two shillings and eight pence English.

A silver ruble is equal to a paper ruble and twenty-five copecs.

It is rather remarkable that the silver rubles, which were coined in the last and present reigns, have no impression of the heads of the last or present emperors.

CHAP. XL 10

RUSTIC URBANITY——WRETCHED VILLAGE——NO. 1——WIBOURG——GREEK RELIGION——A CHARITY SERMON——RELIGION AND EXTORTION——A WORD OR TWO TO FORTIFIED TOWNS——STARVED HORSES——VOLUNTEER JACKET——APPEARANCE OF PETERSBURG——COSSAC——RENOWNED STATUE.

WHILST the peasants were adjusting our horses, four abreast to the carriage, in the yard of our kind and hospitable host, I was amused with seeing with what solemn and courteous bows the commonest Russians saluted each other; nothing but an airy dress and a light elastic step were wanting to rank them with the thoughtless, gay, and graceful creatures of the Boulevards des Italiens: here the Russian exterior was more decisively developed; but I should wish to postpone a more particular description of it until we reach the capital; it is now sufficient to observe, that the men in complexion and sturdiness resembled the trunk of a tree, and that the women were remarkably ugly: I saw not a female nose which was not large and twisted, and the dress of the latter, so unlike their sex in other regions, was remarkable only for filth and raggedness. Travelling is very cheap in Russian Finland: we paid only two copecs for each horse per verst, except for the last post to Petersburg,

when we paid five copecs.   In Russian Finland the comfort of send
ing an avant-courier to order horses ceases.   On the road we met
with several kibitkas, such as I have described.

After we left Uperla, those extraordinary detached rocks, and vast
stones, which hitherto had lined the sides of the roads and were scattered over the fields, began to assume a redder tint, and to shew a
greater portion of friability than their hard and savage brethren
which we had left behind, and gradually disappeared in deep sand :
the country presented a scene of extreme wretchedness.   To the
squalid inhabitants we might have said in the beautiful language of
Cowper :

> " ——————— Within th' enclosure of your rocks,
> Nor herds have ye to boast, nor bleating flocks ;
> No fertilizing streams your fields divide,
> That shew, revers'd, the villas on their side ;
> No groves have ye ; no cheerful sound of bird,
> Or voice of turtle, in your land is heard ;
> No grateful eglantine regales the smell
> Of those that walk at evening where ye dwell."

We halted at a village of old crazy hovels, composed of trunks
of trees, rudely thrown across each other, and perched upon granite
rocks ; every one of these forlorn abodes was out of the perpendicular, whilst, from a little hole which feebly admitted the light,
the smoke issued.   The inhabitants were nearly naked, and looked
like a race of animals formed in the anger of heaven.   Instead of
the green refreshing blade, parched hoary moss covered the earth ;
where the limpid brook ought to have rippled, a narrow, slimy,
brown stream of reeking offensive water crawled indolently and un-
wholesomely along.   Not a tree was to be seen ; not even a melancholy fir !   Time, that bids the barrenness of nature bear, that ena-
bles the shepherd and his flock to find shelter and rich pasture in
the altered desert, has passed over these regions without shedding
his accustomed beneficence.   These people, or, as they are called,
the Finns, I found always distinguishable in the capital from the proper Russian, by their squalid and loathsome appearance.

Yet, even in this inhospitable spot are to be found what many a
traveller in England has frequently lamented the want of, viz. the
exposition of every diverging road carefully, and intelligibly marked
out by a directing post.   Although the peasantry of the country, in
these immediate parts, are so wretched, a considerable portion of

Russian Finland is considered to be as fertile in corn as any part of the polar empire.

We were prevented from reaching Wibourg on the day we set off from Fredericksham, on account of our being detained, for want of horses, at Terviock, which forms the last stage to the former place. Here, as it was too hot to admit of two sleeping in a chaise, I entered a sorry post-house; the room contained only a crib and a sheet, as aged, and as brown, and as filthy, as the post-master's face and hands, who, after having given me to understand that I might use the bed after he had done with it, very composedly jumped into it with his cloaths on, and soon made this black hole resound with one of the loudest, and least tuneable, nasal noises, I ever heard. Sleep sat heavy upon me, and with my pelisse for a bed, and my portmanteau for a pillow, I closed my eyes upon the floor, which appeared to be the favourite promenade of flies, fleas, and tarrakans. Necessity, like

"Misery, acquaints a man with strange bed-fellows."

At three in the morning, I was awakened by the jingling of the bells of our horses, which the peasants very merrily gallopped up to the door. The sun was up, and threatened very speedily to destroy the refreshing coolness of the air. At five we passed the bridge, and were at the gate of Wibourg, the capital of Russian Finland. It is a large, handsome, fortified town, a place of considerable commerce, and has been much improved since the terrible fire which happened in 1793. Like mice, who find no difficulty in getting into a cage, but know not how to return, we were admitted within the gates of this town with perfect facility, but were detained no less than nine hours for a new post order, which must be signed by the governor or his deputy. It was Sunday, and whilst this was negociating, I visited the Greek church, which stands in a corner of the area where the parade is held, and is an elegant structure of wood, painted light yellow and white, with a roof and dome of copper, painted green. It had a very light and pleasing effect. Every Russian, before he ascended the steps which led to the door, raised his eyes to a little picture of the Virgin, fixed to the cornice, and having uncovered his head, inclined his body, and crossed himself with his thumb and fore-finger. The Virgin was framed and decorated with a projecting hood of silver. If she had not been produced by the coarse and

S

crazy imagination of the painter, it might have been supposed that one of the nymphs, which we saw between Fredericksham and this place, had sat for the model. She was a brunette of the deepest mahogany, and bore no resemblance whatever to any branch of Vandyke's holy family.

In the Greek church images, musical instruments, and seats, are proscribed. Even the emperor and empress have no drawing-room indulgence here. No stuffed cushion, no stolen slumbers in padded pews, inviting to repose. Upon entering the church, these people again crossed and bowed themselves, and then eagerly proceeded to an officer of the church, who was habited in a rich robe; to him they gave one of the small pieces of money, and received in return a little wax taper, which they lighted at a lamp and placed in a girandole, before the picture of the saint they preferred amongst the legions enrolled in the Greek calender. Some of them had a brilliant homage paid to them, whilst others were destitute of a single luminary. In the body of the church were inclined tables, containing miniatures of some of these sanctified personages in glass cases, adorned with hoods, of gold, silver, and brass, looking very much like a collection of medals. The screen, composed of folding-doors, at the back of the altar, to which a flight of steps ascended, was richly gilded and embellished with whole-length figures of saints of both sexes, well executed. In one part of the service the folding doors opened, and displayed a priest, called a Papa, in the shrine or sacristy, where lovely woman is never permitted to enter, for reasons that an untravelled lover would wonder to hear, without caring for, and which I leave to the ladies to discover. The priest always assumes his pontificals in this place, whilst it constitutes a part of the privileges of a bishop to robe in the body of the church. The sacerdotal habit was made of costly silk and rich gold lace; and the wearer, who appeared to be in the very bloom of life, presented the most mild, expressive, evangelical countenance, I ever beheld, something resembling the best portraits of our Charles I; his auburn beard was of great length, fell gracefully over his vest, and tapered to a point. Seen, as I saw him, under the favour of a descending light, he was altogether a nobly study for a painter. After reading the ritual in a low voice, during which his auditory crossed themselves, and one man, near me, in a long and apparently penitential gown of sackcloth, repeatedly touched the basement with his head: the congregation sung in recitative, and with their manly voices produced a fine effect. This will suffice for a description of the Greek church; as to its abstract mysteries, they are but little known, even to its followers, who recognise the authority of their own priests only, and renounce the supremacy of the Roman pontiff.

From this place we proceeded to a reformed catholic church, where the preacher was delivering, with apparently great pathos, a charity sermon, in German: every avenue was thronged almost to suffocation; whenever the orator had made a successful appeal, his hearers testified their approbation in savage acclamations, and the proper officers seized these impressive moments to collect from the congregation the fruits of their bountiful dispositions, received in a little silk bag, fastened to the end of a long stick, from which depended a small bell, shaken whenever charity dropped her mite.

I had good reason to believe that our landlord, who was a thorough-paced Italian, had been a devotee here, and wished to supply by extortion the vacancy which a sudden impulse of beneficence had occasioned in his purse; for the fellow had the impudence to charge us ten rubles and fifty copecs for a breakfast, a plain dinner, and a bottle of claret. " Gentlemen," said he, in reply to our remonstrance, (which by the by was a successful one) " why do you object to high " charges? they are the inevitable consequences of approaching the " capital." There are some who, thinking with less respect than I do of the Russians, would have thought that they had inoculated this native of the south with knavery, but I was satisfied from his tone, look, and gesture, that he took it in the natural way; so wishing that we might never see his face, nor that of a fortified town more, we mounted our carriage and proceeded to the gate leading to Petersburg, where we were again detained at the guard-house three quarters of an hour, because it was necessary that the deputy governor should once more see his own wretched scrawl at the bottom of our post-order, not then even perfectly dry.

In what a situation would English travellers in their own country have been, with all their accustomed irritability and impatience, if the sound sense of a single vote had not overpowered the fortifying phrenzy of a certain illustrious engineer! How many governors, gates, and guards, would have been wished at the devil a thousand and a thousand times? The gratitude of those who are fond of loco-motive facility, should long since have raised a monument to Wolfran Cornwall. However, our stoppage reminds me to mention a characteristic which I had forgotten: before all the guard-houses in the

north there is a raised platform of wood, upon which are little posts;
against these the soldiers on duty recline their pieces.

Thank heaven! we are out of the town, although the road is very
sandy and hilly. We travelled all night, and in attempting to ascend a long and steep hill, our cattle began to flag. There is a very
material difference between the Swedish and Russian Finn horses;
the latter are much larger, but very weak; indeed they appeared to
be nearly in the situation of the hack of an eccentric genius, who resolved to see whether his beast could not serve him without food; for
seven days the poor thing fasted, but just as his master had taught
him to live without eating, *he died*. Upon observing the stoppage,
our peasant (for in Russia only one takes charge of the post-horses)
descended, and breaking a sapling fir, would have belaboured his
miserable animals most unmercifully, had we not interfered: famine
or excess of labour had fixed them to the earth, and they had less
motion than the firs of the dark and hideous forest in which the accident befel us. I would not have answered for the perfect patience
of Job, had he been obliged to drive four in hand in Russian Finland.

In spite of the military jokes and sparkling philippics of Mr.
Windham in the senate, I was resolved to see if a volunteer uniform
had really nothing of value in it, but to excite a jest. I speedily
mounted my jacket, and with the peasant walked forward to the next
post-house, distant about two miles and a half. It was in the dead of
a cloudy night; as we approached the house, I saw upon a dreary
heath six or seven sturdy peasants lying on each side of a great
blazing fir-tree, fast asleep:

> " Allow not Nature more than Nature needs;
> " Man's life is cheap as beasts."

The moment the post-master opened the door and beheld my regimentals, he bowed most respectfully, and upon the peasant's explaining the condition of our horses, he awakened the peasants by their
fir fire, and dispatched four of them to assist in drawing the carriage,
and the remainder to catch the horses in the adjoining woods for the
next post; he then very civilly placed three chairs in a line, and
gave me a pillow, looking tolerably clean, and thus equipped, I was
preparing to lay down, when a *marchand de liqueur*, who lived in an
opposite hotel, uncovered, with a large beard, a great bottle of quass
in one hand, and a glass in the other, entered the room, and after
crossing himself and bowing before me, he pressed me to drink; all
these marks of distinction, to which let me add four good courier
horses for the next stage, were the happy fruits of my volunteer

jacket. Thus satisfied, I enjoyed two hours of delicious sleep, until
the jingling bells of our poor post-horses announced the arrival of
the vehicle, and of all the cavalcade.

The following day we beheld the shining cupola and spires of the
capital, about ten versts from us, just rising above a long dark line
of fir-forests. At twelve o'clock we reached the barrier, a plain lofty
arch of brick stuccoed white, from each side of which a palisado ran,
part of the lines of this vast city. There is no custom-house here,
but we were detained nearly an hour, owing, as we afterwards found,
to the officer of the guard, a very fine looking young man, and I dare
say very brave withal, being somewhat of a novice in the mystery of
reading and writing: our passports appeared to puzzle him dreadfully, at length a serjeant, who doubtless was the literary wonder of
the guard-house, was sent for, and in two minutes relieved his officer and the Englishmen at the same time. A fair-complexioned Cossac of the Don, habited in a pyramidal red velvet cap, short scarlet
cloak, with a belt of pistols, a light fuzee slung across his shoulders,
and a long elastic spear in his hand, mounted upon a little miserable
high-boned hack, was ordered to attend us to the governor of the
city, and with this *garde d'honneur* we posted through the vast suburbs
of Wibourg, and at length ascended the emperor's bridge of pontoons
or barges; here the most magnificent and gorgeous spectacle burst
upon me, and for a time overwhelmed me with amazement and admiration.

The sky was cloudless, the Neva of a brilliant blue, clear, and
nearly as broad as the Thames at Westminster bridge; it flowed
majestically along, bearing on its bosom the most picturesque vessels, and splendid pleasure barges; as the eye rapidly travelled several miles up and down this glorious river, adorned with stupendous
embankments of granite, it beheld its sides lined with palaces, stately buildings, and gardens, whilst at a distance arose green cupolas,
and the lofty spires of the Greek churches covered with ducat gold,
and glittering in the sun. Immediately before us extended the magnificent railing of the summer gardens, with its columns and vases of
granite, a matchless work of imperial taste and splendour.

In the capacious streets of this marvellous city, we passed through
crowds of carriages drawn by four horses at length, and a variety of
rich equipages, and of people from all parts of the world, in their
various and motley costume. At the governor's office we presented
our passports, and the cossac left us. The cossacs have a curious ap-

pearance upon their little shabby horses, which have the reputation, however, of being remarkably fleet and-hardy; their riders hold their spear, which is from fifteen to eighteen feet long, vertically rest-.ing upon their stirrup. It is said that they have the faculty of calculating from the appearance of trodden grass, the number of men and of cattle that have passed over it, and even to ascertain the period of their passing. The cossacs are never trained to attack in squadrons : they are always placed in the rear of the army, and act only in a desultory manner upon the retreat of an enemy. At the governor's we were questioned by the officer upon duty, as to our motives of travelling, names, &c. &c.; a description of his room will serve to give a general idea of the arrangements which constantly occur in the Russian houses: the apartment was divided by a partition of wood, of about three-fourths of the height of the room, indented at the top, and ornamented with little crescents; behind this screen was his bed, and in a corner, suspended near the top of the cieling, was the framed and glazed picture of his favourite saint, before which a lamp was burning; this economy of space gave him the convenience of two rooms.

Amidst the tumult of ideas which the scenes around us excited, we drove into the yard of Demoth's hotel, I believe the best in Petersburg ; it is kept by some civil Germans, and stands on the side of the Moika, a beautiful canal, having a rich iron railing and an embankment of granite. It may be as well now to caution the traveller against the free use of the Neva water, which, like that of the Seine, is very aperient.

Our hotel was upon a scale with all the surrounding objects, and very crowded ; it was with great difficulty that we obtained two uncomfortable rooms, which, according to the custom of the place, we were obliged to hire for a week certain. One of these apartments was divided as I have described, and afforded a place to sleep in for the servant. The walls were covered with a complete crust of our old tormentors the flies, which in Russia, at this season of the year, are little inferior to the plague of Egypt. After discharging the dust of Finland in a copious ablution, and partaking of a good dinner, at which, for the first time since we left Stockholm, we tasted vegetables, I sallied forth, but the day was far gone.

After hesitating some time, amidst such a blaze of novel magnificence, what object I should first investigate, I resolved to present myself at the base of the statue of Peter the Great. All the world has heard of this colossal compliment paid by the munificence of

Catherine II, and the genius of Falconet, to the memory of that wonderful man, who elevated Muscovy to the rank of an European empire. Filled, as I was, with admiration of this glorious work of art, I
could not help regretting that the artist had so much reduced and
polished the granite rock, which, with great grandeur of conception,
forms the pedestal of the statue. The horse, in the act of ascending
its acclivity, is intended to illustrate the difficulties which Peter had
to encounter in civilizing his unenlightened people. Had this rock
retained the size and shape which it bore when, as if propelled by
some vast convulsion of nature, it first occupied its present place,
with only a few of its asperities removed, it would have encreased the
dignity and expression of the horse and his rider, and would have
astonished every beholder with a stupendous evidence of toil and enterprise, which since the subversion of the Roman empire has no
parallel. A gentleman, who saw this rock in Carelia, before its removal, describes it to have been forty feet long, twenty-two broad,
and twenty-two high. It is of granite and onyx, and has a mixture of
white, black, and grey colouring; if I may judge of it by a seal,
which the learned Dr. Guthrie presented to me, it is susceptible of
a very fine polish. In six months the rock was removed from its
native bed to the spot where it now stands, partly by land and water,
a distance of eleven versts, or forty-one thousand two hundred and
fifty English feet, and cost four hundred and twenty-four thousand
six hundred and ten rubles. So indefatigable has been the labour of
the chisel upon its enormous magnitude and rugged coating, that its
history is its greatest wonder. The genius of Falconet was evidently
jealous of the rude but stupendous powers of nature, and was fearful
that *her rock* might engage more attention than *his statue ;* hence he
reduced the former, until he rendered it disproportioned to the colossal figures which it supports; but he has thereby succeeded in
bringing his work nearer to the eye of the beholder. Had he been
content to have divided the homage with nature, he would not have
been a loser. The head of Peter, which is very fine, was modelled
by madame Collot, the mistress of Falconet. The figure and the
drapery are admirable, and the horse is worthy of being ranked next
to his *Venetian brethren,* those matchless works of art, which now
adorn the gates of the Thuilleries. The spot where this statue is
raised is always very much thronged, on account of its being central, and leading to one of the bridges.

I bestrode one of the little droshkas which I have described ; my

driver, who emitted a most pestiferous atmosphere of garlic, with a
tin plate upon his back, marked with his number, and the quarter to
which he belonged (a badge which is used by all the fraternity, to
facilitate their punishment, if they behave ill), drove me with uncommon velocity. His horse had a high arch of ash rising from his
collar, more for ornament than use. I was much struck with the
prodigious length and breadth of the streets, and with the magnitude
and magnificence of the houses, which are built in the Italian style
of architecture, of brick stuccoed, and stained to resemble stone.
They are mostly of four stories, including the basement, in the centre of which is generally a large carriage gate-way : the roof slopes
very gently, and is formed of sheets of cast iron, or of copper, painted red or green ; and behind there is a great yard, containing the
out-houses, and ice-houses, and immense stores of wood. The vast
number also of chariots, each of which was drawn by four horses,
the leaders at a great distance from the shaft horses, very much
augmented the effect. The postilion is always a little boy, habited in
a round hat, and a long coarse coat, generally brown, fastened round
the middle by a red sash, and, strangely reversing the order of
things, is always mounted on the off horse, and carries his whip in
his left hand. The little fellow is very skilful and careful, and it is
pleasant to hear him, whenever he turns a corner, or sees any one in
the road before him, exclaim, or rather very musically sing,
" paddee! paddee! paddee!" The coachman, or, as he is called, the
Ishvoshick, is dressed in the same manner, and wears a long venerable beard; behind the carriage are one or two servants in large,
laced, cocked hats, shewy liveries, military boots and spurs. What
an equipage for St. James's-street on a birth-day ! The beard of the
Russian charioteer would here produce as strong a sensation as did
the neat, formal, little bob wig of lord Whitworth's coachman in the
streets of Paris. The carriage and horses in attendance are standing
the greater part of the day in the court yards, or before the houses of
their masters; the horses are fed in harness, and the little postilion
is frequently twenty-four hours in the stirrup, eats, drinks, and sleeps
on horseback, and the coachman does the same upon his box. A
stranger immediately upon his arrival, if he wishes to maintain the
least respectability, is under the necessity of hiring a coach or
chariot and four, for which he pays two hundred rubles a month.
Without this equipage a traveller is of no consideration in Petersburg.

CHAP. XI.

PETERSBURG is worthy of being the capital of an empire as large as the half of Asia, more than twice the size of Europe, and covered with a population of forty millions of people. Its boundaries measure about twenty English miles, but the circumference of the ground actually built upon is considerably less. The vast space of its streets and areas will ever give it superiority over every other European capital; but its principal beauty arises from its being the result of *one mighty design.*

In almost every other city, the buildings at once display the progress of its prosperity and taste. In some dark and narrow lane a palace rears its head; or, in a handsome street, the eye is suddenly offended, by beholding the little squalid abode of a *marchand de liqueur.* Most towns, in their progress, have resembled the house of the Cornish fisherman, who at first thriftily built his little abode of one story; becoming prosperous, he resolved upon raising it, and accordingly sent for a neighbouring carpenter: the village architect, to whom, I suppose, the names of Holland, Wyatt, and Cockerell were as foreign as that of Palladio, upon being informed of the object of his employer's wishes, the builder very judiciously begged him to stand up, took measure of his height, and raised his simple chateau one story higher, in which the owner and his wife could very comfortably walk without stooping. In process of time, the

X

fisherman became rich by privateering; the house must be enlarged; the roof was removed, and two rooms, twice the height of those below, occupied the place of the garret, which was promoted one story higher.

In the capital before us, time has been actively and ardently employed in filling up one grand outline. What death prevented Peter the Great from executing, successive sovereigns, and particularly Catherine II and the present Emperor, with great taste and encouragement, have nearly accomplished. So rapidly has this city risen, that a traveller might think that one mind had planned, and one hand had executed the whole. Very few of the ancient wooden houses remain; and those which have not yet fallen a prey to time, are lost in the splendour of the buildings that surround them.

Of the magical celerity with which buildings are constructed in Petersburg the reader may judge, when he is informed that five hundred noble houses were erected in the last year; yet, though building so rapidly advances in the city, its population, by the last estimate, it appears, has rather declined, whilst that of the country has encreased. I have before stated the amount to be forty millions, in which two females are averaged to one male.

' To all great national works, the government and the genius of the country have been propitious. Unbounded power presents an Emperor of Russia with the lamp of Aladdin: at his nod a temple of ice rears its chrystal front, or a rocky mountain floats upon the deep.* At Petersburg there is no public to consult, the public buildings are therefore the result of one man's will. In England the public is every thing, and the variety of its taste appears in the variety of its buildings.

Petersburg is divided into three grand sections by the Neva, and a branch of it called the Little Neva, which issues from the Ladoga lake, and disembogues in the gulf of Cronstadt: this division resembles that of Paris by the Seine. The first section is called the Admiralty quarter, situated on the south side of the river, and com-

* The pedestal of Peter the Great, which was floated up the Neva on vast rafts.

prises the largest and most superb part of the city, and is the residence of the imperial family, the nobility, a principal part of the
merchants and gentry, and nearly the whole of the trading community : this part is formed into a number of islands by the intersections
of the Moika, the Fontanka, the Katarina, and Nikolai canals. The
second section is named the Vassili Ostrof, situated on the north-
west of the river, where there are many public buildings and elegant
streets; this part coincides with the Fauxbourg St. Germain of
Paris : and the third is called the Island of St. Petersburg, standing
on the north side of the river, and is distinguishable for containing
the fortress and some good streets.

The country about the city is very flat and sterile ; but the gardens in the suburbal part have been much improved by the introduction of vast quantities of vegetable mould, which have been brought
from distant parts of the country, and also by ship ballast. The
morning after our arrival was spent in delivering our letters of introduction; and such is the spirit of hospitality here, so frequently and
so justly extolled, that it became necessary to chronicle down the
invitations that flowed in upon us from all quarters.

In our walk upon this occasion, it was with astonishment that we
beheld the bank and pavement of hewn granite, which we first saw
in the English line in the Galeerenhof : figure to yourself a parapet
and footpath of the hardest rock which nature produces, of great
breadth and thickness, gracing the southern side of the river, and
running parallel with a line of magnificent palaces and splendid
mansions for near two English miles !

In the evening I visited the summer gardens that face the Neva,
the palisade of which, unquestionably the grandest in Europe, is
composed of thirty-six massy Doric columns of solid granite, surmounted by alternate vases and urns, the whole of which, from the
ground, are about twenty feet high, connected by a magnificent
railing, formed of spears of wrought iron, tipped with ducat gold.
The decorations over the three grand entrances are also exquisitely
wrought, and covered with gold of the same superior quality. As
near as I could ascertain by my own paces, the length of this magnificent balustrade must be about seven hundred feet. The pillars

would certainly be improved were they thinner or fluted. It is customary to attend a little more than ordinary to dress in this promenade, as the imperial family frequently walk here. The walks are very extensive, umbrageous, and beautiful, though too regular; they are all of the growth of Catherine the second's taste and liberality. Here only the chirping of the sparrow is to be heard; not a thrush, linnet, or goldfinch, are to be found in Russia. Amongst the women, who were all dressed à la mode de Paris, there were some lovely faces; but, to prevent incense being offered upon a mistaken altar, let me hint that they were Polish beauties: to each of the group one might have said,

> " ———You are the cruell'st she alive,
> If you will lead these graces to the grave,
> And leave no copy."

A young officer of the imperial guards approached one of them and kissed her hand, and, as he raised his head, the lady kissed his cheek: it is the custom in Russia. Is it possible, thought I, that this spot, in no very distant day, owned a Swedish master? Can a little paltry bridge make all this difference between the belles of the two countries? But I will leave this point undecided. Be it as it may, the salutation was the most graceful I ever witnessed: it was politeness improved by the most charming gallantry; bows, curtsies, and salams are icicles to it. Whilst France furnishes us with caps and bonnets, and Egypt with dusky side-boards, may the Russians fix the universal mode of friendly meeting between the sexes for ever and for ever!

This captivating characteristic, and as the sun descends, the gentle sounds of lovers whispering in the shade, and the beauty of the spot, entitle the Summer Gardens to the name of the Northern Eden. Where the parties are not familiar, the lady *bows*, never curtsies: the attitude is very graceful. As I am upon the subject of kissing, and quit it with reluctance, I beg leave to state, that in Easter every Russian, be his rank in life however humble, and his beard as large, long, and as bristly as ever graced or guarded the chin of a man, may, upon presenting an egg, salute the loveliest woman he meets, however high her station: they say, such is the omnipotence of the custom, that, during this delicious festival, the cheek of the lovely Empress herself, were she to be seen in the streets, would not be exempt from the blissful privilege.

As I approached the Summer Gardens, to which a great number of equipages were hastening, it was curious to observe the prodigious fulness of the horses' manes and tails, which are never cropped: to the former the Russians pay a religious attention; they even carry it so far as to adorn them, as many of the British fair decorate themselves, with false hair. To shew the various prejudices of mankind, it is only a short time since that mares were rode. On the appearance of a friend of mine, some years since, mounted upon one of them, the men expressed their astonishment, and the women tittered. Geldings are prohibited as useless animals. In the streets it is very common to see pairs of Russians, who in their dress much resemble the boys of Christ's Hospital, walking *hand in hand*, never arm in arm.

The Russian language sounded very sweet to my ears, and peculiarly so as it flowed from the lips of madame Khremer of the English line. There is something very musical in the following expression: "*Pazar vleita, padeta suda*," Pray, sir, come and sit by me. French is chiefly spoken amongst the well-bred Russians, who are said to be imperfectly acquainted with their own language: this is one of the foolish effects of fashion. The Russians always add the christian name of their father to their own, with the termination of *ivitch* or *evitch*, which denotes the son, as *ovna* or *eona* does the daughter.

It requires some interest, time, and trouble, before a stranger can see the palaces and public buildings; I therefore recommend him, through the medium of his ambassador, to be speedy in making the arrangements for this purpose. Whilst these matters were negociating in our favour, I resolved to make the best of my time in seeing what lay expanded before me. Accordingly, a friend of mine ordered his Russian servant to drive us to the fortress: when the man received his orders, he curled up his beard, took off his hat, scratched his head, and expressed by his manner, some reluctance

and disgust, which arose, as we afterwards found, from the horror
with which the common Russians regard the citadel, on account of its
containing the state dungeons, and of the horrible stories to which
they have given birth. As we galloped all the way, the usual pace in
Petersburg, we soon crossed the Emperor's bridge, and passed the
drawbridge and outer court of this melancholy place, which is built
of massy walls of brick, faced with hewn granite, of the same materials as the five bastions which defend it. We were set down at the
door of the church of St. Peter and St. Paul, remarkable for being
the burial-place of the Russian sovereigns, and for its lofty and beautiful spire, two hundred and forty feet high, richly covered with
ducat gold. The inside of the church was damp and dreary, and
had no beauties of architecture to recommend it. In oblong square
sepulchres of stone, raised and arranged in lines on the right of the
shrine, and covered with velvet richly embroidered with gold and
silver, repose the remains of Peter the Great, his Empress Catherine, the celebrated peasant of Livonia, of Alexey, Anne, Elizabeth,
and Peter III and Catherine II; and, on the other side of the church,
at a distance, is the tomb of Paul, the late emperor, opposite to a
whole length painting of the saint of his name, covered like the
others, but with more cost and grandeur. An inscription in copper
informed us, that the unhappy Emperor died on the *eleventh* or
twelfth of March, 1801. On each side of the church, very carelessly
arranged, are banners of war; truncheons, keys of cities, and arms,
taken in battle by the Russians: amongst the former were some
Turkish colours taken by count Orloff, or rather, if merit had its
due, by the British admirals, Greig and Dugdale, in the celebrated
engagement of Tscheme, when the whole of the vast Turkish fleet,
except one man-of-war and a few galleys were burnt, so that " the
" sun at its rising saw no more of its flag."

The view from the belfry is one of the grandest spectacles I ever
beheld: below flowed the Neva; before us lay the whole city expanded, from the Couvent des Demoiselles to the end of the Galeern-
hoff, a line of palaces and superb houses, extending nearly six English miles; immediately facing us was the marble palace, the palace of Peter the Great; the hermitage, the winter palace, crowded

with statues and pillars; and the admiralty, its church, and the dome
of the marble church; in the fortress from this height we could
discern a number of gloomy prison yards and the gratings of dungeons, than which nothing could look more melancholy; and also
the mint, which appeared a handsome building, where the gold and
silver from the mines of Siberia are refined and converted into coin.
Here also we had a fine view of the country over the Wibourg
suburbs, and in a distant part of the citadel was pointed out the court
of the prison in which the unfortunate young princess, who was en-
snared from Leghorn by the treacherous stratagems of Orloff, and
afterwards confined in this place, is said to have perished. The
story of this devoted young personage is still wrapped in some obscurity: After the burning of the Turkish fleets near Tscheme, a
beautiful young Russian lady, attended by an elderly lady, appeared
at Leghorn; although she appeared without show, or the means of
making any, her society was much courted on account of the sweetness and accomplishments of her mind, the attractions of her person,
and a certain air of majesty which particularly distinguished her.
To some of her most confidential friends she communicated the fatal
secret, that she was the daughter of the Empress Elizabeth by a private marriage, and that her pretensions to the throne of Russia were
superior to those of Catharine II, to whose suspicious ear the communication was imparted with uncommon celerity. Allured by the
deceitful solicitations of a Russian officer, who was an agent of count
Orloff, who promised to espouse her cause, and to gain over the
count, she came to Pisa in the beginning of the year 1775, where
Alexey Orloff then resided in great magnificence during the repairs
of his fleet. Upon her arrival the count paid his respects to her
with all the deference and ceremony due to a reigning sovereign,
affected to believe her story, and promised to support her pretensions.
At length, after appearing with her at every fashionable place during
the carnival, and paying her the most marked and flattering attentions, he avowed, in the most respectful manner, a tender passion
for her, and submitted to her the glittering prospect of her mounting
with him the throne to which she was entitled. Intoxicated with
the idea, she gave him her hand. A few days after the nuptials, the

count announced a magnificent marine entertainment in honour of
the marriage. The young personage proceeded to his ship in all
imaginable naval pomp; as soon as she entered the cabin, gracious
heaven, what a display of treachery was developed! Orloff upbraided
her with being an impostor, and, the more barbarously to degrade
her, ordered her delicate hands to be fastened by handcuffs, which
had been prepared for the purpose, and quitted the ship, which immediately sailed for Cronstadt, fom whence she was brought to the
fortress in a covered barge, where she was immolated, and never
heard of more. It is supposed that she was drowned in her dungeon, which was rather deep, during one of the inundations of the
Neva. In a part of this fortress is a little boat, which is said to be
the father of the Russian marine, by having furnished Peter the
Great, when a child, with the rudiments of naval architecture, which
he afterwards so passionately pursued at Sardam. It was brought
from Moscow, and deposited here with great pomp, in 1723, and
was called by Peter " *the Little Grandsire.*"

Upon our return from the fortress, I took a view of the celebrated
street called the Grand or *Nevski* Perspective: it runs in a direct
line from the church of the admiralty, from which the principal
streets of the admiralty quarter branch like radii, to the monastery
of St. Alexander Nevski: its length is about four miles, and its
breadth not quite equal to that of our Oxford-street; it is lined with
very noble houses, and what will afford the most delight to the liberal and reflecting observer, with elegant churches, in which the de-
vout man, without restraint, may worship his God after the dictates
of his own habits or persuasion. Here sectarian fury never disfi-
gures the temple of the Almighty : the Greek and the Protestant,
the Armenian and the Catholic, here quietly pass to their respective
places of devotion, and unite in sending up to the throne of Heaven
the hallowed, though varying, sounds of their grateful adoration,
which, blending as they ascend, charm the Divine ear, with the
most acceptable homage, the *harmony of religion.*

The late Emperor very materially affected the beauty of this
street, by destroying the foot-paths which were formerly on each
side, and forming a very broad path in the centre of it, which he

planted with Linden trees, and guarded by a low railing. The idea
was evidently taken from the beautiful Linden walk at Berlin, which
originated in the exquisite taste and genius of Frederic, so justly
called the Great. The trees look very sickly, and, for want of soil
and moisture, never can flourish, and cannot atone for the violation
which is offered to taste. If this great nuisance were removed, the
perspective would be one of the finest in Europe. The great bee-
hive of the city, called the *Gostinnoi dvor*, is in this street; it is a
vast building, wholly dedicated to trade, containing two piazza stories, and presenting three unequal sides, the longest of which is upwards of nine hundred feet: under this roof is an immense number
of shops and stores: the neatness of the shops, and the dexterity
and activity of the shopmen, cannot but impress a stranger. The
haberdashers here, as in England, are fine lusty fellows, but add to
their athletic appearance a prodigious bushy beard; this said beard
is the pride and glory of Russian manhood:

> " It is the equal grace
> Both of his wisdom and his face,"

which the churches of the north and of the east protected with uncommon zeal and contumacy, whilst the razor of ecclesiastical discipline committed sad ravages upon it in the southern and western
regions: at one time, as if in derision, this venerable growth of the
human visage was cut into a tapering cone; it next assumed the
gravity of the scollop; then it alarmed the ladies in whiskers, and
afterwards tickled their cheeks with a few monkish hairs upon the
upper lip; till at length the holy scythe, pursuing its victory, cleared
every hair, until the chin assumed the polish and smoothness of an
alabaster statue.

The Russian beard struck terror into the soul of Peter the Great;
he dared not attack it. It was not surprising that Catherine wished
to see its honours shorn, but amidst her mighty and resplendent
conquests, the beard remained not only unassaulted but unassailable;
and if a smooth chin is one of the characteristics of high civilization,

Y

I believe the Russian will implore his saint to let him live and die a barbarian.

The following anecdote is an authentic one: A nobleman having laid a wager upon the subject, offered a common Russian, one of his slaves, freedom and two thousand pounds to part with his beard; the reply of the poor fellow was, " I had sooner part with my life." To return to the shops: before the door of each of them parades a shop-boy, whose duty it is to importune every passenger to walk in and buy: this little fellow seems to partake of the same spirit which so indefatigably moves his brethren, who mount guard before the old clothes and slop shops of Monmouth-street.

The acuteness, frugality, and perseverance, of these people, virtues which never fail to raise for their fortunate possessor a pyramid of wealth, is surprising. Most of these tradesmen have been rasnoschiks, or ambulatory venders of little merchandizes in the streets, who, by a judicious application of the golden rule, " take care of the " *copecs*, and the *rubles* will take care of themselves," well digested with black bread and a little quas, a common antiscorbutic acidulous beverage, produced by pouring hot water on rye or barley, and fermented, have become *marchands des modes*, or successful followers of other trades; the fruitful principle of getting and saving has enabled them to purchase houses, and commence money brokers and lenders, in which capacity many of them die immensely rich.

These shopkeepers have also their phrases of allurement. The haberdasher says: " Walk in, my fair one, we have straw bonnets " which will very much become that pretty face; oh! how well " they would look upon you! how much more your lover would " admire you in one!" In an adjoining shop, the shoemaker is seen sweeping the pretty foot of some fair customer with his long beard, as he adjusts the glossy slipper. Upon tables, before the doors of the upholsterers, in which all descriptions of furniture may be purchased, plaster-of-Paris busts of Alexander and his lovely consort are presented to the eye: " Sir, I am sure you like the Em- " peror and the Empress; they are exactly like the originals; you " shall have them for twelve rubles; I cannot sell them apart, they

" must not be separated, they always go together, sir; they are, you
" may rely upon it, exactly like the originals."

The consummate knowledge which the Russian shopkeeper possesses of the most complicated calculation, and the entangled caprices of that cameleon-coloured goddess who presides over the exchange, is absolutely astonishing. If he cannot write, he has
recourse to a small wooden frame, containing rows of beans, or little
wooden balls, strung upon stretched wires, and with this simple
machine he would set the spirit of Necker at defiance. It has been
the fashion amongst travellers to assert, and they seem to have
alternately received and imparted the prejudice, without the trouble
and the justice of making their own observations, that the Russians
are the greatest cheats in the universe. If the worthy shopkeepers
of London, of Paris, and of Vienna, had never been known to consider that the

> " ———— value of the thing
> Is just as much as it will bring,"

then, indeed, might Mercury, invested with his least favourable attribute, regard the shop-boards of Gostinnoi dvor as his chosen altars.
Accustomed to obtain wealth in the detail, and to have their reservoirs filled by partial drops, and not by copious showers, they display that little trick, which may be seen in all other countries under
similar influences. It is related of Peter the Great, that, when a
deputation of Jews waited upon him, to solicit permission to settle at
Petersburg, he replied: " My good friends, I esteem you too much
" to grant you that favour, for my people will outwit you."

The Russian has an apology for *his* craft; nature furnishes him
with it: he is doubly a slave, first to his immediate master, and se-
condly to his Emperor. It is the policy of the poor fellow to conceal, as cautiously as he can, not from the latter, for he is the fond
father of his people, although constitutionally his paramount owner,
but from his *immediate* lord, the amount of his profits: he does,
what I have heard has been done in another country, where, thank
God, petty legalized tyranny has never yet had an inch of ground to

rest upon! he makes an inaccurate *return of income* to avoid an augmented imposition upon his profits.   Men, whilst they have wigs upon their heads, and robes upon their shoulders, may perhaps blame him, but when these grave and impressive habiliments of morality are quietly placed upon their respective pegs, their own-ers will, I am confident, pity, smile upon, and pardon, this hard and much injured toiling son of traffic.   In so severe a degree does this sort of subordinate, and ever the most grinding and pernicious of all slavery exist, that it is no unusual thing for a peasant to be ex-changed for a horse, and even a favourite dog.   A certain Russian countess used to make her Calmuc girls read to her till she slept, and, under the pain of severe flagellation, continue to read afterwards, to prevent her being awakened by the effect of *sudden silence.*

I one day saw a Russian, distinguished only from the commonest sort by the superiority of the cloth of his long coat, who had paid fifteen thousand pounds for his freedom, and had amassed by inde-fatigable industry, a fortune of one hundred thousand pounds : and not far from my hotel resided a Russian, who, in the short space of twelve years, with a fair character, had amassed nearly a million sterling.

I am ready to admit that the petty stratagems of the counter can never be justifiable, and that a propensity to conceal may increase them.   The more assailants morality has, like every other assaulted power, the less is her security, and if she withstand, the greater her triumph ; whilst she is expelling knavery at one gate, falsehood may enter at another, and this contentious combination frequently termi-nates in the restoration and victorious settlement of both.   Upon the mausoleums of few may justly be recorded the beautiful epitaph which appears upon the tomb of the brave and generous Philip de Villiers de l'Isle d'Adam, in the imperial museum of monuments in Les Petites Augustines, at Paris :

" Here lies Virtue, vanquishing Fortune."

But do not let us think, that the Russian is naturally worse than his brethren in other parts of the globe.   Heaven has scattered our infirmities pretty equally; and I must again repeat, that the little stratagems of our northern brother find considerable palliation in the law, that secures not the fruits of his labour, but exposes him to the iron grasp of rapacious and unrelenting oppression.

The late Catherine thought, that the glory of government did not consist alone in military triumphs; alarmed, as she most assuredly was, yet wholly uninfluenced, by the terrible storms of the French revolution, it was the anxious aim and the cordial desire of her long and splendid reign to civilize her people, by gradually unfolding to them, through a soft corrected medium, the glorious light of freedom. Her sagacious mind taught her to know, what Cowper has so exquisitely described, that

> " ———————————— all constraint
> Except what wisdom lays on evil men,
> Is evil; hurts the faculties, impedes
> Their progress in the road of science; blinds
> The eye-sight of discovery; and begets
> In those that suffer it, a sordid mind
> Bestial, a meagre intellect, unfit
> To be the tenant of man's noble form."

The modern Semiramis made some, though inconsiderable advances in the abolition of this odious vassalage, and, during its continuance, checked its wanton abuses by some wholesome corrections. The same wise and benign desire exists in the breast of the reigning Emperor. Yet the labours of so noble an undertaking are immense. Genius and patience, firmness and perseverance, unextinguishable enthusiasm and heroic philanthropy, must possess the head and heart of that being who accomplishes so glorious an achievement. Alas! baronial pride and hereditary prejudice, and that invincible attachment of man to property, have opposed, and will long oppose, this " consummation so devoutly to be wished." When once the Russian peer shall talk of his estate by its quantity and quality, and not by the degrading enumeration of so many heads of peasantry; then, and not till then, can civilization make any rapid and extensive progress in this vast empire.

To say that Nature has irreversibly doomed the Russian to be a barbarian, is an assertion as digraceful as it is unjust, and such as Nature has herself contravened.   Amidst all the oppression that weighs him to the earth, that half associates him with the rugged bear of his forest; and taught, as he is, that his condition can never know amelioration, this poor slave of the north has displayed the most heroic valour in the field, the most gentle moderation in success, and the mildest unrepining philosophy in suffering : such as would have done honour to a Roman.   If you ask whether the sensibilities of nature ever softened the Russian breast, read what the poor exiles have expressed in the desolate wilds of Siberia, and it will put the feelings of your own heart to their fullest proof.   In those regions of gloom, the poet may catch some of the finest subjects for his muse.

Let us not endeavour to convert the law of climates into the ruthless decrees of immortal vengeance. Well did the poor African say, " Ah! massa, a good Negro is like a chesnut, all *white* within; and " a bad Englishman is like an apple, thought perfect when it has many " little black grains in its heart." No! no! the breast of the Russian is not unimpressible. The granite of his inclement region is hard and rugged, harder than any other rock; but under its rough surface gems are sometimes found, and time and toil have proved that it is susceptible of a high polish.

No one who has remarked the Russian with candour, who judges from what he sees, and not from what he has heard or read, will hesitate to pronounce him one of the best tempered creatures in the creation.   He will bear the curse and scorn, and frequently the blows of his superior, with mildness.   Revenge, almost sanctioned by insults, never maddens his blood; and knowing, perhaps, how hard it is to suffer without resisting, he is scarcely ever seen to strike the animal over which he has power.   His horse is seldom propelled by any other influence than a few cherishing and cheerful sounds ; if this encouragement encreases not his pace, he does not, heated with savage fury, dissect the wretched beast with the scourge, beat out an eye, or tear out the tongue; no! his patient driver begins to sing to him, and the Russians are all famous singers, as I shall hereafter tell; if the charms of music have no influence on his legs, he then begins to reason with him : " You silly fellow ! why don't you " go on faster? come, get on, get on, don't you know that to-mor- " row is a prashnick (a fast day) and then you will have nothing to " do but to eat?" By this time the sulky jade has generally had her whim out, and trots on gaily. His horse is the object of his pride and comfort; well observing the wisdom of a Russian proverb, " It is not the horse but the oats that carry you:" as long as the animal will eat he feeds him; and his appearance generally honours, and his grateful services remunerate, the humanity of his master. A Russian, in the ebullition of passion, may do a ferocious thing, but never an *ill-natured* one. No being under heaven surpasses him in the gaiety of the heart. His little national song cheers him where- ver he goes. Where a German would smoke for comfort, the Russian sings. There is nothing cold about him but his wintry climate; whenever he speaks, it is with good-humour and vivacity, accompa- nied by the most animated gestures; and although I do not think that the Graces would at first pull caps about him, yet in the dance, for spirit and agility, I would match and back him against any one of the most agile sons of carelessness in the *Champs Elysées*.

In his religious notions the Russian knows not the *meaning* of bigotry, and what is better, of *toleration*. He mercifully thinks that every one will go to heaven, only that the Russians will have the best place. When these simple children of Nature address each other, it is always by the affectionate names of my father, my mother, my brother, or my sister, according to the age and sex of the party. To these good qualities of the heart let me add the fa- vourable and manly appearance of the Russians, I mean the proper Russian: during my stay in their residence I never saw one man that was either lame or deformed, or who squinted, and they are re- markable for the beauty of their teeth. Their dress is plain and simple, consisting of a long coat of woollen cloth, reaching to the knees, and folding before, fastened round the middle by a sash, into which his thick leather gloves are generally tucked, and frequently it holds his axe; his drawers are of the same stuff with his coat, and his legs are usually covered with heavy boots, or swathed round

with bandages, for they scarcely ever wear stockings, and for shoes
he uses coarse sandals made of cloth and the matted bark of linden
or birch; his hair is always cropped: the dress of the common
women did not appear to me to vary much from that of our
own females of the same degree; it consisted of a tunic, generally
of some shewy colour, with the sleeves of the shift appearing. The
milk-women looked very well in this dress; and the manner in
which they carry an ashen bow, from the ends of which are suspended little jars covered with matted birch bark, resting upon one
shoulder, gives them an uncommonly graceful appearance. When
the tradesmen's wives go out, they generally cover the top of their
caps with a large red silk handkerchief, which falls behind: this appeared to be a very favourite decoration.

Prudence demands some little knowledge of a character before
we associate with it, and it is with great pleasure that in this early
stage I present the Russian.

What of good he has he owes to himself; his foibles, and they
are few, originate elsewhere: he is the absolute slave of his lord,
and ranks with the sod of his domains; of a lord whose despotism
is frequently more biting than the Siberian blast. Never illumined
by education, bruised with ignoble blows, the object, and frequently
the victim of baronial rapacity, with a wide world before him, this oppressed child of nature is denied the common right of raising his shed
where his condition may be ameliorated, *permitted* only to toil in a
distant district under the protection of that disgraceful badge of vassalage, a *certificate of leave*, and upon his return compellable to lay the
scanty fruits of his labour at the feet of his master; and, finally, he
is excluded from the common privilege which nature has bestowed
upon the birds of the air, and the beasts of the wilderness, of chusing
his mate;- he must marry when and whom his master orders. Yet
under all this pressure, enough to destroy the marvellous elasticity
of a Frenchman's mind, the Russian is what I have depicted him.
If the reader is not pleased with the portrait, the painter is in fault.

CHAP. XII.

PEDESTRIANS, HOW CONSIDERED—THE SCAFFOLDING OF THE NEW KAZAN
CHURCH—GREAT INGENUITY OF COMMON RUSSIANS—THE MARKET—
THE KNOUT—CRUELTY OF THE EMPRESS ELIZABETH—PUNISHMENT
OF TWO LOVELY FEMALES.

AS I have described that focus of trade, the Gostinnoi-dvor, I must
not omit to mention that in the continuation of the perspective towards
the admiralty, an Englishman, of the name of Owens, carries on a
prodigious trade, chiefly in English manufactures ; his house, which
is a very magnificent one, has twenty-five rooms *en suite*, which are
filled with the most beautiful merchandize ; each room is a separate
shop, and attended by persons who are solely attached to it : the promenade, through magazines of music, of books, of jewels, of fashions,
&c. is very agreeable, and I believe perfectly novel. The respectable and enterprising proprietor is said frequently to receive one
thousand pounds sterling in one day : it is the constant and crowded
resort of all the fashion of Petersburg.

In the streets I rarely ever saw a Russian above the lowest degree
walking ; the very taylor bestrides his droshka to take measure of his
customer, and even many of the officers ride to the parade : this
may arise from the great extent of the city, and the distance which
one place is from another. If a gentleman is seen on foot he is immediately considered to be an Englishman, who wishes to examine
the city ; protected by this consideration, and this alone, he is regarded with tokens of courtesy, should a Russian noble of his acquaintance gallop by in his chariot and four. An Englishman is the
only privileged foreigner who may, with safety to his own dignity,
perambulate the streets, and investigate the buildings of Petersburg.

As I walked down the Linden footpath of the Grand Perspective,
I observed almost every passenger, with whatever hurry he seemed
to be moving, stop short before a church on the right hand, a little
below the shops, take off his hat, bow, and touch his forehead, and
either side of his breast, and then proceed. This building was the
church of the Mother of God, of Kazan, which, although an inferior
building, is, in religious estimation, the most considerable of the
Greek churches, on account of its containing the figure of the Virgin. Upon all public occasions, the emperor and court assist, with

Z

great splendour, in the celebration of divine worship here. Behind it
was a vast pile of scaffolding, raised for the purpose of erecting a
magnificent metropolitan church, in the room of the one which I
have just named. This place of worship, when completed, will surpass in size and splendour every other building in the residence; and,
if I may judge from the model, will be little inferior in magnitude
and grandeur to our St. Paul's. . The emperor has allotted an enormous sum for its completion: all the holy utensils are to be set with
the richest diamonds; even the screen is to be studded with precious
stones. The scaffolding of this colossal temple is stupendous, and
most ingeniously designed and executed, and would alone be sufficient to prove the genius and indefatigable labour of the Russians.
Most of the masons and bricklayers who were engaged in raising the
New Kazan, as well as those who are to be seen embellishing the city
in other parts, are boors from the provinces. The axe constitutes the
carpenter's box of tools : with that he performs all his work. No one
can observe with what admirable judgment, perspicuity, and preci-
sion, these untutored rustics work, and what graceful objects rise
from their uncouth hands, without doing them the justice to say, that
they are not to be surpassed by the most refined people in imitation
and ingenuity: from me they have drawn many a silent eulogium,
as I passed through the streets.

Whilst I was gazing upon the New Kazan, the foundation of
which, as well as the pedestals of the columns, are already raised, on
a sudden all the hats flew off about me, in compliment to the empress
dowager, and her lovely daughters the grand duchesses, who, with
their attendants, were passing in two very plain carriages of a dark
olive colour, drawn each by four horses, with two footmen behind, in
liveries of the colour of the carriages, with a red cape, large cocked
hats, and military boots: upon the pannels were merely the letter
E. and the black eagle. This august family, like that of the sovereign of England, but with less show, frequently ride about the city,
and pay friendly visits.

Strolling nearly to the end of the Perspective, I found myself in
the market-place, and saw lying near the great market, scales, the
apparatus to which delinquents are fastened, when they receive the
punishment of the knout, that terrible scourge which Peter the
Great, and the empress Elizabeth, were perpetually raising over the
heads of their subjects, but which the mercy of the present emperor

never, except for crimes of the deepest dye, permits to be exercised with fatal violence.   The last man who perished by it broke into the cottage of a family consisting of five persons, in a dark night, and butchered every one of them with a pole-axe.   An act of such wanton barbarity, and so alien to the character of the Russian, did not fail to excite the highest sensations of horror.   After a fair trial, the murderer was twice knouted; and, upon receiving his last punishment, was, in the language of the Russian executioner, "*finished,*" by receiving several strokes of the thong dexterously applied to the loins, which were thus cut open: the miserable wretch was then raised, and the ligaments which united the nostrils were terribly lacerated by pincers: but this latter part of his punishment, as I was informed by a gentleman who was present, created no additional pang to the sufferer, for the last stroke of the scourge only fell upon a breathless body.   When a criminal is going to receive the knout, he has a right, if he chuses, to stop at a certain kabac, and drink an allowance of liquor at the expense of government.

I question if the cruelty of punishment is to be determined by the quantum of unnecessary agony which it causes, whether the infliction of death by suspension is not almost as barbarous as the knout : sufferers in the former mode have been seen to display, for eight and ten minutes, all the appearances of the most horrible torment.   There is no mode of putting a capital offender to death so swift and decisive as decapitation.   The scaffold, the preparation, the fatal stroke, the blood, are pregnant with exemplary and repulsive horror: the pang of the sufferer is instantaneous—all the substantial ends of justice are effected with all possible humanity.

In Russia, ladies of rank have suffered the punishment of the knout: the Abbé Chappe D'Auteroche relates the circumstance of an execution of this nature which took place in the reign of the cruel Elizabeth.   He states that madame Lapookin, who was one of the loveliest women belonging to the court of that empress, had been intimately connected with a foreign ambassador who was concerned in a conspiracy against Elizabeth, and, on this account, his fair companion was denounced as an accessory in his guilt, and condemned to undergo the knout: the truth was, madame Lapookin had been indiscreet enough to mention some of the endless amours of her imperial mistress.   The beautiful culprit mounted the scaffold in an elegant undress, which encreased the beauty of her charms, and the interest of her situation. Distinguished by the captivation of her mind and person, she had been the idol of the court, and wherever she moved she was environed by admirers : she was now surrounded by executioners, upon whom she gazed with astonishment, and seemed to doubt that she was the object of such cruel preparations. One of the executioners pulled off a cloak which covered her bosom, at which, like Charlotte Cordey, as she was preparing for the guillotine, her modesty took alarm, she started back, turned pale, and burst into tears. Her clothes were soon stripped off, and she was naked to the waist, before the eager eyes of an immense concourse of people profoundly silent. One of the executioners then took her by both hands, and turning her half round, raised her on his back, inclining forwards, lifting her a little from the ground; upon which the other executioner laid hold of her delicate limbs with his rough hands, adjusted her on the back of his coadjutor, and placed her in the properest posture for receiving the punishment. He then retreated a few steps, measuring the proper distance with a steady eye, and leaping backwards, gave a stroke with the whip, so as to carry away a slip of skin from the neck to the bottom of her back; then striking his feet against the ground, he made a second blow, parallel to the former, and in a few minutes all the skin of the back was cut away in small slips, most of which remained hanging to her chemise: her tongue was cut out immediately after, and she was banished to Siberia.

It is impossible to reflect upon this savage scene, in which the empress betrayed all the qualities of a ruthless barbarian, without equal horror and indignation. History represents Elizabeth as the most indolent, voluptuous, and sensual, of her sex, which her portraits fully confirm. An anecdote is related of her, which proves, if any thing further were wanting, that she was a total stranger to feeling. One of her ladies in waiting, who was far advanced in years, and laboured under a great weakness in her legs, one day very nearly fainted in the presence of the empress from the fatigue of standing. Elizabeth observing her situation, enquired the cause; and, upon being informed, she coolly replied: " Oh, is it so? then lean a " little against those drawers, and I will *make believe* that I don't " see you. "

The late empress Catherine exercised her vengeance upon a similar occasion with more lenity, but in a very mortifying manner. A lovely young woman, who had married the count M———, one of her discarded favourites, obtained from her husband some singular. particulars respecting his intimacy with the empress, which she very injudiciously related to some of her female friends at Moscow, where she resided. Not long after, just as the lady and her husband were resigning themselves to sleep, they were awakened by a loud knocking at the door of their chamber, which the husband unbolted, when a stout police officer entered with a large rod in one hand, and an imperial order in the other. The husband was commanded to kneel on one side of the bed, and make no resistance or noise, as in the next room there were several brethren of this summary minister of justice in waiting. The lady was ordered, just as she was, to descend from the bed, and lay herself upon the floor; the officer then tied her hands and feet, and gave her a severe whipping : when he had finished the discipline, he loosened her, raised her up, and said, " This is the punishment which the empress inflicts upon tattlers ; " the next time, you go to Siberia." The story was soon buzzed abroad, and the poor young lady could not appear for some time after in Moscow without exciting a titter.

In her pleasures, Catherine only reflected upon the unbridled indulgences of the sovereigns of the opposite sex, which she cherished as precedents of indisputable authority. As an *Empress*, she considered herself above those restraints with which the protective code of society has environed the delicacy and chastity of women, the bright lustre of which cannot be breathed upon without being sullied. It is not likely that I, who belong to a country which female modesty has selected for her favourite residence, and in the diadem of which she has fixed her whitest plume, should advocate the licentiousness of Catherine; yet it is but justice to her memory to say, that she endeavoured to conceal her faulty pleasures under a surface of refinement; that she punished, with efficacious severity, every inclination to depravity in her court ; and that she laboured only to make the better parts of her character exemplary.

The present empress dowager, though past the meridian of beauty, exhibits very powerful traces of her having been one of nature's favourites. Her complexion is very fine, her face full, her eyes of hazel colour, sweet and expressive ; her person somewhat corpulent, but very majestic. Her manners are in a peculiar degree soft, benign, and captivating. She devotes herself to the education of the younger branches of her august family, to the superintendence and encou-

ragement of benevolent institutions, and to a very tasteful cultivation of the arts. One of her pursuits is somewhat singular: she is
an excellent medalist. I have seen some of her works in this elegant
branch of art, as well as some of her chasing in gold, which would
do honour to any artist. Her needle-work is also very beautiful, and
must be admired even by those who have beheld the exquisite per-
formances of a Linwood.

The present emperor Alexander is about twenty-nine years of
age, his face is full, very fair, and his complexion pale; his eyes
blue, and expressive of that benificent mildness which is one of the
prominent features of his character. His person is tall, lusty, and
well proportioned; but, being a little deaf, to facilitate his hearing,
he stoops: his deportment is condescending, yet dignified. In the
discharge of his august duties he displays great activity and acuteness, but without show and bustle: the leading features of his mind
are sound discretion and humanity, qualities which cannot fail to
render an empire flourishing, and a people happy. He is so much
an enemy to parade, that he is frequently seen wrapped up in his
regimental cloak, riding about the capital alone, upon a little common droshka: in this manner he has been known to administer to
the wants of the poor. It is his wish, if he should be recognized in
this state of privacy, that no one will take off their hats; but the
graciousness of his desire only puts the heart in the hand as it un-
covers the head. I have many times seen him in a chariot, perfectly
plain, of a dark olive, drawn by four horses, driven by a bearded
coachman, a common little postilion, and attended by a single footman. Soldiers are always upon the look-out for him, to give timely
notice to the guard of his approach; without this precaution it would
be impossible, amidst the crowd of carriages which is to be seen in
the residence, to pay him the honours due to his rank. The emperor is very much attached to the English, numbers of whom have
settled in the empire, and have formed, under the auspices of the
government, a sort of colony. The emperor has often been heard to
say, that " The man within whose reach heaven has placed the
" greatest materials for making life happy, was, in his opinion, an
" *English country Gentlemen.* "

Although the emperor has never visited England, he is perfectly
acquainted with its character and manners, as he is with its language. A very amiable and respectable English gentleman, Mr. G.

of the treasury, was, by the wish of Catherine, brought up with him, and was the play-mate and associate of his early years. The incidents of boyish days, so dear to every feeling and generous mind, left their accustomed impressions upon the heart of Alexander; and though time placed him at an immeasurable distance from his early companion, he has never ceased to honour him with the most gracious regard; in the display of which he exhibited the emperor only in the munificent proofs of his friendship. I heard another instance of the strong partiality of Alexander for England. When an English gentleman, who, a short time before the death of Paul, had frequently played duets upon the flute with the grand duke, was preparing to quit the empire for his own country, in consequence of the sudden antipathy which the former had taken to our countrymen, after the close of the last piece they ever performed together, Alexander thus feelingly apostrophized the flute of his friendly musician, as he held it in his hand: " Adieu, sweet instrument! you " have charmed away many an hour of care; often and deeply shall " I regret the absence of your enchanting sounds; but you are " going to breathe them in the best and happiest country in the " world. " These are trifling anecdotes to record; but they conduct the reader to the heart.

" Man is most natural in little things. "

How much, and how justly, the emperor is beloved by his people, will occasionally appear as I proceed. The Russians, who have had so many foreign princes to govern them, behold with enthusiastic fondness an emperor born in Russia. The face of the reigning empress is very sweet and expressive; her person is slight, but very elegant, and of the usual height of her sex; she is remarkably amiable, and diffident, even to shyness. Her mind is highly cultivated, and her manners soft, gracious, and fascinating. Her sister, the queen of Sweden, if there be any fidelity in the chisel of Sergell, must be a model of female beauty. The emperor and empress have no family. They were united at an extraordinary early age, from a wish of Catherine to contemplate as many of her posterity, who were destined to succeed to the throne, as she could before she died. The two grand duchesses, who are grown up, do honour to the care of their imperial mother, and excite the attachment and admiration of all who approach them. The youngest of the two was married to the prince of Saxe Weimar, during my stay in Petersburgh; and as the ceremony of their nuptials will illustrate the manners and customs of the Russians, I shall hereafter give a brief description of it.

From the place of execution in the market place, I made my way to the monastery of St. Alexander Nevsky, at the very extremity of the eastern part of the city. In the street were several carts standing, filled with peas in pod, with their roots just as when they were pulled up from the garden, and with their stalks, which the poor people bought, sometimes for themselves, and sometimes for their horses; to both, the vegetable, which was eaten shell and stalk together, appeared a dainty. The monastery occupies a vast space of ground, is moated round, and contains a magnificent church, surmounted by a vast copper dome, a chapel, the cells, refectories, and dormitories for sixty monks, a seminary and the residence of the metropolitan archbishop. The front of the basement of the buildings, which are all connected together, is painted of a deep crimson colour, and, from the immense quantity and size of the windows, resembles a collection of colossal hot-houses.

In the church, which is very elegant, I saw the shrine of St. Alexander Nevsky, the tutelar saint of Russia, formerly one of its sovereigns, who was raised to that distinguished honour in consequence of his having most gallantly repulsed the Swedes, or Finns, some centuries since, on the banks of the Neva. The monument, and military trophies which adorn it, as well as the pillars and canopy under which it stands, are of wrought massy silver, made from the first ore of that metal ever discovered in Russia. One of the columns, which forms the back of the space allotted for the imperial family, is a whole-length portrait of the late empress, well executed. The altar, screen, and decorations, are very superb. There are cloisters round the whole of the buildings, formed almost entirely of double windows, by which in winter every house in Russia, of the least respectability, is protected against the terrible severity of the cold; the joists, and all other avenues of air, being either covered with pasted paper or felt. Every part of the monastery appeared to be very neat and clean, and the mansion of the archbishop handsome. The chanting of some fine deep-toned voices attracted me to the chapel, where the monks, assisted by the priest, were at their devotion. The dress of the former is singularly gloomy; on their heads they wore a high hat, covered with black crape flowing down the back: the habit, which fell below the ancles, was black cloth lined with a sombre dark blue stuff, their beards were of a great length, and each monk carried a rosary of brown or black beads. As I was returning, several beautiful monuments in the church-yard attracted my steps; they appeared to be constructed and arranged as in England. While engaged in examining them, an elderly lady, in deep mourning, apparently about sixty years of age, with a pale but dignified face, leaning upon the arm of a graceful youth, clad in the same suit of sorrow, slowly passed by me, and at some distance stopped before a small but elegant tomb, which, from its unsullied whiteness, had the appearance of having been but very lately erected. I noticed them unobserved. They stood under the shade of a wide spreading silver birch, and turning towards the church of the monastery, the youth pulled off his hat, and they both prostrated and crossed themselves, according to the forms of the Greek faith; the female then, clasping her hands, dropped her head upon the pedestal of the monument, and appeared to be lost in profound and affecting meditation. The young man knelt by her side, and, if I mistook not the cause which moved his hand, he wept. Some minutes elapsed, they then arose, tenderly surveying the spot, ascended a hillock of grass, and kissed a little marble urn, which surmounted the monument. My conjecture enclosed in it the heart of some long-loved husband and father. They then withdrew in the same sad, solemn, and impressive manner, with which they entered, and I approached the object of their melancholy regard. The pedestal which supported the urn was embellished with two medallions; one represented Resignation, with the face of a beautiful female, upon which the most angelic sweetness appeared to triumph over languor and pain; the other depicted Hope, modestly, yet ardently looking to heaven. There was a small inscription between the two heads, in Russ, and underneath, the figures 1804. The Russians, like wise people, always bury their dead in the suburbs. The late empress never permitted burials in the day; she thought, with some reference to the popular prejudice, that the gloom of the spectacle ought to be confined, as much as possible, to the relatives of the deceased; and I should suppose that her ukase, regulating this awful ceremony, still continues, for I never saw a funeral during my stay in Russia.

A A

The reader will, I am sure, be pleased with the beauty and pathos of the following stanzas, which form a part of the hymn recited over the body previous to its inhumation.

" Oh, what is life ? a blossom ! a vapour or dew of the morning !
" Approach and contemplate the grave. Where now is the graceful
" form ! where is youth ! where the organs of sight ! and where the
" beauty of complexion !

" What lamentation and wailing, and mourning, and struggling,
" when the soul is separated from the body ! Human life seems alto-
" gether vanity ; a transient shadow ; the *sleep of error ; the unavailing*
" *labour of imagined existence.* Let us therefore fly from every cor-
" ruption of the world, that we may inherit the kingdom of heaven."

" Thou Mother of the Sun that never sets ; Parent of God ; we be-
" seech thee intercede with thy divine offspring, that he who hath
" departed hence may enjoy repose with the souls of the just. Un-
" blemished Virgin ! may he enjoy the eternal inheritance of heaven
" in the abodes of the righteous."

The superstition of the Russians is very great. Upon the ceremony of blessing the waters in the winter, when a large hole is per-
forated in the Neva, a woman supplicated a priest to immerse her
new-born child ; the priest consented ; but in dipping the miserable
little sufferer, his fingers were so benumbed, that he irrecoverably
dropped it under the ice ; the parent, with a smile of delight, exclaimed, " He is gone to heaven."

In one of the churches I saw a woman doing penance for the following crime : She had not long been married before she polluted
the bed of her husband, whom she used to keep in an almost constant
state of intoxication. One day, whilst she was indulging herself in
her adulterous attachment, her husband unexpectedly appeared perfectly sober : stung with jealousy by what he saw, he sprang upon
his guilty rival, and with a knife stabbed him to the heart. The laws
of England would have protected the miserable man, but by those of
Russia he was knouted and sent to Siberia ; and his wife, who was
the authoress of this bloody tragedy, was ordered by her priest to
prostrate herself six hundred times a day for two years, before the
Virgin. Her conscience and her bigotry enforced punctual observance of the prescribed mortifications. By the Russian laws, if the
husband is of a tyrannical and violent temper, a woman may
commit adultery with impunity.

The Russians are fanatically attached to the very stone, brick, wood, and plaster, of their churches: they have a remark, that whilst the Russians build their churches first and their towns afterwards, the English never think of a temple until they have erected their own dwellings.

It is somewhat singular, that with all their religious enthusiasm, the Russians pay their priests more miserably than we do our curates; but perhaps it may be traced to the extreme ignorance of the former. After wealth and birth, knowledge awakens respect, and perhaps the Russian populace would revolt at the idea of making their ministers independent before their minds were cultivated; to their saints they would devote their lives; to their priests they give black bread.

That the Greek faith admits of confession, the following anecdote will prove: A priest came to hear the confession of a great man: "Holy father," says the count, "have you a good memory?" "Yes." "Then you remember what I told you at my last confession; since "that I have had the same temptations from without; the same "weaknesses from within; and here is the same number of rubles."

Another reason was now assigned for Paul's having introduced the magpie colour, which I have before mentioned: it was that the soldiers, raw recruits, and boors, employed for government, might the more readily distinguish the buildings which belonged to it.

As I crossed the drawbridge of the Ligova canal, the latter appeared to be almost choked with barks of a prodigious length, filled with billets of birch-wood, for the immediate use of the kitchen, and for a winter-stock of fuel; this and the rent of houses, and necessary equipages, and bread, constitute the most expensive part of housekeeping in Petersburg, which in most other respects is moderate. These vessels, in which not only wood but charcoal is brought from the shores of the nearest rivers, or of the Ladoga lake, never return, but are broken up and sold, for building houses for the poor, or for fuel. These barks, unavoidably necessary, sadly disfigure the beautiful canals which form the pride and comfort of this capital; and here, as upon the sides of the Seine, the washerwomen are the principal water nymphs. Most of the canals are finely embanked with granite, and have a rich iron railing running on each side. The Fontanka canal is eminently beautiful. These intersections of water assimilate Petersburg in some degree to Venice. As I returned through the Grand Perspective, I took a peep at that part of it which is called the *Yemskoi*, answering to the Long Acre of London, where there is a long row of carriage builders' shops ; here are droshkaes, calashkies, chariots, sledges, and all sorts of carriages, many of them very neat, some of them very heavy, but none very lasting ; yet there is no knavery ; those who build them use the best materials the country will afford, and in shape and fashion, where the carriage will admit of it, they imitate us very closely, and a stranger may buy a very comfortable calashka for about five hundred rubles, for which, a little more elegantly and substantially made, if calashkies and rubles ran in England, he would at least pay one thousand of the latter. This depot, or the yards of the coachmakers, amongst whom there is an English one, in the second line of the Galeerenoff, are the best places for a foreigner to purchase a carriage when he is about to quit Russia.

As I walked along I observed, on each side of the street, several stands, each attended by a reverend looking long-bearded Russian, with piroghi, or little pies filled with meat, next to which were eggs, and salted cucumbers, of which the Russians are particularly fond, and in a third were pyramids of berries, much resembling a mulberry in shape, but of a light yellowish colour, called the maroshki; the cranberry, called the glukoi ; wild strawberries, whortleberries, and cloudberries, said to be excellent antiscorbutics. I cannot say much of the attractive cleanliness and delicacy of the *patissier*, but a Russian stomach is not squeamish ; and for a very few copecs it may be, in the estimation of its owner, substantially and completely filled. The fasts of the Russians are very frequent, and very rigidly observed.

As a *fast* in England always reminds me of a *feast*, I will just give a brief sketch of a Russian dinner, which is seldom later than three o'clock. Upon a sideboard in the drawing-room is always placed a table filled with fish, meats, and sausages, salted, pickled, and smoked, bread and butter, and liqueurs ; these airy nothings are mere running footmen of the dinner, which is in the following order : a cold dish, generally of sturgeon or some other fish, precedes, followed by soup, a number of made dishes, a profusion of roast and boiled meats, amongst which the Ukraine beef is distinguishable, and abundance of excellent vegetables; then pastry, and a desert of very fine melons, and sour flavourless wall fruit; the table is covered with a variety of wines, and excellent ale and beer. The master of the house or a took carves, and slices of every dish are handed round to the guests. One of the most gratifying things that I always saw upon the table was a large vase of ice broken into small pieces, with which the guest cools his wine and beer. In the yard every Russian house has two large cellars, one warm for winter, and the other filled with ice for the summer. The soup, and coffee, and chocolate are frequently iced. One day at dinner, I sat by a *lovely Russian* lady, that is, born in Russia, but of German parents: the explanation will save me a remark embarrassing to gallantry, and which I wish to avoid, respecting the beauty of the *proper* Russian women, at least of those whom I saw. This accomplished woman, in my own language as pure as ever it fell from an English lady's lips, requested some salt; upon my presenting it she said, "Whenever you give salt, never fail to *smile;* it is a superstitious custom in Russia." A *smile* is in this country considered as a charm against *poison.* Heavens! surely they have not yet to learn that

"A man may smile, may smile, and be a villain."

They have a beautiful proverbial expression:

"Banter, but never make the cheek red."

Nature has less to do with climate than library gossips suppose: at least I thought so when I committed the following blunder: "You "never saw my Sophinka before," said Madame L———, pointing to a fine little girl at table, about ten years of age; "She is your "*daughter*, I presume?" "Madame L———'s daughter!" exclaimed a gentleman, "surely that cannot be; she is more like your *sister.*" The fact was, the child was neither daughter nor sister, but a little visitor. The result was, that the principal part of Madame L———'s enchanting conversation during dinner was withdrawn from me, and addressed to the gentleman whose error was the most fortunate. After a few glasses of delicious wines, champagne included, the lady rises, and the company retires to coffee in the drawing-room. The rooms of respectable houses are never papered, but, where the sides are not covered with silk or cotton, they are coloured in a brilliant and beautiful manner to resemble papering. In this act the natives are uncommonly tasteful and rapid.

The hospitality of this place cannot be surpassed: When a stranger is introduced, the family mention the days of the week when they receive their friends, and expect that he will include himself in the number: the invitation is frank and *cordial,* and is seldom re-

peated; where it is understood there is no occasion for it. The frip-
pery and formality of forced, and frequently treacherous ceremony,
is not known here.

At the back of the Gastinnoi-dvor are the fruit, bird, and poultry
markets, in a street of wooden sheds, like those at a fair in England.
Apples, pears, rasberries, currants, peaches, excellent melons, and
pine apples, are temptingly presented to the eye, and are all intole-
rably dear, even when you are permitted to buy for half the price at
first demanded; for the custom of asking double the sum intended to
be taken prevails in all this neighbourhood; but as it is well known,
it seldom answers. In the bird quarter were pigeons, sparrows,
hawks, birds of the rock, and a few others, in greater numbers than
variety: upon a beam in this place was suspended the image of a
favourite Saint, with a lamp burning before her. In the poultry department very fine geese, ducks, and fowls, were in great abundance.
The bank next attracted my attention: it is a large and very beautiful building of brick, stuccoed, containing a centre and two wings, and
adorned in front by a very handsome and elegant iron railing. The
whole of this neighbourhood is filled with kabacs, and public-houses,
where dinners are dressed, and beer, and mead, and brandy sold.

At the end of the Grand Perspective, the church of the admiralty
with its lofty spire, plated with ducat gold, having a vane in the form
of a ship, presents itself, and, like a haughty female, ashamed in her
proud attire of her mean origin and humble relations, seems scorn-
fully to lift herself above the long gloomy line of low brick buildings
which, with the yards behind, constitute the admiralty, and disfigure
this part of the capital. Time has proved that Peter the Great acted
wisely in chusing the situation for his city. The shallowness of the
Neva presents an insuperable barrier to the fleets of Sweden, and a
noble river, so clear that it is drank without filtration, divides and en-
riches the quarters of the city with the beauty and purity of its
waters: but, with the powerful facilities of building ships at Cronstadt, a large impregnable island at the mouth of the Neva, in the
gulf of Finland, and the grand naval arsenal of Russia, I must confess, in my poor opinion, he has not been equally judicious in establishing an admiralty at Petersburg. So little is the depth of water,
at the latter place, that whenever a ship of war is launched, she is
obliged to be floated down to Cronstadt upon camels. Of the trouble
and expense of such a removal let the reader judge, when I inform

him that I saw this stupendous machinery mounted upon thousands of wedges of wood, in a meadow, about half a mile from any water in which they could be floated. My astonishment could not have been exceeded, had I beheld a first rate seventy-four upon the top of Saint James's palace! Suppose the clear shell of a larger ship than ever yet was built were cut in two, and each part put into an outer case, but at such a distance from it as to leave throughout a hollow space of from eight to ten feet: such was the appearance of the camels. But how they are removed from the place where they lie in ordinary, supposing any number of men were employed, surpasses my imagination; however, like every thing else in Russia, when they are wanted they make their appearance, and come when they are called to the admiralty, where each takes its station on either side of the ship which they are destined to carry to Cronstadt. By the means of vast moveable weights, and by opening several apertures in the external sides of this mighty section of a ship, to admit the water, they are sunk, drawn close together under the curve of the ship, and braced with cables; a work fit for a race of giants! To see them moved and directed by men, must present the image of the recumbent body of Gulliver covered with Lilliputians. But whilst the frame of man becomes diminutive by the side of his own works, his soul expands, and rises with his labours. The admiralty is a vast oblong square: the side towards the river is open, and far from being ornamental to the adjoining palaces: that towards the city is defended by earthen ramparts, fortified with cannon and secured by drawbridges. The storehouses appeared to be well arranged: there were two ships, one of seventy-four, and the other of sixty guns, ready for launching. An Englishman cannot fail being struck with the prodigious waste which occurs in the dock-yards, in consequence of the carpenters using their hatchets instead of the saw in dividing timber. The chips form the perquisite of the workmen; but the government would save an immense quantity of valuable timber would it give an equivalent, and insist upon the use of the saw. In the naval constitution of Russia there is a regulation which cries aloud for reform; it is balloting for rank, and the right of blackballing; terms which sufficiently explain the nature and abuses of an arrangement so degrading and odious to merit, and detrimental to the service. It appears also injudicious to send a young marine cadet to England, to learn navigation, upon a salary of from one hundred and eighty to two hundred

arrived with the first merchant vessel that ever sailed upon the Neva, and was the bearer of a letter of introduction to the captain of the port from a friend of his in Holland, requesting him to use his interest to procure a freight for him.   Peter the Great was working like a common labourer in the admiralty as the galliot passed, and saluted with two or three small guns.   The emperor was uncommonly delighted, and having been informed of the Dutchman's business, he resolved to have some frolic with him, and accordingly commanded the port captain to see the skipper, as soon as he landed, and direct him to the emperor as a merchant just settled there, whom he intended to personate ; the better to carry on the joke, Peter repaired to this cottage with his empress, who, to humour the plan, dressed herself in a plain bourgeois habit, such as suited the wife of a merchant. The Dutchman was introduced to the emperor, who received him with great kindness, and they sat and ate bread and cheese, and smoked together for some time, during which the Dutchman's eye examined the room, and began to think that no one who lived in so mean a place could be of any service to him : presently the empress entered, when the skipper addressed her, by observing that he had brought her a cheese, a much better one than she had ever tasted, for which, affecting an awkward manner, she thanked him.   Being much pleased with her appearance, he took from his coat a piece of linen, and begged her acceptance of it for shifts. " Oh !" exclaimed the emperor, taking the pipe from his mouth, " Kate, you will now " be as fine and as proud as an empress ! there, you are a lucky " woman ; you never had such shifts as you will now have, in your life " before. This was followed by the stranger begging to have a kiss, which she coyly indulged him in. At this moment Prince Menzikof, the favourite and minister of Peter the Great, who represented him upon matters of state, entered with all his orders, and stood before the emperor uncovered. The skipper began to stare with amazement, whilst Peter, by winking and making private signs, induced the prince immediately to retire. The astonished Dutchman said, " Why you appear to have great acquaintance here ?" Yes," replied Peter, " and so may you, if you stay here but ten days ; there are " plenty of such needy noblemen as the one you saw ; they are al- " ways in debt, and very glad to borrow money of any one, and they " have even found out me ; but, sir, beware of these fellows ; resist " their importunity, however flattering, and do not be dazzled by

" their stars and garters, and such trumpery." This explanatory advice put the stranger a little more at his ease, who drank and smoked on very cheerfully, and made his bargain with the *Imperial Merchant* for a cargo. Just as he had settled this point to his wish, the officer of the guard, which had been changed, entered to receive his orders, and stood with profound respect uncovered, and before Peter could stop him, addressed him by the title of Imperial Majesty. The Dutchman sprang from his chair, fell on his knees before the emperor and empress, and implored forgiveness for the liberties he had been taking. Peter enjoyed the scene, and laughing heartily, raised up the terrified supplicant, and made him kiss the empress's hand, presented him with fifteen hundred rubles, gave him a freight, and ordered that his vessel, as long as her timbers remained together, should be permitted to enter all the Russian ports free of duty. This privilege made the rapid fortune of the owner. A friend of mine frequently saw her, some years since, at Cronstadt. On the right hand side of the cottage is a boat, built by the hands of Peter the Great. It resembles a large Thames wherry, and does honour to the skill of the princely boat-builder. As I sat in the carriage, waiting for some of my companions, I made a sketch of the house, boat, a droshka, and a group of Russians and an American, who were there. Upon our return the evening was advanced, and the night watch was set ; we met the police-master mounted upon a droshka, drawn by two horses in full gallop, followed by two of the police on horseback, dressed in light green, and armed with sabres; they were going their rounds through the city, to see that order was preserved, and that the nocturnal guards, amounting to five hundred, were at their respective posts. Soon after, we met with a patroling troop of Cossacs on horseback. In no city is there greater safety and tranquillity preserved than at Petersburg, which for this purpose is divided into ten departments, and these divided into several smaller parts, each of which has its proper chief and subordinate officers, who, by a very simple organization, preserve the capital, at all hours of the night, in a state of quiet and security, that cannot fail to excite the admiration of foreigners, and particularly of Englishmen. Those detestable agents of government, spies, have no existence in Petersburg; without their baneful assistance, the police is so admirably and powerfully extended, that, like a spider's web, whatever comes in contact with it, is felt from the centre to the extremities.

The commanding officers of the police do not rank with the officers of the army, nor are they received with much respect in society.

I one evening saw an instance of severity which surprised and disgusted me; but probably it was intended to strike terror, and to abbreviate the labour of the police, by commanding an instantaneous submission to its functionaries. A quarrel had taken place between two men in the street through which I was passing, and before the third exchange of imprecations, two of the police appeared, and ordered these disturbers of the peace to walk before them to the nearest sieja, or little watch-house, but one of them refused to go, upon which an officer drew his sabre, and cut him in the face; the man, like a true Russian, more affected at the sight of the blood, than by the pain of the wound, submitted himself to the law, and marched off without further delay.

It would be well for the safety and tranquillity of the inhabitants of London, and more particularly of its immediate neighbourhood, if its police were more *extended, swift* and *powerful*. In this respect we are assuredly inferior to most nations. I am aware that arbitrary governments have, hitherto, displayed the most perfect systems of police; but is this the reason why the genius and constitution of a *free* one cannot admit of its extending domestic protection to its subjects? Is civil liberty incompatible with preventive policy? Is the freedom of the country'gone, when murderers and robbers cease to be free? or is it to preserve our chartered privileges, that a band of superannuated watchmen, who, to protract their becoming an additional burden upon the poor-rate, beyond the ordinary era of eleemosynary aid, are helmeted in flannel night-caps, and with a *rattle* and a *lanthorn*, admirable equipments for *second childhood*, and *eyes dim with age!* are sent forth to guard the lives and property of the inhabitants of the most crowded, populous, and wealthy city in the world? To find fault is an easy and an odious office. But a traveller, like a bee, should never be upon the wing without bringing home some sweet to encrease the honey of his native hive. Neither at night, nor by day, are the streets infested by women of the town; they live in a quarter by themselves, and I believe are not very numerous; some of them are Polish, of course handsome; some Germans, of course fascinating; and some, and the most of them, fair and frail wanderers from the upper parts of Finland, which, although the portion of the province that we saw was so destitute of every thing like beauty, is said to possess many pretty faces and good persons amongst the females. If it be true, as Mr. Justice Colquhoun's register asserts, that the prostitutes of London amount to fifty thousand, I should not suppose, from all that I could learn, that the frail sisterhood of Petersburg exceeds a tenth of their number. Where these unhappy beings abound, it is always a compliment to the chastity of the purer part of the sex. There was some portion of sagacity in the remark made by a poor little night wanderer, in a city on the continent which shall be nameless, when a traveller, who pitied and relieved her distress, observed, that he was surprised to see so few of the sisterhood in such a capital. " Alas, sir," said the unfortunate, " we cannot live for the *virtuous* " part of our sex." One morning presented a very singular spectacle. A number of well-dressed women, walking in pairs, fastened by the arm to each other with cords, with their band-boxes in their hands, and each couple attended by a police officer, were very quietly and decorously marching to the emperor's cotton-mills, which are correctional houses of industry for ladies of this description. There were no repining looks amongst them, not a pouting lip, so great in general is the constitutional submission to the law in the north. Upon enquiry, I found that a man had been violently ill-treated in the haunts of these Idalian goddesses, and that upon the affair being represented to the emperor, he ordered three hundred of them to be marched off for a few months, as above mentioned. How the list was filled up, whether by ballot, or promiscuously, I know not. Passing by the senate in which the nobles assemble to digest and discuss such laws as the emperor may chuse to submit to their consideration, the image of justice, which adorns the right hand side of the grand entrance towards the statue of Peter the Great, attracted my notice ; she was blindfolded as usual, but the equipoise of her scales was destroyed : a wag, who some time since had lost his cause, in consequence, as he thought, of the venality of his judges, between frolic and pique had dexterously cast a copec into one of them, and had thus kicked up the beam.

It would be unfair and invidious to investigate the present laws of Russia ; the emperor is convinced of their radical defects, and it is intended, with all possible speed, to bless the empire with a new code. The brilliant elementary outline of legislation, which Catherine II, with the most imposing pomp and solemnity, submitted to the deputies from all parts of the empire, in which she professed to give equitable laws to all her subjects, from Lapland to the Caspian, and from the Baltic to the wall of China, which excited the homage, how sincere I know not, of Frederic, and, what she valued more, of Voltaire, has never been acted upon. At this meeting, the following curious incident happened: Two Samoid deputies were directed by the empress to state those legislative provisions which they thought were best adapted to their own nation. One of them replied, " Our laws are few, and we want no more." " What ! " exclaimed the imperial legislatrix, " do theft, murder, and adultery, " never appear amongst you ? " " We have such crimes, " answered the deputy, "and they are punished : the man who deprives " another of his life wrongfully, is put to death."—" But what," said her majesty, interrupting him, " are the punishments of theft and " adultery ? " " How!" said the Samoid, with great astonishment, " are they not sufficiently punished by detection ? " Many events have conspired to prevent the accomplishment of the magnificent plan of Catherine ; and heavily oppressive indeed would the present laws of Russia be, if an appeal to the emperor did not lie from the most abject of his subjects.

The courts of the grand police-office opposite the admiralty are crowded every day, where the laws are expounded and administered, according to the discretion of the judicial officers appointed to preside over them. Whilst England might borrow some ideas from the police of Russia, she is enabled to present to the latter the sublimest spectacle of justice. Let us press for a moment through the crowd, into a British court of criminal justice ; see that emaciated tattered wretch at the bar! he is without friends and without money ; he can bring no witnesses ; he can retain no counsel. What then ? Is all the force of the law and the powers of eloquence against him? Listen : the judge before whom he stands is *his* advocate ! Hear that acute and favourable interrogation to the witness that presses against the culprit's life ; mark that benign exposition ; the miserable being is saved : tears gush from his eyes ; he falls upon his knees, and in broken accents blesses Heaven that he was born in a country whose laws befriend the friendless and the persecuted.

I have hitherto omitted to mention the terrible annoyance of the bells of the Greek churches, the most deep-toned of any I ever heard : those of one very near my chamber used every morning to curtail that little portion of sleep which legions of flies had allowed me. To a stranger, the alternate clashing and jingling of these deep-mouthed tenants of the steeple, for an hour without any interval, is very harassing ; the bells, like saleable horses going to a fair, are tied in succession, and by pulling the rope which connects them, the agreeable harmony of clashing is effected, whilst the melody of chiming is produced by striking the particular bell with a wedge of iron. The Russian saints are said to be very fond of this matin music; and many was the time and oft that I wished it confined exclusively to their ears.

Amongst the other early sounds of the busy morning, with which you are saluted, some are very foreign, and others very familiar, to an Englishman, and might, if the flies would permit, half induce him to think that he were in the capital of his own country : amongst the latter I was particularly delighted with the cry of the fruiterer, who, with a reverend beard, carried upon his head an oblong board, on which, in little baskets of birch bark, very neat and clean, the choicest summer fruits of Russia were disposed. Nothing could be more grateful than a block of ice, brought in every morning, to chill the water of the Neva with which we washed ourselves : I am at a loss to conjecture how the natives of tropical climates can survive their sultry summers without ice. Soon after our arrival we dined at the elegant and hospitable country house of Mons. B——, upon the Peterhoff road, where we sat down, about thirty, to dinner, and after coffee retired to the gardens, formed of little romantic islands rising out of a small lake, the whole surrounded by a wood. When we were weary of rowing some pleasure boats, an amusement of which the Russians are very fond, we returned to the house, and the rest of the evening was spent in cards and waltzing. The day following we were introduced to the English club by a member, where the company is very select, consisting of Russian and Polish noblemen, foreigners of respectability, and that truly *dignified charac-ter, an English merchant.* The dinner is always excellent, and served up in the English fashion : adjoining are rooms for billiards and reading, where the principal foreign papers are taken in. The porter was ornamented with a very broad sash of velvet, richly embroider-ed with silver, thrown over the left shoulder, and held a staff tipped with silver, as do most of the porters of the principal nobility. The building on the outside is far from being handsome ; but the apart-ments are good, and particularly the eating-room, which is very lofty,

and has two enormous stoves made of brick, covered with blue
Dutch tiles: upon the whole, its appearance is very inferior to the
club-houses of Stockholm. About two o'clock, the dinner hour at
this place, the court-yard is crowded with carriages and equipages.

A fortunate removal of people from the hotel, enabled me to
change my apartment for another more pleasantly situated; the
price was the same, *viz.* seven rubles, or nineteen shillings English,
per week. This room was divided, *à la Russe*, by a screen, behind
which my bed, or crib, was placed. The windows looked upon the
Moika canal, where of an evening I used to be serenaded by the
common bargemen, and sometimes by the rowers of the pleasure-
barges. Of the Russian song and music I will speak by and by : I
shall only now, as some modest barristers say, *humbly insist* upon it,
that barbarians have not a natural and ardent taste for music and
singing. One evening, while amusing myself with a young bear in
the court-yard of the house of a friend, my ears were gratified by some
wild notes, which, upon turning round, I found issued from an instrument resembling a guitar, upon which a native of Archangel was
playing very sweetly: the tenderness of the scene improved the
music. The poor fellow was weeping as he played, to mitigate the
sufferings of his wife, upon whom death had fixed his seal, and who,
with her head reclining upon her hand, sat at an open window in the
basement floor to enjoy a little air. The rude and sorrowful musician,
and his pale and interesting wife, formed a subject for the painter.
This sensibility, which would have charmed a traveller, had he
beheld it in the love-inspiring groves of Italy, was the produce of
the frozen regions of the White Sea! The natives of Archangel are
looked upon as more civilized than their more southern brethren,
and servants from this part of Russia are preferred for their integrity,
intelligence, and activity.

Although I have expressed my attachment to the Russian, and
like the good-humoured fellow prodigiously, yet I must admit that
he has no objection to improve his notions of earthly felicity by a
little occasional inebriation. At a house where I passed the evening,
previous to supper we had been drinking some ale, which in this
country is prized on account of its being both excellent and forbidden,
having left a couple of bottles, about half full, upon the table when
supper was announced, a most demure looking menial, with a long
beard, who stood behind my chair, was ordered to bring them in :

after some little hesitation, he informed his master " that he was " very sorry for it; but that, as he passed through the room, by " *mere accident* he had emptied the bottles. " Nature, by some of her odd freaks, very soon confirmed the truth of one part of this statement. This propensity is much encouraged by the extraordinary number of festivals which occur in this country, particularly at the end of Lent; almost as many as the feasts of the civic corporation of London, which, it is said, would present, if they were duly observed, one for every day in the year, and some over.

One day whilst I was at Petersburg, as the emperor was returning from Cronstadt, when the weather was most oppressively hot, he halted at a little village about twenty versts from the residence, in consequence of the relay of horses not being immediately ready. An English merchant who had a country house adjoining, with that warmth of heart which forgets and surpasses all etiquette, ran out, and presented to the emperor, who appeared to be in great heat and covered with dust, a glass of excellent Burton ale, for which his majesty, with his usual affability, thanked his attentive host, and drank. Both the emperor and the merchant forgot that the beverage was prohibited, or secretly relished it the more on that account. A German, who was present, and was struck with the frank and cordial avidity with which the emperor emptied the glass, observed, " that " had a Frenchman offered it, his majesty would have made one of " his horses taste it first. "

Upon another occasion the emperor exhibited the native goodness of his heart: some British bottled porter, which is also prohibited, was shipped for an Englishman whose lady was very much indisposed, and to whom it was recommended by her physicians. Scarcely had it reached Petersburg from Cronstadt, before it was seized by the custom-house officer: upon the emperor hearing of it, he sent to the customs, declaring it to be his own (for such, in truth, the law of confiscation had made it) and immediately forwarded it, with some very kind expressions, to the fair invalid.

The princely magnificence in which some of the Russian nobility live is prodigious. Having occasion one day to find out a person who occupied a suite of rooms in one of the great town hotels of count Sherametoff, the Russian duke of Bedford, we had an opportunity of seeing this enormous pile, in which a great number of respectable families reside; and the rent, amounting to twenty thou-

C c

sand rubles, is applied by its munificent lord to the relief of the
poor.   Exclusive of another superb mansion in the city, which he
inhabits, the count has a town on the road to Moscow, called Paulova,
containing about two thousand five hundred houses, and five churches:
this place is the Birmingham of Russia, all the inhabitants of which
are his slaves, who carry on an extensive trade on the Caspian Sea.
In the neighbourhood of this place, he has a palace rivalling Versailles in extent and splendour.   Many of his slaves, all of whom
adore him, have realized vast fortunes, and display at their tables
sumptuous services of plate, every costly luxury, and have foreign
masters to teach their children.   Though rolling in unwieldy revenues, the count is frequently embarrassed, from his princely munificence; yet he never replenishes his exhausted treasury, by exer-
cising the sovereign right which he has to raise the capitation-tax
of his peasantry.   What additional blessings might not such a nobleman bestow upon his country, by converting his vassals into
tenants:—how great and immediate would be the influence and
example of a spirit so liberal:—with what power has fortune invested him to accelerate the civilization of his country!   One of the
count's slaves advertised, during my stay in Petersburg, for a family
preceptor, with an offer of two thousand rubles per annum, and six
rubles per day for his table, and a cook!   The count was under severe
domestic affliction at this time, having just lost his amiable lady who
had formerly been one of his slaves: she left behind her a little son
to console him, whom the emperor elevated to the rank of nobility;
a measure rendered necessary in consequence of his mixed birth, to
enable him to enjoy his father's wealth and honours.   Prince Sherametoff, who is the lord of one hundred and forty thousand slaves,
lost eighty thousand rubles one night at the gaming-table: not having so much money at immediate command, he offered to transfer
to the winner an estate of slaves of that value.   As soon as the unfortunate vassals heard of the intended assignment, dreading to have
another master, they immediately raised the money amongst them,
and sent it to their lord.   Many of the nobles have three hundred
servants; and one of that order, it is reported, had thirteen thousand
in constant attendance.

   The manners of the Russian nobility very much partake of the
manners of the old school of France, and, in complimentary profession, perhaps a little exceed it.   They are acute observers of human

nature; and knowing that their urbanity, on account of their polar
situation, is generally suspected, they are even anxious to make a
profuse display of it. They are remarkably hospitable, and very attentive to strangers. Connubial happiness amongst the higher orders seldom endures eleven months after the honey-moon, when the
parties generally kiss, pout, part, and afterwards are happy. Divorce
is not recognized by the laws of Russia. The road to Moscow frequently exhibits a singular spectacle of lords and their ladies, taking
a half-yearly glance at each other as they meet, in exchanging their
residences in the two cities, for their mutual accommodation and
amusement: this is the nearest point of contact. The education of the
young nobility very frequently suffers from the free and unguarded
manner in which they receive every needy adventurer in the capacity of domestic tutor, particularly, if he be an Englishman: English
taylors, and servants out of livery, and travelling valets, frequently
become the preceptors and governors of children. A fellow of this
description said one day: " In summer I be clerk to a butcher at
" Cronstadt, and in winter I teaches English to the Russian nobi-
" lity's children." I knew a lady whose valet left her at Petersburg,
in consequence of having been appointed to the superintendence of
the children of a Russian nobleman of high distinction, with one
thousand rubles per annum, a table, and two slaves. The Russian
nobility are in general very extravagant, and consequently frequently embarrassed: their bills are often at a discount of sixty and even
seventy pounds per cent.

Soon after our arrival, we visited the grand imperial theatre, or
opera house, called the Stone-Theatre, which stands in a large open
place, nearly in front of the marine garrison, formerly the new jail,
and the Nicolai canal. At four angles, in this spacious area, are four
pavilions of iron, supported by pillars of the same metal, resting upon
a circular basement of granite, within which, in winter, large fir fires
are constructed, the wind being kept off by vast circular moveable
shutters of iron, for warming and screening the servants of those who
visit the theatre in the winter. Previous to the erection of these
sheds, many of those unfortunate persons were frozen to death. The
government, attentive to the lives of the people, has interdicted per-
formances at the opera, when the frost is unusually severe. The
front is a noble portico, supported by Doric pillars; the interior is
about the size of Covent-Garden, of an oval shape, and splendidly but

rather heavily decorated. The lower tier of boxes project from the sides, at the back of which are pilasters, adorned with appropriate decorations, richly gilded, above which are three rows of boxes, supported by Corinthian pillars, each of which, as well as those below, contain nine persons. Nothing less than the whole box can be taken. It frequently happens that servants stand behind their masters or mistresses in the boxes, during the performance, and present a curious motly appearance. The imperial box is in the centre of the first tier, projecting a little, is small, and very plainly decorated. The pit has seven or eight rows of seats with backs to them, in which a commodious portion of space for each spectator is marked off by little plates of brass, numbered upon the top of the back seat; this part is called the *fauteuils*. Such is the order observed here, and in every theatre on the continent, that however popular the piece, a spectator may, during any part of the performance, reach his seat, in this part of the theatre, without any difficulty. Behind, but not boarded off, is the pit and the parterre. The price of admission to the boxes and *fauteuils* are two silver rubles, little more than five shillings. There are no galleries. The massy girandoles, one of which is placed at every pilaster, are never illuminated but when the imperial family are present; on which occasion only, a magnificent circle of large patent lamps is used, descending from the centre of the roof; at other times its place is supplied by one of smaller dimensions, when the obscurity which prevails induces the ladies generally to appear in an undress. Although this gloom before the curtain is said to be advantageous to the effect of scenery, yet the eye is saddened, as it runs its circuit in vain for forms adorned with graceful drapery, the glittering gem, the nodding plume, and looks of adorned beauty, that give fresh brilliance to the gay galaxy of light. This theatre is furnished with a great number of doors and passages, reservoirs of water, and an engine in case of fire, and with concealed flues and stoves, to give it summer warmth in winter. It is always strongly guarded by a detachment from the guards, as well as by the police officers, who preserve the most admirable order among the carriages and servants. It is not an ungratifying sight, after the opera, to pause at the doors and see with what uncommon skill and velocity the carriages, each drawn by four horses, drive up to the grand entrance under the portico, receive their company, and gallop off at full speed; pockets are very rarely picked, and accidents seldom happen.

Owing to the size and quantity of decorations, and the spacious arrangement of the boxes, I should not think the theatre could contain
more than twelve hundred persons. Its receipts have never yet exceeded one thousand six hundred and eighty rubles, or two hundred
and forty pounds. How different from a London theatre, which, on
a crowded night, when a Siddons or a Litchfield delight their audience,
is lined with faces, and the very walls appear to breathe !

The first opera I saw was Blue Beard, performed by Italian performers ; the subject of which varied but little from the representation of it in England, except that the last wife of Blue Beard has a
lover, who in the concluding act lays the sanguinary tyrant breathless
with his sword. The catastrophe was finely worked up, and drew
from the Russians successions of enthusiastic acclamation. Do these
sentiments of tenderness, these noble notions of retributive justice, denote an immutable barbarism? The processions were in the first style
of magnificence, the dresses and ornaments were very costly, and it is
not unusual to introduce, on these occasions, one thousand men, selected from the guards for the expression of their faces and symmetry
of their figures, to swell the scene of pomp. The orchestra was very
full, and combined the first-rate powers of music. The scenes were
handsome and well managed. A room was formed of entire sides,
and well furnished ; and a garden was displayed with all its characteristics. The emperor contributes very munificently to the support
of this theatre ; and as all the machinists and workmen are his slaves,
they are all under admirable discipline. The introduction of a tree
into a study, or fringing the top of a forest with a rich cieling, scenic
blunders, which frequently occur on the English stage, would hazard
the backs of the Russian scene shifters. This theatre has a very
beautiful set of scenes, which is never displayed but on nights when
the imperial family honour it with their presence. The silence and
decorum of the audience cannot but impress the mind of any one, who
has witnessed the boisterous clamours of an English audience. The
curtain ascends at six o'clock precisely. No after-piece, as with us,
only now and then a ballet, succeeds the opera, which is generally
concluded by nine o'clock, when the company go to the summer
gardens, drive about the city, or proceed to card and supper parties.

This theatre is as much dedicated to the Russian muses as to those
of more genial climates. In this respect Catherine II pursued the
same plan of domestic policy, so wisely adopted by Gustavus III ; but

the plan, since her demise, has never been encouraged by the higher circles. A Russ play has the same effect upon fashion in Russia as George Barnwell has upon the same class in England. Although in the former there are some inimitable performers, as in the hero of the latter, one of the most perfect and affecting imitations of nature, in that walk of the drama, ever exhibited upon any stage, is display-ed by Mr. Charles Kemble.

I went one evening, in company with my amiable and gallant friend, captain Elphinstone, to see a Russ opera, called " The School for Jealousy :" it is not much esteemed. As it proceeded captain E. explained it to me : the sentiments were frequently coarse, sometimes very obscene ; the actors, who were Russians, appeared to perform with great ability ; the heroine of the piece was represented by a very pretty and interesting girl, who was taken from the hospital of foundlings : she manifested grace, and a be-witching *naïveté*, and played and sang most sweetly. I am sorry I have forgotten her name ; she is the principal Russ actress, and is a very great favourite. In the course of the play, to my astonishment, was introduced a scene of the inside of the mad-house at Petersburg, in which, amongst a number of horrible grotesque figures, a mad periwig-maker threw a handful of hair-powder into the face of a frantic girl, who ran raving about the stage with dishevelled locks, which excited strong risibility amongst the audience. I was so dis-gusted at the spectacle, and the applause, that I wished it had not happened ; but as it did, I record it. Although an English audience has been delighted at a dance of undertakers, laughed at the feats of skeletons in pantomines, and in Hamlet has expressed great mirth at seeing a buffoon grave-digger roll human skulls upon the stage, and beat them about with his spade, it could not endure a sight in which those objects, whom pity and every tender feeling have consecrated, are brought forward with ridicule. But let it be remembered that madness is less frequent in Russia than in milder regions ; and hence the people, for they are very far from being strangers to feel-ings which would do honour to the most civilized of the human race, are less acquainted with, and consequently less affected by its ap-pearance ; and when it is thus wantonly displayed upon the stage, it appears under the mask of buffoonery. The government would do well to suppress this and every similar exhibition, calculated only to imbrute a civilized mind, and postpone the refinement of a rude one.

I was much more pleased with the Russ opera of the Nymph of the Dnieper, which is so popular and attractive, that it never fails to fill the seats of fashion. It is chiefly intended to display the ancient costume and music of Russia. The story is very simple : A prince has sworn eternal constancy to a nymph, who is violently attached to him ; his father, a powerful king, wishes him to marry a princess of an ancient house ; the prince consents, but the nuptials are always interrupted by the stratagems of the jealous nymph, who appears in various disguises. The first scene was singularly beautiful: it displayed a river and its banks, and nymphs swimming ; the manner in which they rose upon the water was admirably natural ; the music of the ancient Russ airs, in which the celebrated Cossacka is introduced, were exquisite ; the scenery was very fine, and displayed a number of pantomimic changes.

The Russian noblemen are fond of the drama ; almost every country mansion has a private theatre. Those of the nobility, who from disgust to the court, or some other cause, confine their residence to Moscow and the adjacent country, live in the voluptuous magnificence of eastern satraps: after dinner they frequently retire to a vast rotunda, and sip their coffee, during a battle of dogs, wild bears, and wolves ; from thence they go to their private theatres, where great dramatic skill is frequently displayed by their slaves, who perform, and who also furnish the orchestra. These people are tutored by French players, who are very liberally paid by their employers.

CHAP. XIV.

A GLOOMY CATASTROPHE.

IT is with deep regret that I approach the delicate and awful subject of this chapter. Humanity would gladly cover it with the pall of oblivion; but justice to the memory of an unhappy monarch, and to the chief of the august family of Russia, demand a candid though careful development of the events which preceded the fall of the last emperor. The original source of my information is from one who beheld the catastrophe which I am about to relate, whom I can neither name nor doubt; a catastrophe which is too near the period in which I write, not to render an unrestrained disclosure of all the particulars with which I have been furnished unfair, if not imprudent. The causes that first created those well-known prejudices which Catherine II cherished against her son, have perished with her; but all the world knows, that, during the many years which rolled away between the grand duke's arrival at the age of maturity and his elevation to the throne, his august mother never admitted him to any participation of power, but kept him in a state of the most abject and mortifying separation from the court, and in almost total ignorance of the affairs of the empire. Although Paul, by his birth, was generalissimo of the armies, he never was permitted to head a regiment; and although, by the same right, grand admiral of the Baltic, he was interdicted from even visiting the fleet at Cronstadt. To these painful privations may be added, that when he was recommended, that is *ordered*, to travel, during his absence Catherine seized and sent to Siberia one of his most cherished friends, because she discovered that he had informed her son of some inconsiderable state affair. Thus Paul beheld himself not only severed from the being who gave him birth, but from all the ordinary felicities of life. The pressure of his hand excited suspicion; peril was in his attachment, and in his confidence guilt and treason. He could not have a friend, without furnishing a victim.

A gentleman nearly connected with me, now no more, a man of talent and acute observation and veracity, had several years since the honour of spending a short period at the little secluded court of Gatchina, upon which, as the dazzling beams of imperial favour

never shone, the observer was left in the tranquillity of the shade, to
make a more calm, steady, and undiverted survey. At this time, Paul
displayed a mind very elegantly inclined, and without being brilliant,
highly cultivated, accomplished and informed, frank and generous,
brave and magnanimous, a heart tender and affectionate, and a disposition very sweet, though most acutely and poignantly susceptible :
his person was not handsome, but his eye was penetrating, and his
manners such as denoted the finished gentleman. In his youth he
was seen by the bed-side of the dying Panin, the hoary and able
minister of Catherine, and his tutor, kissing and bathing his hand
with tears. As an evidence of his intellectual vigour, let the elaborate and able ukase, by which he settled the precedence and provision of the imperial family, unquestionably his own unassisted composition, be referred to. He loved his amiable princess, and his
children, with the most ardent, the most indulgent fondness, and it
was the labour of their love, as well as of his servants, who were devotedly attached to him, to requite his affections and graciousness,
and to endeavour to fill up with every endearing, every studied attention, the gloomy chasm which had been formed by an unnatural and
inexplicable neglect ; but this chasm was a bottomless abyss, upon
the brink of which his wounded spirit was ever wandering ! Paul
possessed a high martial inclination, and, reflecting that he might
one day mount the throne of a military empire, he made the art of
war the principal object of his studies ; but neither this pursuit, so
copious, so interesting, nor the endearments of those who surrounded him, could expel from his mind the sense of his injuries. He beheld himself, the second personage and the destined ruler of the empire, postponed to the periodical favourite of his mother, the minister
of her unbounded voluptuousness, not unfrequently elevated to the
presidency of the hermitage from the ranks, with no other pretensions than vigorous health and a mighty frame ; whilst, on the other
hand, the bleeding shade of his father was for ever, in his morbid
imagination, pointing to his wound, and whispering revenge. Thus
exiled from the heart of his mother, is it a matter of surprise that he
should exclude her from his own ?

Catherine more than once observed, that her son would not long
occupy the throne after her decease ; and it has been the fashion to
say, that her alienation from him was justified by the events which
succeeded her death. With this prophetic spirit, she devoted all her

D D

care to the education of her grandsons, Alexander and Constantine, and exercised all the powers she possessed towards the consummation of her prediction. She foretold that the flower which she had planted would wither early: she shook it till every blossom fell, and shaded it so, that the dew of heaven should never visit it more: she pressed and pierced the delicate and ardent mind of her son until she subverted it. Was it then a proof of inspiration, to prognosticate the brevity of his reign over an empire, the history of which has too often and fatally proved, that however despotic its government, and there is not one under heaven more absolute, a cautious and dexterous cultivation of the interest, feelings, prejudices, and affections, of the people, is inseparable from the safety of the ruler?

A short time before her demise, Catherine committed to P——Z——, her last favourite, whom she highly esteemed, a declaration of her will, addressed to the senate, purporting that Paul should be passed over in the succession, and that the grand duke Alexander should mount the vacant throne. As soon as the favourite was acquainted with the sudden death of the empress, he flew to Pavlovsk, about thirty-five versts from the capital, where Paul occasionally resided, whom he met on the road, and, after a short explanation, delivered up to him this important document. Paul, charmed with his zeal and loyalty, preserved him in all his honours and fortunes, whilst a general and rapid dispersion, to all points of the compass, instantaneously succeeded amongst the members of the *male seraglio* of the Hermitage. The emperor ascended the throne without difficulty, but a total stranger to his subjects. One of the first measures of his reign displayed, in a very singular manner, the native goodness of his heart, under the clouds that rapidly began to overshadow it, in an act of piety towards his murdered father, whose remains he removed from the church of St. Alexander Nevski, called the Monastery; and having exhibited them in great funeral state, he consigned them to the sepulchre of Catherine II, in the cathedral of St. Peter and St. Paul. The latter part of this extraordinary transaction has often induced me to think that Paul did not believe that his mother issued the order for the assassination of his father. At this eccentric solemnity; he compelled count Alexey Orloff, and prince Baratynski, under whose hands the unhappy monarch is said to have perished, to stand on each side of the body as it lay in state, and afterwards to follow it to the tomb, as the principal mourners.

Not long after this event, his mind began occasionally to display the most fearful symptoms of distraction; but when his reason was restored, the hapless emperor never failed to endeavour, with the most affecting sensibility, to repair the ruin and havoc which his delirium had occasioned. The deposed Stanislaus, the broken-hearted king of Poland, partook alternately of his beneficence and severity; but with what demonstration of respect and genuine grief did the emperor attend the obsequies of this last of the Sarmates? On that gloomy occasion, he commanded in person the guards who assisted at the funeral; and uncovering himself, with the most affecting emotions, saluted the coffin as it passed. To the memory of the hoary and heroic Suvaroff, who fell a broken-hearted victim to the distraction of his imperial master, in periods of agonized and compunctious reflection, he raised a colossal statue of bronze, in the vast area behind Benskoi's palace, opposite to Romantzoff's monument; and, on the days when he reviewed his troops there, he used to order them to march by in open order, and face the statue, which he said represented one of the greatest and bravest generals of his own or any other age.

Notwithstanding the important service which P—— Z—— had rendered him, the emperor could never separate him, in his mind's eye, from the caresses of his mother, and speedily became disgusted with him; spoke of him with great asperity to his friends, and at length, converting the bounty of Catherine into a robbery, he denounced him as a defaulter to the imperial treasury of half a million of rubles; and, convinced of the justice of the allegation, proceeded, without loss of time, to sequester the vast estates which belonged to him and to his two brothers. Driven to desperation by such conduct, one of the sufferers, the second brother, one day boldly walked up to the emperor upon the parade, and, with manly eloquence, represented the injustice of his measures. Paul received him without anger, heard him without interruption, reflected, and restored the property: but the original disgust rapidly returning, he ordered P—— Z—— to reside upon his estate, to which he submitted for a considerable time. But the mind of the exile was too ardent to endure seclusion; ambitious, bold, active, and enterprising, he determined upon releasing himself from the unjust constraint imposed upon him by his sovereign, the delirium of whose mind now frequently burst forth with all the fury and desolation of a convulsed volcano. Messrs. Otto, Sieyes, and Talleyrand, who, at that time, formed a diplomatic trio, or rather were spies, at the court of Petersburg, with the dexterity of talent, and the subtilty of Frenchmen, resolved to turn the gathering storm to the advantage of their own country, by means, which, extending beyond their calculation and their wishes, finally and rapidly led to the overthrow of the emperor. Under their tuition, a French actress was introduced on the boards of the French theatre at Petersburg, and placed in such situations of allurement, that the eye of the emperor could not but notice her. The ruin of domestic happiness furnished these politicians with the means of their success. A French actress was destined to estrange the emperor from his family, and to create a temporary and terrible change in the affairs of Europe. Madame Chevalier possessed that style of face, which, without being regularly handsome, was more sweet, expressive, and captivating, than the exact symmetry of a finished beauty. Her person was small, but delicate, and rather *enbonpoint:* her manners were of the highest order, and enchanted every one who approached her. The emperor was fond of music: madame Chevalier excelled upon the harp, and sang to it some sweet and crafty verses, composed by one of her three employers, and which she herself had set to music; the subject of which was, the martial skill, valour, and generosity, of the emperor. She had not spread her witcheries long, before an evening was appointed for a private gratification of the musical taste and passion of the emperor. This syren very soon became the sole idol of his shattered mind, which she moved according to the direction of her secret principals, until the emperor withdrew himself from his alliance with Austria, recalled Suvaroff and his army covered with glory, crowded the roads to Siberia with British subjects, and filled with terror and consternation the exchange of the British empire. I mean not to enumerate all the calamities which followed: they were too signal not to be widely known, too recent not to be well remembered; and, from their very nature, incontestably proved the aberration of those faculties which could alone, by their presence, render the emperor responsible for all the misery, dismay, and ruin, which threatened the very existence of the empire. P—— Z—— resolved upon availing himself of the influence of the fair favourite, to whom he addressed himself with all the insinuation of person, manners, wit, and money: having engaged her in his favour, he made her acquainted

with count K——, a man, who, from having been about the person
of Paul in the menial capacity of a valet, at last obtained a high place
in his affection, distinguished honour, and great wealth. The more
firmly to bind ·K—— to his interest, P—— Z—— feigned an
honourable passion for the daughter of the former, who was, like all
the sudden favourites of fortune, much pleased at the prospect of an
alliance with a very distinguished family. Count K——, and madame Chevalier, conceived many plans for prevailing upon his
majesty to restore Z—— to his favour. At length, one evening,
when she had tranquillized the mind of the emperor, and excited in
him an appearance of gaiety by the vivacity of her wit, and some of
her most successful songs, she artfully insinuated that P—— Z——
was the most unhappy man alive in being deprived of the emperor's
favour, and of the power of promoting the interests of one of the
greatest geniuses that ever mounted the Czarian throne, to whom
he was most inviolably attached. The emperor paused, and expressed
some doubt of the truth of the statement; but upon her re-assuring
him of its sincerity, accompanied by some of those little blandish-
ments which no woman ever knew how to display with more finished address than madame Chevalier, Paul granted her petition, and
recalled Z—— to the residence, where he flew with the celerity of
a courier, and threw himself at the feet of the emperor, by whom
he was graciously received, and from whose presence he withdrew
to present his fair advocate with the stipulated reward, a magnificent
aigrette of diamonds, valued at sixty thousand rubles. What private
pique Z—— might have cherished against his imperial master, I
believe that it was wholly lost in his review of the deteriorated and
dreadful condition of the empire, and in those awful measures of
restoration which were afterwards resorted to. Z—— gradually
and warily unfolded his mind to K——, who as cautiously entered
into his views, until their confidence was completely established.
The result of their deliberations was, that to save the empire, it
was necessary that the emperor should be removed. They next prevailed upon count P——, the governor of the city, and count P——,
a very young nobleman, but of considerable family interest, the son
of the celebrated general, count P—— P——, who so eminently
distinguished himself in the Turkish war, and also the prince Y——,
and some other persons of great rank and consequence. All of these
noblemen were actuated by no other motive than to prevent the

final ruin of their country, and for this purpose they determined to place in peril their lives and their fortunes.

In their conferences, which were managed with admirable discretion, it was resolved that Paul should die; and, like Cæsar, it was destined that he should perish in the ides of March, on the day of the festival called Maslaintza.

I think I hear the voice of humanity exclaim, " Why not provi-" sionally remove the unhappy Monarch from the throne?" Alas! the constitution of Russia possesses none of those mild and beneficent provisions, which endear our own constitution to us a thousand and a thousand times. When the ruler is once mounted on the throne, an abyss opens below, and the descent from the last step is into eternity. I am endeavouring to illustrate motives, not justify them; the record is before another tribunal! It is scarcely necessary for me to observe, that the august family of Paul were wholly unacquainted with the meditated blow.

The emperor, from an aversion he had taken to those palaces, which formed the favourite residence of Catherine, resolved upon building a palace for himself. The gorgeous magnificence of Zarsko Želo, and of the Winter palace, and all the oriental voluptuousness of the Hermitage, were hateful to him; indeed, to such an elevation had his abhorrence of these places attained, that he had determined to reduce them to the dust, that only

" ———— The blackness of ashes should mark where they stood."

His fate, which was fast approaching, prevented the accomplishment of this irretrievable act of delirium. The emperor and his family resided, at the time when the confederacy had resolved upon his removal, in the new palace of Saint Michael. It is an enormous quadrangular pile, of red Dutch brick, rising from a massy basement of hewn granite; it stands at the bottom of the Summer Gardens, and the lofty spire of its Greek chapel, richly covered with ducat gold, rising above the trees, has a beautiful appearance.

As Paul was anxious to inhabit this palace as soon after he was crowned as possible, the masons, the carpenters, and various artificers, toiled with incredible labour by day and by torch-light, under the sultry sun of the summer, and in all the severity of a polar winter, and in three years this enormous and magnificent fabric was completed. The whole is moated round; and when the stranger surveys its bastions of granite, and numerous drawbridges, he is naturally led to conclude, that it was intended for the last asylum of a prince at war with his subjects. Those who have seen its massy walls, and the capaciousness and variety of its chambers, will easily admit that an act of violence might be committed in one room, and not be heard by those who occupy the adjoining one; and that a massacre might be perpetrated at one end, and not known at the other. Paul took possession of this palace as a place of strength, and beheld it with rapture, because his imperial mother had never even seen it. Whilst his family were here, by every act of tenderness endeavouring to soothe the terrible perturbation of his mind, there were not wanting those who exerted every stratagem to inflame and encrease it. These people were constantly insinuating, that every hand was armed against him. With this impression, which added fuel to his burning brain, he ordered a secret staircase to be constructed, which, leading from his own chamber, passed under a false stove in the anti-room, and led by a small door to the terrace.

It was the custom of the emperor to sleep in an outer apartment next to the empress's upon a sopha, in his regimentals and boots, whilst the grand duke and duchess, and the rest of the imperial family, were lodged at various distances, in apartments below the story which he occupied. On the tenth day of March, O. S. 1801, the day preceding the fatal night, whether Paul's apprehension, or anonymous information, suggested the idea, is not known, but conceiving that a storm was ready to burst upon him, he sent to count P——, the governor of the city, one of the noblemen who had resolved on his destruction: " I am informed, P——," said the emperor, " that there is a conspiracy on foot against me; do you think it " necessary to take any precaution?" The count, without betraying the least emotion, replied, " Sire, do not suffer such apprehensions " to haunt your mind; if there were any combinations forming " against your majesty's person, I am sure I should be acquainted " with it." " Then I am satisfied," said the emperor; and the governor withdrew. Before Paul retired to rest, he unexpectedly expressed the most tender solicitude for the empress and his children, kissed them with all the warmth of farewel fondness, and remained with them longer than usual; and after he had visited the centinels at their different posts, he retired to his chamber, where he had not

long remained, before, under some colourable pretext, that satisfied
the men, the guard was changed by the officers who had the command for the night, and were engaged in the confederacy.   An hussar, whom the emperor had particularly honoured by his notice and
attention, always at night slept at his bed-room door, in the anti-
room.   It was impossible to remove this faithful soldier by any fair
means.   At this momentous period, silence reigned throughout the
palace, except where it was disturbed by the pacing of the centinels,
or at a distance by the murmurs of the Neva, and only a few lights
were to be seen distantly and irregularly gleaming through the windows of this dark colossal abode. In the dead of the night, Z——— and
his friends, amounting to eight or nine persons, passed the drawbridge, easily ascended the staircase which led to Paul's chamber,
and met with no resistance till they reached the anti-room, when the
faithful hussar, awakened by the noise, challenged them, and presented his fusee.   Much as they must have all admired the brave
fidelity of the guard, neither time nor circumstances would admit of
an act of generosity, which might have endangered the whole plan.
Z——— drew his sabre, and cut the poor fellow down.   Paul, awakened by the noise, sprang from his sopha : at this moment the whole
party rushed into his room : the unhappy sovereign, anticipating
their design, at first endeavoured to entrench himself in the chairs
and tables, then, recovering himself, he assumed a high tone, told
them they were his prisoners, and called upon them to surrender.
Finding that they fixed their eyes steadily and fiercely upon him, and
continued advancing towards him, he implored them to spare his life,
declared his consent instantly to relinquish the sceptre, and to accept
of any terms which they would dictate.   In his raving, he offered to
make them princes, and to give them estates, and titles, and orders,
without end.   They now began to press upon him, when he made a
convulsive effort to reach the window : in the attempt he failed, and
indeed so high was it from the ground, that had he succeeded, the
expedient would only have put a more instantaneous period to his
misery.   In the effort he very severely cut his hand with the glass ;
and as they drew him back he grasped a chair, with which he felled
one of the assailants, and a desperate resistance took place. So great
was the noise, that notwithstanding the massy walls, and thick double-
folding-doors, which divided the apartments, the empress was disturbed, and began to cry for help, when a voice whispered in her ear,

and imperatively told her to remain quiet, otherwise, if she uttered another word, she should be put to instant death. Whilst the emperor was thus making a last struggle, the prince Y—— struck him on one of his temples with his fist, and laid him upon the floor. Paul, recovering from the blow, again implored his life; at this moment the heart of P—— Z—— relented, and, upon being observed to tremble and hesitate, a young Hanoverian resolutely exclaimed, " We have passed the Rubicon: if we spare his life, before the set- " ting of to-morrow's sun we shall be his victims!" upon which he took off his sash, turned it twice round the naked neck of the emperor, and giving one end to Z——, and holding the other himself; they pulled for a considerable time with all their force, until their miserable sovereign was no more; they then retired from the palace without the least molestation, and returned to their respective homes. What occured after their departure can be better conceived than depicted: medical aid was resorted to, but in vain, and upon the breathless body of the emperor fell the tears of his widowed empress and children, and domestics; nor was genuine grief ever more forcibly or feelingly displayed than by him on whose brow this melancholy event had planted the crown. So passed away this night of horror, and thus perished a prince, to whom nature was *severely* bountiful. The acuteness and pungency of his feeling was incompatible with happiness: unnatural prejudice pressed upon the fibre, too finely spun, and snapped it.

> 'Tis not, as heads that never ache suppose,
> Forgery of fancy, and a dream of woes;
> Man is a harp, whose chords elude the sight,
> Each yielding harmony, dispos'd aright;
> The screws revers'd (a task which, if he please,
> God in a moment executes with ease),
> Ten thousand thousand strings at once go loose,
> Lost, till he tune them, all their power and use.

COWPER.

The sun shone upon a new order of things. At seven o'clock the intelligence of the demise of Paul spread through the capital. The interval of time from its first communication to its diffusion over every part of Petersburg was scarcely perceptible. At the parade Alexander presented himself on horseback, when the troops, with tears rolling down their rugged and sun-browned faces, hailed him with loud and cordial acclamation. The young emperor was overwhelmed, and, at the moment of mounting the throne of the most extensive empire under heaven, he was seen to turn from the grand and affecting spectacle, and weep.

What followed is of very subordinate consideration; but perhaps it will be eagerly asked, to what extremity did the avenging arm of justice pursue the perpetrators of the deed? Mercy, the brightest jewel of every crown, and a forlorn and melancholy conviction, that the reigning motive was the salvation of the empire, prevented her from being vindictive. Never upon the theatre of life was there presented a scene of more affecting magnanimity; decency, not revenge, governed the sacrifice. P—— Z—— was ordered not to approach the imperial residence, and the governor of the city was transferred to Riga. As soon as madame Chevalier was informed of the demise of her imperial patron, she prepared, under the protection of her brother, a dancer, for flight, with a booty of nearly a million of rubles. A police officer was sent to inspect and report upon her property: amongst a pile of valuable articles, he discovered a diamond cross, of no great intrinsic value, which had been given by Peter I to a branch of the imperial family, and, on that account, much esteemed; it was to recover this that the officer was sent, who obtained it, after the most indecent and unprincipled resistance on her part. Passports were then granted to madame Chevalier and her brother. Thus terminated this extraordinary and impressive tragedy.

CHAP. XV.

SIR JOHN BORLASE WARREN—THE POLIGNACS—THE PARADE—THE BANE-
FUL EFFECTS OF PASSION—THE EMPEROR—A PICK-POCKET—A TRA-
VELLER'S MEMORANDUMS—UNPUGILISTIC BRUISERS—DOCTOR GUTHRIE
—VISIT TO THE TAURIDA PALACE—THE COLOSSAL HALL—THE WINTER
GARDENS—THE BANQUET—PRINCE POTEMKIN—RAW CARROTS—FLY-
ING GARDENS—THE HOUSE OF CHARLES XII, AT BENDER, DISCOVERED.

IT was impossible for an Englishman to visit Peterburg when I did,
without feeling a justifiable national pride in finding his country represented by one of her most distinguished naval heroes, who, to
the frankness and sincerity so peculiar to that character, unites the
graceful attractions of the most courteous and polished manners.
From the intrepid minister, and his elegant and enlightened lady, I
experienced that urbanity and attention which eminently distinguished their conduct, and endeared them to the Russian court, and to
their countrymen. The emperor, in his private circles, has often
extolled the nautical skill and undaunted valour of Sir John Borlase
Warren, and honoured him with his friendship. In no period of
those political storms which have so long shaken, and still continue
to convulse, the continent of Europe, has the cabinet of Russia manifested a more propitious and cordial disposition to the cause and
interests of Great Britain, than during the diplomacy of the gallant
admiral.

The house of embassy, a noble mansion, in the English line, was
fitted up with great taste, and the hospitality which prevailed in it
was truly *Russian*. The parties which assembled there were very
select and agreeable. Amongst the most frequent visitors I met
the Duc de Polignac and several of the members of that illustrious
house, who, from the highest rank, and an influence equal to that of
their sovereign, have been cast into the regions of the north, by the
terrible tornado of the French revolution, where, in the sensibility
and munificence of the emperor, they have found protection.

The noble fortitude of the Polignacs, and particularly the heroic
and affecting eloquence of one of the brothers before the tribunal
of Bonaparte, created at this period a strong sensation in the public
mind, and in no part of the world more forcibly than at Petersburg.

In another age, when passion and prejudice shall repose in " the tomb of all the Capulets," the calm investigating historian may perhaps, but in better language, describe their crime, as I have ever considered it, a conspiracy of Bonaparte against himself, to enable him to assume the imperial purple.

Sunday is always at Petersburg a day of great festivity, but it only manifests itself after the hours of devotion. On this day the parade is well worthy the traveller's notice; it commences at ten o'clock, in that great area which lies between one side of the winter palace and the magnificent crescent, which formerly constituted the palace of Catherine's most cherished favourite, Lanskoi. The men amounted to four thousand, and presented a very noble and martial appearance; their uniform consisted of a round hat, with only a rim in front, and green feather, a short green coat, buttoned tight round the body, and white duck breeches cut very high, so that no waistcoat is necessary. The belly of the soldier is tightly strapped in, for the purpose of giving an artificial breadth to the chest. With an exception to the English and consular guards, I never saw finer men in my life, nor greater neatness in dress and person. The emperor came from the palace, mounted upon a beautiful grey charger, attended by two or three officers; he wore an amazing large cocked hat, fastened under his chin by a black leather strap, and buttoned to prevent the wind from occasioning that accident, for which a cruel disciplinarian (Frederick the great) once severely flogged a poor Prussian soldier. The rest of his dress was a short coat of dark olive-green colour, decorated with a small star and the cordon bleu, white leather breeches, and high military boots, with very long projecting spurs. Upon this occasion there is always a great concourse of the commonalty, and a great muster of officers to pay their respects to the emperor, who rode at an easy canter down the line. As he passed I was much surprised to hear each company salute him with deep-toned voices, and highly gratified when I was informed that the salutation was, " Good day to our emperor." The words seemed to bring down the haughty disdain of military discipline to its proper level, and to place the hearts of the emperor and his brave soldiers in contact with each other. Upon his return he alighted and took his station in the centre, when the regiments passed the emperor (who stood uncovered all the time) in open order, the band playing and officers saluting. As the imperial colours passed, which time or war, or both, had reduced to a few shreds of silk, all the officers and spectators bowed. As the last company was marching off the ground, a lane was formed to the palace through the people, who gazed upon their young emperor with enthusiastic delight.   The whole was a very interesting spectacle, for which, by the by, I had nearly paid rather dearly. Thinking, perhaps, that I was far removed from the nimble-fingered disciples of London, or what is more likely, not thinking about the matter, I carelessly carried my pocket-book to the parade: a common Russian had for some time, it appeared, watched me with a cat-like eye, and at the moment the emperor passed me, he affected to relieve me from the pressure of the mob, and at the same time *really* endeavoured to relieve me of my letter of credit, some ruble notes, and what I fear the critics will wish I never had recovered, many of the memorandums from which I am now writing.   A German valet, belonging to a gentleman who was with me, instantly seized him by the throat, ere his hand could leave my pocket, when he as speedily relinquished his prey.   The attempt was made with a skilful knowledge of *seizing opportunities,* by which some folks become wealthy, others *imperial,* and the dexterity and lightness of his finger would have obtained a medal of felonious honour in the academy of Barrington.   However, as I lost no property by the fellow, I ordered the active servant to dismiss him; and the terrified Russian rushed rapidly from my sight, and was lost in the surrounding crowd.

The Russian is not naturally addicted to thieving: he is seldom seen in hostility to life, in order to obtain the felonious possession of another man's property.   A rare instance of what, however, may be committed in an ebullition of passion, occurred at the preceding parade.   An officer, in consequence of very improper behaviour, was put under arrest; in the bitterness of wounded pride, he slew the centinel who was placed at his chamber door: the emperor, instead of dooming him to death, ordered him to receive twenty-five strokes of the knout, to be branded in the forehead with *vor,* or rogue, and be sent to Siberia.

As I was quitting the throng, two fellows, somewhat tipsy, began to quarrel; and, after abusing each other very violently as they walked along, they at last proceeded to blows.   No pugilistic science was displayed: they fought with the hand expanded, as awkwardly as women play at battledore and shuttlecock; no desperate contusion ensued.   A police officer soon appeared, and, taking out a cord from his pocket, tied the combatants back to back, and placing them upon a droshka, galloped them off to the nearest sieja. The police of England would do well to act with the same spirit and promptitude towards those academic bruisers, who, in the most daring manner, violate the public tranquillity, and bid defiance to the authority of the law.

A short time before my arrival, an affair, which in some degree illustrates the Russian character, had created considerable interest. A gallant English merchant conceiving himself rudely treated at the theatre by a Russian officer, one of the emperor's aid-du-camps, sent him a challenge. The officer declined the combat, and appealed to the emperor, which, according to the custom of his country, he might do without a stain upon his courage. Those martial notions of honour, which reign so imperiously in England and France, are but little known in Russia, where the feudal system, the judicial combat and its chivalrous concomitants, never obtained, and where the sword never forms, and never has formed, a necessary appendage to the dress of the people, which, till lately, has for ages been worn amongst their brethren in more southern latitudes.

It was with great pleasure that I availed myself of an introduction to the venerable doctor Guthrie, physician to the noble land cadet corps, a gentleman of the most amiable manners, a philosopher, and well known to the world for his various scientific and literary productions, and particularly for being the editor, as he has modestly announced himself, of the Letters of his deceased lady from the Crimea, whither she went, but in vain, in search of health. It is very generally believed, that the doctor very largely contributed to this able and beautiful work, which, from fondness to the memory of the departed, he is anxious should be considered as her own.

I found the doctor protected, by his philosophical knowledge, from one of the most sultry days I ever experienced. He was in a little study built of wood, raised upon piles, in a little meadow. Instead of his summer windows being open to admit the air, they were all closed and fastened without; his servant occasionally moistened the branches of the trees, that were suspended over the building, with water from a garden engine; and to prevent, as much as possible, the admission of the flies, the entrance was through an outer door, and an inner one of gauze, and in the centre of the room stood a tub filled with ice. By these means the doctor, whilst every other person was languishing and panting with heat, enjoyed a cool and delightful atmosphere. His collection of Siberian minerals, gems, and precious stones (amongst which is a beautiful riband agate), from various parts of the Russian empire, and a variety of marine fowls from the Russian archipelago, are very curious and interesting. I here saw a fine specimen of the encoustic, or wax-painting, the art of which was discovered a few years since in Herculaneum, by a soldier accidentally holding a flambeau to an apparently naked wall, when the action of the heat created, to his astonishment, a beautiful landscape, by reviving the encoustic colour in which it had been painted. The doctor also obligingly shewed me an opera which was composed by the late empress, in which, with great poetical spirit and genius, she has described the founding of Moscow, and the habits and customs of the Russians. The words of many of the songs were adapted to old Russ tunes, and others were set to music by Sarti. Of this imperial production only four copies were ever printed; as soon as they were struck off, the press, the types of which were made at Paris, was broken. Independent of his merited reputation, the doctor has two other reasons sufficient to make any philosopher proud and happy : he is the father of two lovely daughters ; the eldest is lady Gascoigne, who, to the charms of youth and beauty, unites the most elegant accomplishments and captivating manners. So high was report in her favour, and so little can she be known with impunity, that I felt a sullen satisfaction in learning that she was upon a visit to her friends in Scotland whilst I was at Petersburg; the other daughter is a lovely girl, pursuing her studies in the Convent des Demoiselles.

On account of his long and faithful services, the doctor was ennobled by Paul, who always retained a great partiality for him, even during the temporary disgust which he felt against his countrymen: he is honoured with a hat and feathers, and the rank of a general. It is scarcely necessary for me to observe, that in a military government like Russia, military rank precedes every other. .

From doctor Guthrie's cool philosophic shade, we proceeded to the Taurida palace, built by Catherine II, and given by her to her distinguished favourite prince Potemkin, upon whom she lavished unprecedented dignities and treasure. She bestowed upon him the name of the Taurian, in honour of his conquest of the Crimea, and called this building after him. Upon the death of the prince, the empress purchased it of his family for a vast sum. The grand front of this building, which is of brick, stuccoed white, is towards the street leading to the Convent des Demoiselles, in the east end of the city, consisting of a centre, adorned with a portico supported by columns, and a large cupola of copper, painted green, and extensive wings. A variety of out-offices, orangeries, and hot-houses, reach from the left wing to a prodigious distance: in the front is a court yard, divided from the street by a handsome railing. The exterior of this building is very extensive, but low; and although it has a princely appearance, does not excite the astonishment that a stranger feels in entering it. Through the civility of our countryman, Mr. Gould, the emperor's gardener, who enjoys a munificent salary, and a handsome house on the west side of the gardens, I was frequently enabled to visit this delightful place. The kitchen, fruit, and pleasure-gardens, and hot-houses, occupy a vast space of ground, which are watered by several canals; over one of them is thrown the celebrated model of a flying covered bridge of one arch, which an obscure illiterate Russian constructed, for the purpose of embracing the two sides of the Neva, opposite to the statue of Peter the Great: it is about seventy feet long, and is a wonderful display of mechanical ingenuity. This extraordinary peasant has clearly elucidated the practicability of such a measure; the model is capable of bearing more comparative weight than could ever press upon the bridge itself. The enormous expense which must attend such an undertaking will, in all probability, reserve it for a distant period. The ingenious artist received a handsome pension from the late empress, and the satisfaction of having displayed with what extent of capacity unassisted nature has gifted the Russian mind. In this part of the grounds, Catherine II was in the habit of taking her morning promenade with a male friend; and in the evening attended by her court.

The pleasure-grounds are small, but beautifully laid out by Mr. Gould, who was a pupil of the celebrated Browne; and who, at the advanced age of seventy-two years, beholds this little paradise, which he created from a mephitic bog, flourishing and exciting the admiration of foreigners, and in the shade of which Potemkin, Catherine the Great, and two succeeding emperors of Russia, have sought tranquillity and repose from the oppressive weight of public duty.

This respectable Englishman, who has realized a handsome fortune, the fruit of imperial munificence, for long services, keeps an

elegant and hospitable table, and is visited by persons of the first respectability. The late unfortunate king of Poland, during his resi-
dence, or rather incarceration, in Petersburg, felt a melancholy pleasure in quitting the phantom of royalty, which mocked rather than
consoled him, in the palace of Siberian marble, to pour the sufferings
of his afflicted mind into the breast of the frank, cordial, and ingenuous
Englishman in this abode of privacy.

The pleasure-grounds are very elegantly disposed, and, as we passed the little green palisade which separates them from the kitchen-
garden, we contemplated with pleasure the favourite seat of Catherine the Great, that here presented itself: it was a long, tasteful gar-
den-sopha of iron, interlaced, painted green, and stood under the
branches of an oak. Here she used to take her coffee; and, upon
this very seat she gave private and unrestrained audience to the late
king of Sweden. I am enabled, from indubitable authority, to state,
that the age of Catherine when she expired was seventy-five, although
three years are taken from it in the calendar.

As we descended a little slope from Catherine's seat, we passed
by two birch-trees, revered by the superstitious Russians, on account
of their having been, with a third of the same species, preserved,
when the morass in which they grew was first converted into a garden, and the vegetable patriarchs of the place: we were gravely told,
that when Paul died, the one which is missing perished from *excessive sensibility*. I never knew before, that nature had endued the birch
with acute feelings: I remember, at school, it was admitted, *nem.
con.* that it had the power of exciting them.

The first room we entered from the garden was the celebrated
hall in which prince Potemkin gave the most gorgeous and costly entertainment ever recorded since the days of Roman voluptuousness:
I am not able to communicate to my readers the ideas which this
enormous room excited. If a Pagan were to be transported into it
in his sleep, when he awoke he could not fail of thinking that he had
undergone an apotheosis, and had been conducted to the banqueting-
room of Jupiter. It was built after the unassisted design of Potemkin, and unites, to a sublime conception, all the graces of finished
taste. This prodigious room is supported by double rows of colossal Doric pillars, opening on one side into a vast pavilion, composing
the winter-garden, which I saw prepared for the emperor, who resides here for a short time every year, just before I left Petersburg.

F F

This garden is very extensive: the trees, chiefly orange, of an enormous size, are sunk in the earth in their tubs, and are entirely covered with fine mould: the walks are gravelled, wind, and undulate in
a very delightful manner, are neatly turfed, and lined with roses and
other flowers: the whole of the pavilion is lighted by lofty windows:
from the ceiling depend several magnificent lustres of the richest
cut glass.

Here, whilst the polar winter is raging without, covering the world
in white, and hardening the earth to marble; when water tossed in
the air drops down in ice, may be seen the foliage, and inhaled the
fragrance of an Arabian grove, in the soft and benign climate of an
Italian spring. The novelty and voluptuous luxuriance of this green
refreshing spectacle, seen through a colonnade of massy white pillars,
and reduplicated by vast mirrors, is matchless. Between the columns,
now no longer incumbered with boxes for spectators, as they formerly were, are a great number of beautiful statues and colossal casts:
the two celebrated vases of Carrara marble, the largest in the world,
occupy the centre of the room leading to the winter-garden. The
dying gladiator, Cupid and Psyche, a recumbent hermaphrodite,
and many other exquisite productions of the chisel, afford ample gratification to the man of taste. Amongst the busts, is that of the
right honourable Charles James Fox, by Nollekens; an admirable
likeness of that distinguished orator. Paul, during his temporary
aversion to the English, ordered this bust into the *cellar:* whether he
intended that his spleen should carry the marks of some humour, I
know not. His august successor removed it from the region of the
Tuscan juice, and the depths of darkness, and ordered it to occupy its
present station, where, by the side of Grecian and Roman virtue, the
sun of heaven shines full upon it. Opposite to the winter-garden is
a beautiful saloon, divided from the hall only by the colonnade, which
is filled with rare antiques, principally busts. Amongst them a head
of Achilles, and a small Silenus, are justly regarded as the most
precious. During the darkened hours of Paul, he converted this
palace into a garrison; and the hall, pavilion, and saloon, into a riding-
school for his troops!

· The rest of the rooms, which are upon the ground-floor, have been
elegantly, but very simply, fitted up by the present emperor, and all
their gorgeous hangings, furniture, and decorations, have been removed, and deposited in magazines. In one of the rooms there is a

set of superb lustres, every drop of glass in which may be set in
motion by clock-work, concealed in the centre, when it presents the
appearance of a little cascade.   The theatre, which has been much
reduced, is still spacious and very handsome.

It may not be uninteresting to give a very brief description of the
entertainment which I have before alluded to, as I received it from
Mr. Gould, who contributed his talents to augment the rich variety
of that resplendent festival: Soon after prince Potemkin's return
from the conquest of Crim Tartary, under the influence of a gloomy
prepossession that it would be the last time that he should have it in
his power to pay due honour to his imperial benefactress, he resolved
upon giving a banquet, which, in modern Europe and Asia, should
have no parallel.   What the expenses attending it amounted to were
never known, but they must have been prodigious.   For several
months previous to the gala, the most distinguished artists were invited from distant countries to assist in its completion.   The grand
outline was designed by the prince, and so various as well as vast
were the parts, that not one of the assistants could form any previous
idea of the whole of it.   In the general bustle of preparation, the
following anecdote, that proves the natural taste of Potemkin's mind,
is related: He had ordered a statue of Catherine to be formed of
alabaster, which he intended should be raised upon a pedestal, in a
temple of precious stones, in the winter-garden; for the motto upon
its intablature he wrote: " To the Mother of my Country, and to
me the most gracious."   In his design, the artist had extended the
hand and elevated the sceptre, in the formal style of our queen
Anne's appearance in wax-work; the critical eye of this prince, although he has been termed, and in some instances justly, a splendid
barbarian, in a moment perceived the deficiency of grace in the attitude, and ordered the sceptre to be inclined: the artist retired to another room in chagrin, and exclaimed, " This great savage has more
" taste than I have, who have been brought up in the lap of the arts."
Upon giving another direction, the artist stared, and remonstrated
upon the enormous sum which it would cost: " What, Sir!" said
Potemkin, " do you affect to know the depth of my treasury? Be
" assured it stands in no need of your sensibility."   After which his
orders were obeyed without any reference to expenditure.

Nothing could exceed the public sensation which this fête excited.
At length the evening arrived, when the prince was to appear, in all

his pomp and glory, before his fond and adored sovereign.   The
walls of these splendid apartments were most richly and beautifully
illuminated, and decorated with various exquisite transparencies;
and the stairs, hall, avenues, and sides of the rooms were lined with
officers of state, attached to the household of the prince, and servants,
in the most costly dresses, and magnificent liveries.   The orchestra
exceeded six hundred vocal and instrumental musicians, and announced the entrance of the empress and her court, richly attired,
by a grand overture and chorus, which reverberated through the
colonnades and saloons.   Potemkin conducted his imperial visitor
to an elevated chair glittering with gold and diamonds: midway between the columns were boxes gilt with pale gold, and lined with
green silk, filled with spectators in gala dresses.   The festivity commenced with a dance of youths of both sexes, habited in white, and
covered with pearls and jewels, at the head of whom were the present emperor and the grand duke Constantine his brother.   After
the dance, and the most costly refreshments, the party repaired to
the theatre, at the other end of the palace, where an occasional
piece, composed in honour of the empress, was performed, in which
all the powers of singing, acting, dancing, dress, scenery, and decorations, were displayed.   Upon the conclusion of the drama, the audience rose, and, as if impelled by magic, the benches, touched by
springs, moved and formed into tables and little seats, which were
almost instantaneously covered with the richest viands, served up in
gold and silver.   The curtain again rose, and discovered a hall of
mirrors, from which descended globular lustres of crystal, and a table
appeared covered with the rarity of almost every region, splendidly
served in gold; and at the head, upon a throne gilded and glittering
with precious stones, sat the empress surrounded by her court, the
most brilliant in Europe.   Such were the arrangements in this place,
that every one could see and be seen.   In the colossal hall were
spread tables filled with delicacies and the most costly wines, and at
the head of it was a prodigious massy cistern of solid silver, containing sterlet soup, which is said alone to have cost ten thousand rubles.
During this splendid repast, in every room the softest music was
heard, which rather enlivened than restrained the current of conversation.   Universal decorum and hilarity prevailed; every wish was
anticipated, every sense was gratified.

The banquet was followed by a succession of magnificent exhibitions, and the empress did not retire till midnight. As she proceeded to her carriage, it was observed that she appeared much affected by the homage which had been paid to her, encreased, perhaps, by the tender remembrance of departed hours; and as she turned to bid the prince adieu, she could scarcely support herself: at this touching moment, Potemkin fell upon his knees, and covered her hand with his tears and kisses: it was destined that he should never more behold her under that roof, and his mind seemed to be fully possessed of the idea. A short time afterwards, as he was proceeding from Yassy to Nicolaief, he was seized with a violent cholic; which it is supposed was produced by his singular irregularities; he alighted from his travelling carriage, supported by his nieces, with difficulty reached a bank on the side of the road, and expired in their arms. His remains were interred with magnificent honours, at Cherson, on the banks of the Dnieper, and a splendid mausoleum was raised to his memory by the order of her czarian majesty.

The dislike which Paul ever bore towards Potemkin, principally on account of his being the favourite of his imperial mother, induced the emperor, during the dreadful subversion of his mind, to order the body of the prince to be raised and exposed, and the mausoleum destroyed. A lady whom I met, and who was obliged, during this fearful period, to take refuge in the Crimea, beheld the ruins of the tomb, and the remains of the prince exposed to the birds of the air.

To what trifles do many persons owe their elevation : Potemkin was indebted for his honours and fortunes to a *feather*. In the revolution which gave the late empress sole possession of the throne, she appeared at the head of the Ismailof guards, when Potemkin, a young officer in the cavalry, perceiving that she had no feather in her hat, as she appeared on that momentous occasion *en militaire*, rode up to her and presented his. This extraordinary man experienced, in early life, a disappointment of the heart, which so frequently forces the mind out of its proper sphere, and unsettles it for ever. Potemkin rushed into the field of battle, and in search of death obtained glory. The cruel fair one still rejected him, notwithstanding his scars and honours, became violently smitten with an ugly old man, whom she married, and hated for ever after.

Potemkin very frequently refused to pay his tradesmen. It is said that a very celebrated French veterinary professor went from

Vienna to Petersburg, for the purpose of curing a beautiful charger, that had been presented to the prince by the emperor Joseph II, and which was so ill that the medical world of Petersburg had given it over. The professor built a stable for the animal upon a particular construction, and after the most incessant attention succeeded in restoring it to health. When the horse-doctor waited upon Potemkin with the joyful news, and expected to be profusely paid for the heavy sums of money which he had expended, and for his time and skill, he was forbidden the sight of the prince, never could see him afterwards, and never was paid: yet, notwithstanding these occasional acts of avaricious dishonesty, and although his property was estimated at nine millions of rubles in cash, forty-five thousand peasants, besides two pensions, one of seventy-five thousand rubles, and another of thirty thousand rubles, for his table, such was his prodigality that he was frequently embarrassed. In winter he used to wear a muff of the value of one thousand pounds.

In one of the prince's journeys to the Crimea, Mr. Gould attended him, being at that time his head gardener, and was preceded by several hundred assistants. Whenever the prince halted, if it were only for a day, he found his travelling pavilion raised, and surrounded by a garden in the English taste, composed of trees and shrubs, raised, and carried forward as the cavalcade proceeded, and divided by gravel walks. Yet, strange to relate, amidst this Asiatic pomp, whilst the subordinate attendants fared upon every dainty that wealth could purchase, the poor Englishman, whenever the prince requested him to travel in his carriage, which frequently occurred, was obliged to put up with the most homely fare, which Potemkin, always irregular and eccentric, generally preferred. At a sumptuous entertainment, where every rarity of epicurism invited the appetite, the prince has been known to order a raw carrot, or turnip, and to dine upon it.

I must relate the following little anecdote, and then I have done with Potemkin. One day, in the course of their journey, they halted at Bender, in Bessarabia, where, whilst the prince was alone at dinner, Mr. Gould rambled about the neighbourhood, for the purpose of discovering the scite, or remains, of the house of Chares XII of Sweden, in which, on the twelfth of February, 1713, he and a few followers madly bade defiance to the whole Ottoman army, after having been repeatedly and earnestly entreated to leave the dominions of

the grand Turk. After a diligent search, with the assistance of some
of the natives, the English gardener discovered the ruins which the
eccentric spirit of the Swedish king had rendered so interesting, and
exultingly returned to the prince with the intelligence, who exclaimed, with liberal joy, " The English discover every thing," immediately proceeded to it, and, after regarding its remains with a very
lively sensation, ordered the house to be repaired, and partly rebuilt,
and a garden to be constructed round it, which was accordingly done,
as a monument of his respect for the conqueror of Narva.

CHAP. XVI.

DURING my stay at Petersburg, I paid several visits to the country houses of the English merchants on the Peterhoff road, where
they live in great elegance. In the gardens of one of them, I trod
with delight upon British ground. An ardent love for his country
had induced the hospitable owner, at a great expense, to bring a
quantity of English ballast from British ships to cover his walks with.
Every garden is furnished with large swings, capable of holding two
persons standing, and one between sitting. Of this diversion the Russians are very fond. As I was roving in my friend's grounds I heard
the cry of some hounds in an adjoining kennel, belonging to a Russian nobleman : the nobility are very fond of the sports of the field.
The gentlemen of the English factory have a regular pack and sport-
ing establishment at Garrella. Having assumed a tolerable shabby
dress, no difficult thing for a traveller at any time to command, for
the purpose of qualifying ourselves for the approaching scene, and
to prevent the suspicion of improper motives, we proceeded to the
great national bath on a Saturday, which seems to be a purifying
day every where.

After passing over a raised wooden path, by the side of a long
wooden wall, we halted at a house built of the same materials, which
formed the grand entrance. Here, upon paying five copecs a-piece,
from a hole in a dark shed, or magazine of birch rods with the leaves
on, a hand poked out one of them to each of us, which we took, without, at the time, knowing for what purpose they were to be used.
On the entrance on each side were stalls of black bread, little pies,

quass, and liqueurs. In the first court we beheld men and women indiscriminately mingled together, in a state similar to that which preceded the slightest notion of breeches and waistcoats. They were arranged like so many hounds in a dog-kennel, upon benches tier above tier, where they were wringing their beards, and combing and plaiting their hair. In the middle of the yard was a jet-d'eau playing into a great wooden cistern; as the bathers came out of the vapour-room, red and reeking with heat, they ran to this tank, and filling a bucket with cold water, raised it, and threw it over their heads. When these baths are near a river they plunge into it, and in the winter roll themselves in the snow.

I opened the door of the vapour-room, in which I could not continue above a minute, and in that time a profuse perspiration came over me. The room was capacious, women and men were piled one above another amphitheatrically; the vapour which filled the room, and gave it the atmosphere of a digester, was produced from water being thrown upon a great number of heated stones, some of them red hot. In this place, to assist the cause of perspiration and washing, they exchange the little *tender and delicate offices* of flogging, soaping, and rubbing each other down. The Russians in this, as well as many other customs, bear a strong analogy to the Grecians. These scenes, such is the effect of habit, are seldom productive of libertinism, even amongst the natives; to every foreigner they cannot fail to be offensive and repulsive. If a painter wishes to delineate a Venus, or even any part of the figure, let him go to a Russian bath for a model. My curiosity was soon satisfied; I visited no other part of the building, and right glad was I to quit this disgusting scene. These baths, however, which are to be found in every village, prove that the Russians are naturally clean. After these ablutions, clean shirts and shifts are put on for Sunday.

It is highly interesting to observe how nations differ from each other in their customs, and how frequently they reverse them. As we are upon the subject of bathing, I cannot help mentioning that, as I was walking with some English ladies in the summer gardens one evening, I saw about sixty men and women enjoying themselves in a small canal which runs from the Neva to the Michaeleski palace. Public as this spectacle was, there seemed to be the most perfect innocence amongst all the parties. One man was very desirous that I should see how well his wife could swim; and a Polish servant in

G G

waiting said, with great naïveté, to one of our English ladies (a very amiable and sensible woman, in whose service he was), " Madam, there is a fine seat there," pointing to one upon the side of the water, " where you can have an excellent view, and see the manner in " which the Russians swim." Their manner is somewhat curious ; they swim as if a dog had taught them. As I was one day walking by the side of the canal which runs before the opera-house, I saw two young, and I think I may add, *modest* women, seeking shelter from the sun in the limpid steam. The forms of these Musidoras did more honour to their sex than any which I had before seen.

The Russians beat all the doctors hollow. They have one simple (I know not if certain) cure for every description of disease ; viz. two glasses of brandy, a scourging and soaping in the vapour-bath, and a roll in the Neva, or snow.

The smile of the sovereign has an universal influence ; if you are well at court, it is well with you every where. Impressed with this truth, I resolved to visit the greatest favourite of his imperial majesty. As his sagacity was extraordinary ; as he paid no consideration to exterior himself, nor minded it in others; and, moreover, as his residence was in the neighbourhood of the bath, I made up my mind to avail myself of his liberal notions, and seek an audience without returning to my hotel, a distance of three miles at least, to change my dress. Although, with respect to the appearance of his visitors, he was very accommodating, yet I found him, like all courtiers, inaccessible without a bribe ; and accordingly, the honour of being introduced to him cost me something, it is useless now to say what. Was it not singular ? Upon entering his apartment, which was very lofty, I found him heavily ironed by one leg, and guarded ; yet, strange as this appeared, I was rejoiced to find, for his character stands very high, that he was not in disgrace. The personage I am speaking of was his majesty's elephant, who was at least eleven feet high, and, like his imperial master, majestic, yet gracious; and though fearfully armed with power, most discreet and gentle in its use. His establishment consisted of a faithful Persian, who received and repaid his affections.

In the ground behind the elephant's apartment we saw some Calmuc sheep grazing, distinguishable from the same species of animal in other countries, by a vast bag of hard fat, which grows from the rump. As I was returning from his elephantic majesty, a friend of

mine pointed to a Russian who was crossing a bridge, and informed
me that some years since he was one of the leading characters of a
sect, whose tenets extended eternal rewards of happiness to those
who, crossing the great design of God in creating man, deprived
themselves of the possibility of becoming the fathers of families:
against the spreading fanaticism of these monstrous visionaries, which
aimed at the radical extinction of society, Catherine II directed a
prompt and decisive blow: those of its wretched and deluded followers, who are known, are branded, wherever they appear, with public derision.

Catherine put down a sect still more formidable, and by the following whimsically wise manner saved her people from the baneful con-
tagion of French principles. During that revolution, which portend-
ed ruin to all the sacred establishments of all nations, when in England Pitt trampled out the brightening embers, and saved his country
from the devouring flames, a group of mischievous emissaries from
France arrived at Petersburg, and began, in whispers amongst the mob,
to persuade the poor droshka driver, and the ambulatory vender of
honey quass, that thrones were only to be considered as stools, and
that they had as much right to sit upon one of them as their empress: Catherine, concealing her real apprehensions, availed herself
of the powers with which she was clothed, without shedding a drop
of blood. She knew ridicule to be, in able hands, a powerful weapon,
and resolved to wield it upon the present occasion. One evening the
police officers were ordered to seize all these illuminated apostles of
liberty, and bear them away to the lunatic asylum, where the empress had directed that their heads should be shaved and blistered,
and their bodies well scoured by aperient medicines, and kept on
meagre diet; this regimen was continued for fourteen days, when
their confinement terminated. The common Russians had heard of
their fate, and really believing that they had been insane, neglected
and deserted them upon their re-appearance in the city with shorn
heads, hollow eyes, and sunk cheeks, and all the striking indications
of a recently bewildered mind. If this mild and ingenious project
had failed, Catherine would have let loose all the energy of power,
and for this purpose she rapidly caused to be built that vast edifice,
now used for the marine barracks, which she destined for a state
prison.

The transition from the revolutionists to wild dogs is very simple and natural. About three versts on the left hand side of the Zarsko Zello road, is a wood infested with these animals. To this place dead horses, and all the rank garbage of the city, which a Russian stomach cannot relish, are carried. These dogs never aim at *proselytism*, and are never seen beyond the boundaries of their thicket.

Having thrown aside our bathing dresses, we went to the palace of Saint Michael, where, as I have related, the last emperor perished. As Paul had expressed so much aversion to the imperial mansions in which his mother delighted, I felt a curiosity minutely to examine a palace of his own creation. In addition to what has been before observed, the whole of this enormous pile was built by an Italian, of red Dutch brick, which at a distance has an animating appearance, upon a basement of hewn granite, that resembles a foundation of rock. The grand entrance from the great perspective, through the riding-room and offices, is very handsome. Upon the architrave is written in Russ characters, as it was translated to me, the following singular motto: " May my house endure like the Lord's." The Russians observe, with their accustomed superstition, that the number of letters of this inscription correspond with the number of Paul's years, and that out of them an anagram may be composed, denoting that he who raised the building would perish by a violent death. The interior is vast, but very gloomy. The chambers which were shewn were stripped of their furniture and all their moveable decorations, which are lodged in the cabinet of jewels, but the ornaments which remained exhibited a style of costly magnificence ; the doors, some of which were of various-coloured glass, and richly gilded, were uncommonly superb. We saw the room in which the unfortunate sovereign perished, and his private staircase before mentioned. All the rooms, except those which are used for state, are occupied by persons belonging to the court; amongst others Mr. Cameron, the imperial architect, has a superb suite of apartments, those which were formerly occupied by the present emperor and empress before they ascended the throne ; in one of which is a fire-place which had been encrusted with jewels. To the taste and genius of this gentleman, Russia is indebted for many of her beautiful architectural objects.

From the palace of St. Michael, we went, by a special appointment and permission, obtained after much trouble, to the academy of arts, and in our way stopped at the marble church of St. Isaac, which was erected, but not finished, by the late empress : it is entirely built of Siberian marble, porphyry, and jasper, at an immense cost, has a vast copper dome gilded, and is the most magnificent place of worship in Petersburg ; yet, after all, it has a very *sombre* appearance without.

The late emperor, disgusted, as I have already explained, with every thing which had engaged the care and regard of his imperial mother, raised in ridicule a little tower of brick, covered with a small dome, on the west side of this temple. During the calamitous state of his mind, an indiscreet wag affixed to the door of the church the following pasquinade, in Russ verses : " To Paul the first, emperor, &c."

> " In *marble* should thy mother's mem'ry shine ;
> In perishable *brick* and *plaster* thine."

The writer paid dearly for his wit; he was discovered, knouted, had his nostrils torn, and was sent to Siberia. Upon the accession of the present emperor, application was made by his friends for his release, which was granted, and a miserable mutilated wretch was restored to those who could with difficulty recognize him.

The interior of this building is truly magnificent, being entirely composed of the most precious Siberian marble. Near the altar was an elegant pulpit, the only one that I saw in any of the Greek churches: it was built by the orders of the late empress, who was desirous of enlightening her people in their faith by devotional discourses.

The academy of arts is an enormous pile of quadrangular brick building, in the Vassili-ostroff. In the council-room we were shewn a beautiful golden medal of the head of Paul, by the present empress dowager, which at once proves the taste of her mind, and the powerful affections of her heart. In the hall of statues were a great number of fine casts from the antique, particularly a beautiful one of the Belvidere Apollo: the original, in the imperial museum at Paris, afforded me the greatest delight I ever experienced in contemplating any work of art, and which I greatly preferred to the Laocoon. Amongst the pictures was a perfect and precious piece of painting, in fresco, from Herculaneum. As we passed through a suite of rooms, in which the youngest class of students, from the age of eight or nine years, were drawing (all of whom, as well as the rest of the pupils, are clothed, educated, and maintained, at the expense of the crown), we saw some promising works of art ; but, strange to relate, they were principally confined to the younger artists : the tree looks healthy towards the roots, but weakens as it spreads. I could not help observing, that most of the adult students were occupied in painting whole and half length likenesses of the emperor, in his regimentals, instead of attending to the works of the ancient masters, several of whose productions adorn their galleries. The almighty Disposer of the universe has limited nations, as well as individuals, to their proper share of his beneficence. Whilst he has determined that the vine of the Tyrol shall never bend with its luscious grape upon the shores of the Frozen Sea, he seems to have allotted a more benign region to painting, and to have precluded her from wandering far in the north. To the Russian that god has been bountiful :—but Russia has never yet sent an illustrious painter into the world :—it may be too confident to say, she never will.

In the hall of architecture were some exquisite models ; many in cork, of Roman ruins ; the principal were a prodigious one of St. Peter's at Rome, which entirely filled a large room ; its dimensions admitted two of us to stand under its dome, and another of the kazan. In the hall of statuary we saw several students at their occupations, who displayed considerable ability : there were here some beautiful casts, from Canovre's statues, many of which are in prince Usupoff's gallery. The adjoining rooms to this were for the accommodation of the engravers and medalists.

The late empress lavished enormous sums upon this institution, which, if it does not ultimately reach the perfection of similar establishments in more genial climates, will at least have the merit of having made some advancements. After the profuse magnificence of Catherine, and the thoughtless waste of the imperial treasure during the short reign of his disastrous predecessor, Alexander has most judiciously confined himself to a cautious and scrupulous expenditure. Russia is unquestionably much indebted to the genius and spirit of the late empress; but it was impossible that *extended* civilization could be the fruits of her costly culture. In raising magnificent palaces, she raised so many monuments to her memory, which at first *surprised* the common Russian, but never *informed* him ; and, in doing so, she too much neglected the cottage. If I dare intimate the spot where, in such a country the spirit of civilization should commence her operations, I would point to the hovel of felled trees, where the smoke issues through the same hole which admits the light: *ameliorate the domestic economy of rude and abject nature : take care of the peasantry :* the higher classes are pretty nearly the same all over the world. The reverse of this plan will ever present the hideous spectacle of a voluptuous and vicious nobility, and of a people corrupt before they are refined ; or, in the language of a shrewd observer of mankind, "rotten ere they are ripe." As far as my observation and information extended, I should conceive that the civilization of Russia would be rapidly promoted, after the removal of that most frightful and powerful of all checks, *slavery*, by improving the farms, by establishing colleges for the education of those who are destined to the priesthood, by reducing the number of holidays, by instituting rewards for menial integrity at the end of a given period, and by preventing parents from betrothing their female children before the age of consent, and contrary to their will.

The day when we visited the places before described being remarkable fine, captain Elphinstone, of the Russian navy, proposed a visit by water in his barge to Kammenoi Ostroff, a little seat, and the favourite residence of the emperor, about seven versts from the city. The bargemen were very fine fellows, clean shaved, and dressed in clean shirts. As we rowed round the islands formed by the Petrovka, branching from the Neva, my gallant friend gratified me, by relating the following anecdote of the delicacy and fortitude of Catherine's mind. After the battle between the Russian and Swedish fleets, off Cronstadt, in May, 1790, captain Elphinstone, then a very young lieutenant, was dispatched by his uncle, admiral Creuse, to Catherine, who was at that time at the palace of Zarsko Zelo, with an account of the successful manœuvres of her fleet. For four days and nights preceding the empress had taken no rest, and but little refreshment, the greater part of which time she had passed upon the beautiful terrace near the baths of porphyry ; listening, with the greatest anxiety, to the distant thunder of the cannon, which was so tremendous, that several windows in Petersburg were broken by its concussion. It is said that, anticipating the last disaster, her horses and carriages were ready to convey her to Moscow. Young Elphinstone arrived at the palace late at night, in his fighting clothes, covered with dust and gun-powder, and severely fatigued with long and arduous duty. His dispatches were instantly carried to the empress, who ordered her page in waiting to give the bearer refreshments and a bed, and requested that he might on no account be disturbed. The gallant messenger availed himself of her graciousness, and " Tir'd Nature's sweet restorer, balmy sleep!" never quitted his eye-lids till the dawn had far advanced, during which period Catherine had sent three times to see if he were awake. At length captain Elphinstone, in all his *dishabille*, was conducted to her presence by her secretary, when she commenced an enchanting conversation, in which she complimented the gallantry and many naval achievements of his family ; and after proceeding upon various topics for about half an hour, she said, calling him " my son," " Now let " us proceed to business: I have received the dispatches, which " have afforded me infinite satisfaction. I thank you for your bravery " and zeal; I beg you will describe to me the position of the ships;" which, as captain E. explained, she indicated with her pencil upon a leaf of her pocket-book; and as she gave him her orders to the commander in chief, she presented him with a rouleau of ducats, a beautiful little French watch, and, although very young, promoted him to the rank of captain.

It was during this battle that the Swedish monarch behaved with his accustomed distinguished gallantry. As he was rowing in his barge, and giving his orders, in the thickest of the battle, a shot carried away the hand of the strokesman, and, at this moment, a small Russian vessel of war, discovering the king, bore down upon him. The brave and generous monarch, seeing the accident which his poor bargeman had sustained, and his own personal peril at the same time, calmly took out his handkerchief, and bound it over the wound; then leaped on board one of his gun-boats, and miraculously escaped, by that good fortune which never favours little minds, at the instant when his barge was boarded by the enemy, the cushions of which were preserved in the apartment of captain Elphinstone, in the marine barracks, as trophies of war and of humanity.

A short time after the Swedish fleet had retired, the gallant and venerable admiral Creuse, who commanded the Russian fleet, paid his respects to his sovereign. Owing to the corpulency of the admiral, the narrow plank floor of the presence-chamber shook with his weight, which the hero remarked with some little humour, to Catherine, when she turned this trivial circumstance into the following beautiful compliment:—" My brave Creuse, wherever you go you " make the earth shake under you, and your enemies tremble." As we rowed along we passed several national baths, from which the

people precipitately issued in a stream of perspiration, and plunged
into the river.   They regard these transitions from extreme heat to
extreme cold as conducive to an invigoration of the frame.   As we
turned up the little Nevka, we saw several beautiful country houses
and grounds: the chateau of count Narishkin was of this description;
it had a centre, surmounted by a vast copper dome painted green, and
very extensive wings upon a ground floor; a flight of steps led to the
principal entrance, shaded from the sun by a vast projecting awning
of canvas; the whole edifice was built of wood, and painted of a light
yellow.   Several elegant yachts and pleasure barges with gay stream-
ers, floating green-houses and baths, were moored before it; the
whole had an Asiatic appearance.   A superb pleasure barge with
twelve rowers, covered with a rich awning from stem to stern, passed us, in which was a lady of rank, and a little yellow humpbacked
female ideot, who had the good fortune of being her *pet!* The Russian nobility, whether from whim, genuine compassion, or superstition, I know not, are uncommonly fond of these little, sickly, shape-
less, blighted beings: uniting man to monster, and apparently formed by heaven to mock the proud presuming nature of those whom
he has made after his own image.   The imperial chateau is small,
has a terrace in front towards the water, and a wood behind;
as the emperor was here we did not attempt to see the inside of it,
but I understand most of the rooms are for use and comfort only.
The empress, who is one of the most amiable and the shyest being
that ever wore a diadem, hurries with delight from the gaudy tumult
of a court, to veil herself in the tranquil shades of this sequestered
place; and the emperor exhibits the same love of privacy. Is there
no moral in their choice? Does it not point to the spot where only
genuine happiness is to be found?

   We went on board one of the imperial yachts, a beautiful vessel, the state-room of which was most elegantly fitted up. Soon after
leaving Kammenoi Ostroff, we passed count Stroganoff's gardens,
which are prettily laid out, and embellished with the customary decorations of hillocks, rustic temples, artificial rocks and waterfalls.
The count very liberally opens his garden gates on Sunday to the
public, when the walks are very much crowded, and resemble, but in
miniature, those of Kensington gardens. Upon our return, we rowed
against the stream of the Neva a considerable way, and floated down
with it, for the purpose of enabling our boatmen to take in their oars,

H h

and afford us a specimen of Russian vocal music. They first faced
each other, and sat very close together, and upon a signal being given,
the leader sang a little song alone, which, upon his striking a tambo-
rine, all the party stedfastly gazing upon each other, joined in, and,
although their voices at a distance frequently produce an agreeable
harmony, such was the shrillness on the present occasion, that I
could not help thinking the conclusion of the song by far the best
part of it. When captain E. was lying in his frigate, a few years
since, off Palermo, he invited a party, in which were two Italian
princesses, to a marine breakfast, during which the latter requested
to be indulged with a native Russ chorus, the fame of which had
reached them. The sailors, who were assembled round the cabin-
light, commenced their national song before their fair auditors expected it, who, terrified at the screaming sounds which issued from
the strained throats of these untutored warblers, instantly raised their
hands to their ears, and implored captain E. to stop his men; but,
convulsed with laughter, and overpowered by the din of the chorus,
he was obliged to let them make a natural finale. When they had
stopped, captain Elphinstone said, " Now, ladies, will you have a
little more?" " Not for the world, my dear captain, not for the world,
we are quite content," was the universal cry.

Whilst I was upon a visit at the house of my much respected and
hospitable friend, John Venning, Esq. I used generally to be awakened by a cowkeeper, collecting, Orpheus-like, his cows together, by
a very long pipe, from which he produced some strains by no means
unpleasing. The dress and attitude of this fellow, with his instrument in his mouth, resembled very much some of the figures which
I have seen upon Etruscan vases. For two or three days, whilst the
wind was northerly, we were much annoyed in the city by a dense
smoky atmosphere, arising from a large forest, which had been burning for several days, about thirty versts from Petersburg: to prevent
the spreading of this terrible conflagration, two regiments were
marched to the spot, who, after great exertion, by felling trees, and
digging trenches, succeeded in impeding its progress. Accidents of
this kind are attributed to the reaction of intense heat from the rock,
upon the dry moss which is frequently found upon it.

CHAP. XVII.

COURT CLOCK—WINTER PALACE, HERMITAGE—PLAYERS AND GOVERN-
MENT CARRIAGES—CONVENT DES DEMOISELLES—INSTABILITY OF FOR-
TUNE—GENEROSITY IN A CHILD—THE FOUNDLING HOSPITAL.

IN order to observe engagements with punctuality, it is necessary
that a traveller's watch should be set by the clock of the winter
palace, which is the sun's vice-regent in Petersburg, and is certainly
more sovereign than that of the horse-guards in London. I learned
this piece of important information, as I proceeded with a party of
friends to the hermitage; not the matted cell of an anchorite, but
a magnificent modern palace built by the late empress, and connected by a light elegant gallery with an enormous mass of building,
called the winter palace, built of brick stuccoed, and consisting of a
basement floor, a grand and lesser story, supported with Doric
columns, and adorned with balustrades, and an immense number of
statues, many of which are said to be excellent, but as they are asso-
ciated with the chimneys, their beauties are not discernable to gazers
on the ground. This pile was built by the empress Elizabeth, is
grand from its magnitude, but very heavy: within its walls are
many courts, galleries, and passages, and staircases without number.
In the winter it requires fifteen hundred stoves, or, as the Russians
call them, pitchkas, and the resident English, peeches, to warm it.

What could induce Catherine to call one of the most costly and
elegant palaces in Europe by the name of the hermitage I cannot
imagine; not more preposterous would it be to hear Windsor
castle denominated the Nutshell. Its situation on the banks of the
Neva is very beautiful; the apartments are still magnificent, although
much of their rich furniture has been removed, and are embellished
with the Houghton and other choice collections, to which artists
have free access to copy. One room was entirely filled with some of
the finest productions of Vernet; there is also a great number by
Teniers. Upon the same floor with the picture galleries, which,
with the state-rooms, occupy the second story, is a spacious covered
winter garden, filled with orange trees, and foreign singing birds,

opening into a summer garden upon the top of the palace, in which there is a beautiful long gravelled walk, lined with shrubs and large graceful birch-trees, whose roots I should think must have for some time threatened to make their way through the ceiling of the drawing-rooms below. The whole is adorned with statues, elegant garden sophas, and temples, and on each side are magnificent galleries. In the cabinet of curiosities I was much pleased with a faithful and exquisite model of a Russian boor's farm-house, in wax. In the music room adjoining to this are some large and admirable pictures, by Sneyder, representing fish, fowl, and fruit. In the cabinet of jewels there is a rich display of all sorts of jewelry ; and, amongst others, under a great glass case, are the celebrated mechanical peacock, owl, cock, and grasshopper, of the size of life, which was made in England, at a vast expense, and presented by Potemkin to the late empress. The machinery is damaged : the cock, mounted on a tree of gold, no longer crows, nor hoots the owl, nor does the peacock spread his tail, at the expiration of the hour, but the grasshopper still skips round to denote the moments. This animal is nearly the size of his more animated brethren in Russian Finland, which are said to be an inch and a half long. There were also several ivory cups, the fruits of the ingenuity of Peter the Great, whose versatility was such, that, apparently with equal ease, he could bend from the founding of cities, leading armies into the field, and fighting battles, to building boats, turning wooden spoons and platters, and carving in ivory. Raphael's hall, one of the galleries running parallel with the garden, is superbly painted and decorated, and has a fine collection of minerals : its inlaid floor is uncommonly rich and exquisite.

I searched in vain for sir Joshua Reynolds's celebrated Infant Hercules, purchased by the late empress for the hermitage. Upon enquiry I found that it had been removed into a private apartment below, and was seldom shown; the reason assigned was, that the Russians have a superstitious horror of death, and that as the subject was the strangling of the serpent by the infant god, it was on that account unpopular. Upon our return through the rooms, we went to the court theatre, connected with the hermitage by a gallery over an arch, which crosses a cut of water from the Neva to the Moika canal. The space before the curtain is filled with seats rising amphitheatrically, and the whole, without being large, is elegant.

The performers were rehearsing at the time: afterwards, as we were quitting the palace, my curiosity was excited by a number of imperial coaches, presenting a gradation of qualities; some were tolerably good, some shabby, and others very old and crazy, to which must be added a very long vehicle, such as is used in England for conveying wild beasts, having four horses abreast, all drawn up before that part of the palace where the theatre is situated. Upon the conclusion of the rehearsal, the players descended: the tragedians and genteel comedians occupied the better carriages, the low comedians the more ancient and defective ones, and the chorus-singers, to the amount of about thirty, skipped into the long coach, and were all driven to their respective homes. These machines are kept for the sole service of the players.

Not far from the hermitage, and upon a line with it, is the magnificent palace raised by Catherine II, for Gregory Orloff, and afterwards allotted, by the late emperor, to the last of the kings of Poland: it is built of grey Siberian marble, and adorned with columns and pilasters of the same stone, of brown and reddish colours. The balustrades of the balconies, and the frames of the windows, are of brass richly gilded. All the splendid furniture and moveable decorations have been removed, and the whole is now occupied by persons belonging to the court.

In consequence of the gracious orders of the empress-dowager to that effect, we visited a very interesting institution under her immediate protection, the Convent des Demoiselles. This imperial seminary, which has no equal in Europe, contains three hundred and seventy-two young ladies of nobility; and two hundred and forty daughters of citizens. There is also another institution under the same roof, called that of saint Catherine, in which there are one hundred and eighty-eight children, of the inferior orders of nobility. The age of admission is six years. The noble young ladies are taught German, French, Italian, drawing, music, dancing, geography, embroidery, and every other elegant pursuit. The daughters of the bourgeois are instructed in what is useful alone, and can conduce to their making good tradesmen's wives. Their genius, or bias of mind, whenever it can be ascertained, is always consulted in their pursuits. The building is like a great town; it was formerly occupied by the monks of Smolnoi, who have been removed to accommodate much more useful and lovely members of society. In the centre is a vast neglected church, surmounted with a dome in the centre of four small cupolas, all of copper gilded. This edifice forms a venerable and prominent feature in the city. We were received at the grand entrance by some of the officers attached to the establishment, in full uniform, a dress which is worn by all male persons belonging to imperial institutions, on account of the government being military. We are first conducted to the kitchen, where we saw and tasted a sample of the day's dinner, consisting of excellent soup, boiled beef, vegetables, and pastry. The young ladies are divided into classes of age, and distinguished by brown, blue, and green and white dresses. In the first school we were presented to her excellency madame Adlerberg, the directress of the convent, who appeared, decorated with the order of saint Catherine, a lady of great beauty, and elegance of deportment; her mind and character were explained by the smiles and looks of affection which every where attended her, as we proceeded through the schools. In the sick room there were only three patients, who were most tenderly attended by the proper nurses; the name, age, disorder and treatment of the invalid, is inscribed upon a little tablet fixed over her head to the back of the bed. The dormitories were remarkably neat, and even elegant. Some of the little girls surprised us, by the excellence to which they had attained in drawing. In the Greek church belonging to the convent we were attended by the priest in his full robes, who shewed us a magnificent cup of gold studded with jewels, used in devotion, the work of the empress dowager.

The mortality among the children is very inconsiderable; upon an average only two die annually out of eight hundred, unless after filling up of several vacancies, occurring at the same time, when the children admitted from the provinces sometimes bring diseases with them. In the blue class we saw an instance of the mutability of fortune, in a little girl about eleven years of age, the princess S——, the grand-daughter of the late king of Poland. In the dispersion of the family she was left destitute. Her mother, in a frenzy produced by the dethronement of her father, threw her son, a child, from a balcony into the street, and dashed out his brains. This orphan relic of an august and most unfortunate family was saved from actual want by the humanity and feeling of the princess Biron, with whose daughter she is educated in the convent. The young princess Biron, in the blue dress of her class, underwent an examination in French and writing in our presence, and acquitted herself with infinite credit. In the green and white class, where the eldest young ladies are, we were entertained with some very delightful Russ and French airs and choruses, accompanied by the harpsichord.

In the institution of Saint Catherine, under the direction of madame Bredkoff, an elderly lady of distinguished talents, and sweetness of disposition, the following little circumstance occurred, which will prove that the Russian mind, whatever may have been said of it, is susceptible of feeling and generosity. In this institution, which is supported by the empress-dowager, a limited number only of young ladies are admitted, free of expense, by ballot; but others are received upon paying, as it is termed, a pension. At the last admission, two little girls, the eldest not exceeding ten years of age, the daughters of a naval captain, who in this country is noble, the father of a large family, presented themselves, and drew, the one a prize, the other a blank. Although so young, they knew that fate had, in this manner, resolved upon their separation; they felt it, and wept. Another young lady, to whom the next chance devolved, drew a prize, and observing the distress of the sisters, without holding any communication with their parents, or with any other person, spontaneously ran up to the luckless little girl, presented her with the ticket, and leading her up to the directress, said, " See, madam, I have drawn a " prize; but my papa can afford to pay the pension, and I am sure will " pay it for me: pray let one who is less fortunate enjoy the good that " has happened to me." This charming anecdote was immediately reported to the empress-dowager, who expressed the highest delight, and paid, out of her own purse, the pension of the little benefactress.

An idea has gone forth, that when the period arrives for the fair pupils to quit the convent for the great theatre of the world, so many years of sequestration from it renders them totally ignorant, awkward, and that they enter society with little less surprise than that which a man born blind, and suddenly restored to sight, would express on his first contemplation of objects. But this remark is completely disproved by the good-breeding and polished manners which the young ladies displayed in the convent: in addition to which it may be observed, that every month, or oftener, they have a public and splendid ball, which is always crowded by people of fashion, their relations or friends, with whom, upon these occasions, they have unrestrained intercourse. At Easter, and other festivals, by the order of the empress-dowager, they take a ride round the city, to see the diversion of sliding down the ice-hills, or the various festivities incident to the occasion and season. The empress-dowager takes great pleasure in visiting this institution; and whenever she appears, the young people crowd round her, to kiss the palm of her hand, as if she were their common parent. In other countries there may be institutions upon the same principle, but not one of the same magnitude ; there the sovereign thinks he has discharged a splendid duty if he allot a sum of money for its support, without seeing to its appropriation, or cherishing the establishment by his presence; but here the empress-dowager, the empress, and other branches of the imperial family, are personally and actively assistant. When madame Bredkoff was sent to Moscow, to organize an institution there, similar to that of St. Catherine's, the empress-dowager, during her absence, took possession of her chair, and discharged all her functions.

It is with great pleasure I mention another instance of the munificence of the dowager empress, in an establishment called the Institute of Marie, which is wholly supported out of her private purse, and costs one thousand five hundred pounds per annum. In this seminary, which is under the able direction of madame Luky, fifty-six girls are clothed, maintained, and educated in French, German, Russ, arithmetic, drawing, and embroidery. In the latter, the young pupils have attained to such a high state of perfection, that the state dresses of the imperial family are frequently made by them. At eighteen, the fair *élèves* are provided with respectable situations in genteel families, or married, when a little dowry is presented to them. The qualifications required for the admission of a pupil is, not that she should have interest or friends, but that she should be *destitute* and *friendless!* The whole resembled a large, genteel, and happy family. When the money of an empire is thus expended, it is like the sun drinking up the exhalations of the earth, to return it in refreshing showers of dew.

By the same gracious order of the empress-dowager, we were admitted to the foundling-hospital, one of the most extensive and superb buildings in the residence. In this establishment, six thousand children, the offspring of shame or misery, are received, and protected.—Sublime idea! but let us examine whether the end of this great and benevolent design is answered. The children are

classed according to their age: in the first room were several little
creatures who had been left one, two, or three, days before, at the
office of secrecy, where the wretched mother at night, if nature
will admit, with a trembling hand rings the bell, resigns her child
to a porter, receives a ticket of its number, and in agony retires. When we entered a large room where the nurses were suck-
ling the infants, the result of our enquiry and observation, in which
I was much indebted to a very intelligent lady, who was herself a
mother, and who accompanied us, was that, although the nurses,
generally the wives of boors, were examined by surgeons, and bathed upon their admission, yet many of them displayed the effect of
invincible habit, and were very dirty, notwithstanding the greatest
vigilance and care to keep them clean; and, as many of them had
nursed their own children seven or eight months before upon
wretched fare, their milk was neither rich nor copious; a circumstance which was visibly proved by the meagre and unhealthy appearance of the nurslings. The difficulty of procuring an adequate
number of nurses is great indeed; and with a sufficient quantity of
milk, utterly impossible. The mortality is very great: out of two
thousand five hundred infants received the preceding year, five hundred perished! The conclusion is plain. Whilst the principle of
this infant asylum is unquestionably propitious to libertinism, its
present constitution and economy are ungenial to population. If
this establishment were upon a *smaller scale*, it might possibly
answer; but, extensive *as it is*, it seems to overstep its object by too
large a stride, and to countenance an opinion, that the cause of humanity and policy would be more efficaciously promoted even were
no other barriers opposed to infanticide than nature and the laws.
We repeatedly observed that the boys did not look so healthy as the
girls, which may be owing to the nature and hours of their labour
being somewhat greater: indeed, eight hours toil is too much for
boys of tender years. The gardens are very extensive: we there
saw a recreation which is a great favourite with the young Russians.
A broad flat board, about eight feet long, was placed centrically over
another of the same-size and shape: a girl, about fourteen or fifteen
years of age, stood at one extremity of the upper board, and at the
other end two smaller girls, who, by alternately springing up, tossed
each other to the height of five or six feet, from which they descended with uncommon skill and steadiness. A gentleman of the

I 1

party, at the great hazard of his neck, unsuccessfully endeavoured to partake of the pastime. From the windows of the foundling-hospital, in a sequestered part of the city, we saw the top of a private lying-in-house, where only the patients and nurses are admitted, and the offices of tenderness and humanity are discharged, without curiosity, enquiry, or development.

I was very fortunate in being at Petersburg during two great causes of national festivity: the name day, as the Russians call it, of the empress-dowager; and the nuptials of one of her daughters, the grand duchess Maria, a beautiful and amiable princess, about seventeen years of age, to the only son of the reigning prince of Saxe Weimar, a young man of twenty. It was the wish of the empress-dowager that these events should be celebrated on the same day. This marriage, unlike the severe policy which state ceremony imposes on such occasions in other countries, had been preceded by a course of attentions and tenderness for two years preceding, during which period the young prince had resided with the empress-dowager, who wisely thought with Shakespeare, that

> ——" Marriage is a matter of more worth
> Than to be dealt in by attorneyship.
> For what is wedlock forced, but a hell,
> An age of discord, and continual strife?
> Whereas the contrary bringeth forth bliss,
> And is a pattern of celestial peace."

On the third of August, N. S. I went with a party of friends to the winter palace, the vast area before which was covered with carriages; on our arrival we proceeded up the grand marble staircase, through a suite of superb rooms, to an apartment of the foreign ministers, who were splendidly attired. In this room was the lady of the British ambassador, who in her dress and person did honour to the magnificence and beauty of the British empire. All the rooms were uncommonly crowded with people in full gala dresses, and about one o'clock the procession moved from the empress dowager's apartment: after a long line of marshals and state officers, vying with each other in the splendour of their dresses, appeared the emperor, in a plain suit of regimentals, leading the empress dowager by the hand, the empress, in a superb dress covered with diamonds, walking by his side (the former always takes the precedence of the

latter, by an ukase of Paul); then followed the beautiful grand
duchess, between the young prince of Weimar and the grand duke
Constantine, in a blaze of jewelry: upon her head was a crown of
diamonds, upon her shoulders a long robe of crimson velvet lined with
ermine, the train of which was supported (and the intense heat of
the weather called for all the support that could be afforded her) by
several peers of high rank, and in her bosom she wore a most superb
bouquet of flowers in diamonds; then followed the rest of the imperial family, and a train of lords and ladies closed the whole. As
they passed through the guard-room, which was lined with a detachment of gigantic guards, it was amusing to see how these colossal
images curled their stiff whiskers with delight as their emperor
passed. When the procession entered the Greek church in the
palace, the priests and choristers commenced an anthem: the
young couple stood upon a cloth of scarlet fringed with gold, whilst
two officers of state held a crown on each of their heads, which part
of the ceremony is observed towards the commonest Russians; then
walked three times before the altar, each holding a lighted taper,
exchanged rings, and drank three times out of the sacramental cup,
after which the metropolitan exhorted them: when he had concluded, the bride saluted the archbishop and her family, and the procession returned. Upon the close of the ceremony a rocket was discharged from the granite terrace in front of the palace towards the
Neva, when discharges of cannon announced the happy tidings to the
people. About two hours afterwards a splendid banquet, for the
whole court, was served in the grand marble hall, a room, according to my own stepping, two hundred and fifty feet long, and about
forty feet high, having arched galleries for the accommodation of
spectators, at the end and on the side opposite the windows: the
imperial table was covered with vases of gold, filled with the rarest
flowers, pyramids of pines, and the finest fruits, elegantly arranged.
Soon after the nobility were seated at the tables, which were covered with every delicacy, the grand master of the ceremonies made a
buzzing noise, when the greatest silence immediately followed, the
folding-doors opened, and the imperial family entered, attended by a
suite of state officers, and took their seats; when the pages in waiting, richly attired, each having his right hand covered with a napkin,
served the imperial dinner: a noble band of music played, and several fine airs were sung by a distinguished singer, which, on account

of the vastness of the room and the frequent roaring of the cannon, were very imperfectly heard. When the emperor rose and drank felicity to the young couple from a vase of gold, if my sight erred not, a tear bedimmed the eyes of the beautiful bride. During the banquet one of the pages, from excessive agitation, spilt some soup upon her robe, which she returned with a most gracious smile. In the hall were several running footmen who have the privilege of wearing at all times and in all places their caps and feathers. With great difficulty we reached our carriage, through rooms crowded with cooks, and a great number of sailors in their best dresses, who, upon this occasion, were assistant scullions. Whilst we were at dinner at the hotel, we received a note from our ambassador, informing us that the emperor had appointed half past six o'clock in the evening for our introduction to him, previous to the ball: this honour, at such a time and on such an occasion, we were told, was against the usual etiquette of the court, and therefore the more flattering. A short time before the imperial family appeared, the nobility retired from the room where the presentation was to take place; the names of our party, amounting to six, of whom four were English, were given to the emperor by count Sherametoff, who introduced us. Upon the folding doors opening, a procession similar to that in the morning commenced: when the emperor approached us the whole halted, and the count, calling each by his name, introduced us to the emperor, the empress dowager, and the empress, by whom we were very graciously received. An Italian nobleman, who was presented with us, fell at the feet of the emperor and endeavoured to embrace his knees, which the sovereign recoiled from, with a look that indicated how little a manly generous mind, like his, could be gratified with such servility. After this ceremony, the procession, which we followed, moved to St. George's hall : this magnificent apartment, more rich, though not so vast, as Potemkin's hall, is entirely gilded with various coloured gold, and illuminated by a profusion of richly gilded lustres: on each side were galleries crowded with spectators: on either side of the grand entrance were two enormous mirrors, rising above some exquisite statues of alabaster ; and at the end, raised upon a flight of steps, stood the throne. As soon as the imperial family entered, the band struck up an exquisite polonaise, which is rather a figure promenade than a dance, the weather being too hot for such exercise : the emperor led out the

bride, and walked to the time of the music, the rest of the imperial
family and the court, amounting to about forty couple, following up
and down the room, forming curves, and various other figures. This
recreation continued an hour: a short time before it expired, I was
introduced, through the favour of madame B——, to the chamber
of the bride and bridegroom. In front of the bed, under glass covers,
were the bride's jewels, and a service of gold presented to her by
her august family, and a golden salver containing a *loaf and salt*,
which, according to the Russian custom, is presented by the empress
dowager to her daughter on the night of her marriage, just before
she unrobes: it is intended to express her wishes, that as the connection between parent and child is dissolved by marriage, she may
never want the comforts of life.

The bed was a state one, the robes-de-chambre of the princess
were placed on a stool on the *right hand side*, and the slippers of the
prince on the *left*. Heavens! thought I, what a strange country this
is! the postilions ride their horses on the wrong side, and the husbands sleep on the wrong side; but the remark was no sooner
made than removed: it does not accord with the dignity of the empire that any prince under Heaven should take the right of a grand
duchess of Russia. Hymen had touched the tapers with his torch,
and a band of merry-looking pretty girls, dressed in white, and adorned with flowers, were waiting to receive the happy bride, and let
loose the virgin zone. As I quitted this bower of Eden I longed to
leave behind me the following beautiful recipe for preserving love:

"Cool as he warms, and love will never cool:
Then drop into the flame a tear or two,
Which blazing up like oil, will burn him through;
Then add sweet looks, soft words, some sighs, no pout,
And take my word the flame will ne'er go out."

In the evening the city was magnificently illuminated: the house
of the British embassy shone with unrivalled elegance and splendour.
As we rode up the Neva, after supper, we were uncommonly gratified by seeing the whole of the fortress, down to the water's edge,
illuminated, which presented a spectacle the most brilliant, and
completely novel, I ever beheld. Our bargemen again regaled us
with one of their musical yells, the effect of which was encreased by

the addition of two tamborines struck at random.   In the evening, after the nuptials, the imperial family went to the opera, when the theatre was superbly illuminated, and the court scenes were displayed, which presented the finest specimens of scenic painting I ever beheld.   When the emperor was about to leave his box, the people saluted him with the most enthusiastic applause, with which he was visibly affected.

CHAP. XVIII.

APPLE FEAST—DOG-KILLERS—A BARRIER AGAINST SWINDLING—FES-
TIVITIES OF PETERHOFF—HORN MUSIC—A FAVOURITE BEAR—GER-
MAN THEATRE—VISIT TO CRONSTADT—PRISON—MILITARY PUNISH-
MENT—THE INN—ORANIENBAUM—FLYING MOUNTAINS—THE VALUE
OF A BLOODY BEARD—FASTS, FAMINE AND FIRMNESS.

ON the sixth of August, O. S. the feast of apples commences, in which the common Russians frequently indulge themselves to such excess, that death is the consequence of their intemperance. About this period the dog-killers, called Foornantshicks, go their rounds and destroy every dog they find unprotected by a collar, containing the name of his master. This measure, though apparently cruel, is very necessary: some winters past, before this regulation was made, a number of fierce and voracious dogs assembled together in the gloomy ground which surrounds the admiralty, and at night have been known to attack and devour passengers.

As my time for quitting Petersburg drew nigh, I sent my first advertisement, describing my name, age, and profession, to the imperial gazette office, in which it was necessary to appear three times before I could obtain my post-horse order, without which it is impossible to stir. The object of this ceremony is to prevent persons going away in debt, by giving timely notice to their creditors, and may be accomplished in ten days; or if a traveller is in great haste to depart, upon two householders of respectability undertaking, at the proper office, to pay all the debts he may owe, he may immediately depart. A foreigner may stay one month after the expiration of the first complete notice: if he exceed that period, he must advertise again. Immediately after the nuptials the court removed to Peterhoff, a country palace, about thirty versts from the residence, situate on the shores of Cronstadt gulf, built by Le Blonde, where a magnificent ball and illumination, in honour of the nuptials, took place; at which nearly all the population of Petersburg were present.

As we proceeded in a line of carriages, extending several miles, drawn by four horses a-breast and two before them, we passed a small but memorable public house, on the road side, about eight versts from Petersburg, called the Krasnoi Kabac; the first word meaning red, and the latter, as before related, a public house. It was at this house that the late empress halted, when she was advancing against her husband, and slept for a short time upon the cloaks of her officers in one of the little rooms. Here, assisted by her then confidential and enthusiastic friend, the princess Dashkoff, she consumed a great number of letters. We also passed the holy trinity hermitage of saint Sergius, a small monastery surrounded by quadrangular cloisters, having a church and three chapels. There is nothing in the building worthy of inducing a traveller to quit his carriage. A little farther on we saw the palace of Strelna, a vast building of brick stuccoed, built upon piazzas, and surrounded with indulating woods and pleasure-grounds belonging to the grand duke Constantine, the heir presumptive to the throne.

Upon our arrival we found the rooms, which were fitted up in a style of ancient splendour, and richly illuminated, filled with persons of all ranks and conditions in their best dresses, resembling a crowded masquerade, in which much of the costume of the empire was displayed. I was principally struck with the wives of the bearded merchants, who were rouged, and wore a head-dress of muslin, resembling a sugar-loaf, entirely encrusted with large pearls, with which their gowns were trimmed and their stomachers covered.

The illuminations were beyond any thing magnificent; in front of the palace rolled a cascade of water, over various coloured lamps, which had a very novel effect, into a great pond, which appeared to be in a blaze of light, from the sides and centre of which groups of statues threw columns of water to a great height; a canal, more than a mile long, lined with side lights of various coloured lamps, a glory at the end, and the imperial yachts illuminated in every part of their hull, masts, and rigging, stationed at a distance at sea, formed a brilliant and glowing *coup d'œil*. Every avenue, and every part of these extensive gardens, were in a blaze. In a recess was a large tree of copper, and flowers of the same metal, painted to resemble nature, which threw water from every leaf, and produced a very pretty effect. In another part of the gardens we heard the celebrated horn music. Each performer can only produce one tone from his instrument, consequently the skill and attention requisite to play upon it in concert must be great. At a little distance the effect was very charming. *A certain unfortunate class of miserables* will hear with surprise that the *horn* music is a necessary appendage to the ceremony of *nuptials* of the least respectability.

In Russia, marriages are generally effected through the agency of a third person. During the childhood of their daughter, the parents fix upon a husband for her, a mutual female friend is sent to the gentleman with the proposals: if they are accepted, he presents the fair negotiatrix with a pelisse, according to custom. Many of the lower Russians married, as they frequently are, against their inclinations, make no scruple in taking their wives to such a scene of festivity as the one I have just described, and letting them out to prostitution for hire.

In a corner of the grand saloon, in the centre of the palace, I saw the Georgian court, composed of the prince of Georgia, and two princesses of his house, and their retinue. The prince was obliged to cede his country, a province of Asia, formerly belonging to Persia and Turkey, to the Russian empire, from which he receives a pension. I saw no traces whatever of Circassian beauty in the princesses: one was old, fat, and plain, and the other pale, hollow-eyed, and lean: the prince had a very handsome and noble appearance.

In one of the rooms are four celebrated pictures of Hackert, painted by order of count Alexey Orloff, celebrating the victory over the Turkish fleet commanded by the Capudan Pasha, the merit of which the count unjustly assumed to himself, as I have before observed. Upon the painter observing that he had never seen a ship on fire, Orloff ordered a Russian seventy-four to be cleared and burnt, to enable him to execute the subject with more fidelity.

After the imperial family, glittering with jewels, and resembling a stream of brilliant light, had walked several polonaises, in which the empress was attended by a little dwarf in a Turkish dress, they mounted their laneekas, open garden carriages, resembling Irish jaunting-cars, and visited the gardens; after which they sat down to a superb select supper under an awning, upon the top of one of the wings of the palace, at which I had the honour of being present. The guests were attended by about two hundred servants in full imperial liveries. At five o'clock we returned to Petersburg, much gratified. The houses and gardens that line the Peterhoff road are very beautiful.

K k

Being somewhat fatigued, I was glad to devote a great part of the day to s.eep. In the evening I went to the German theatre, at the back of Lanskoi's palace, now the masquerade rooms: it was a very gloomy place, and was feebly illuminated by a small circular lustre descending from the roof, and a strange transparent clock in the centre of the cornice over the stage. The canopy of the imperial box was covered with black dark green plumes, and had a very funereal appearance. The play was Pizarro, or, as it was called, *Rolla's Tod*. When the old blind soldier enters, and during the time of his continuing on the stage, the sound of the distant battle was heard, which had an excellent effect. In all the close adherences to nature in scenic detail, so auxiliary to grand effect, the theatres upon the continent beat us hollow. The greatest tragedian of the present age (I need not mention the name of Kemble) has, in his visits to the different parts of Europe, forcibly felt the truth of this remark, and is making rapid advances to correct the deficiency at home.

The next morning early, a party of us carried into execution a plan which we had long projected, a visit to Cronstadt; having previously furnished ourselves with letters of introduction to some respectable inhabitants of the island. The day proved very beautiful, and, after passing several country-houses, before one of which was a rustic seat in the shape of a mushroom, about eleven o'clock we quitted our carriages at a little English inn, in the village where the palace of Oranienbaum, or Orange-Tree, is situated, about thirty-five versts from Petersburg, and proceeded to the canal opposite the palace, where we hired an eight-oared barge, for which we paid eight rubles, and put off to the island, seven or eight miles from shore. Upon the sides of the canal men were bathing, and young women washing: the water of the gulf was as fresh as that of the Neva. We were stopped at the merchant's mole, at Cronstadt, where a list of our names was demanded by a young officer, who gave us a great deal of trouble, which induced a young German, of the party, who began to be a little impatient, to jump up and exclaim, " Vat de devil! " dus dat little Russ man take us all for *screws ?*" he meant *spies*. It was at this spot, I was afterwards informed, that Peter III, in the ebullition of that revolution which, in a few days afterwards, elevated his empress, Catherine II, to the sole possession of the throne, and consigned him to an untimely tomb, presented himself in a yacht filled with terrified women, himself more terrified than they; and at the instance of the brave and venerable general Munich, who was also on board, demanded admission into Cronstadt, which, had the unhappy prince secured, he might have speedily turned the tide of affairs. "Who are you?" cried the centinel: "I am your emperor."— "We have no emperor: if you do not put about, we will blow your "vessel out of the water," was the reply.—"Leap with me on shore," cried the brave and loyal Gudovitch; "they will not fire upon you." The weak, irresolute sovereign refused, returned to Oranienbaum, and was soon afterwards dethroned and murdered. At length we were permitted to land. Cronstadt, which is said to be one of the most healthy spots in Russia, derived its name from Peter the great, and means Crown Town, or the crown of the new city, and is seven versts in length. Its population, including a yearly average of foreigners, is sixty thousand souls. On the southern side of it is a little island called Cronslot. Ships drawing more than eight feet water are obliged to discharge their cargoes at Cronstadt, which are sent up in lighters to Petersburg.

The town is one verst long, and well drained, by the indefatigable ingenuity of commodore Greig, and has several churches, amongst which is an English one: there are also a custom-house and several other public buildings. After having, English-like, ordered a good dinner at an inn, whose appearance little accorded with the excellent entertainment which it afforded, we presented our letters, and a very intelligent gentleman attended us over the town. In the dry-docks, which are very spacious, and faced with granite, we saw several fine ships, particularly one which the Russians preferred, built by an Englishman. In the streets we met several groups of convicts, returning from the public-works to their prisons, wretchedly clad, and heavily ironed; many of whom had iron collars with long handles round their necks: the allowance of these unfortunate wretches is black bread and water, and half a copec a day. In their hours of relaxation they make boxes, and other little matters of utility, the sale of which alleviates their extreme poverty.

At night I slept at a private house, the servant of which was a very intelligent little deformed Greek: his head and body were of the ordinary size, his legs and thighs not higher than those of an infant, which made him look like a man running upon casters. This dwarf was a living monument of pride triumphing over drunkenness, as one poison frequently expels another: being frequently seen in liquor, the sailors and inhabitants used to turn him into ridicule, which he felt, and reformed. This house, like every other in Russia, was truly hospitable, and was guarded by some ferocious dogs, of whom the Russians stand in terrible fear.

The next morning we visited the moles of the men-of-war and of the merchant vessels, which, as well as the canals, are faced with granite, and are formed after a plan which we saw, of Peter the great. Amongst the ships of war was one, the largest I ever beheld, pierced for an hundred and forty guns, exceeding in size every other ship in the Russian navy : its magnitude, and a strain which it received in launching, prevents it from being fit for service. So unwieldy is it, that it takes an hour in going about.

A little way out of the town we saw a prison for criminals, than which nothing could be more loathsome and shocking. It was an oblong square of wooden houses built upon piles, and surrounded with a high wall of wood, and appeared unfit for the reception of the most despised animal. As we passed over a plain, we observed that, for a great way, it was covered with rods, which, upon our servant enquiring of some soldiers who were collecting them, it appeared had been used in the morning by a regiment upon a military offender, who had been sentenced to run the gauntlet, when each man holds one of these terrible instruments, composed of five birch sticks, about three feet long, and a quarter of an inch thick, and steeped in salt brine.

We returned to Oranienbaum and saw the palace and gardens. The former was built by prince Menchikoff, in 1727, for his own residence, after whose fall it came to the crown. It is raised upon terraces, and is composed of a small central building of two stories, and two very extensive wings, connected by colonnades : these wings are covered with a treillage, and form a beautiful walk in the summer : the apartments are very neat and comfortable, one room is lined with thin taffeta satin of pale lilac and white, plaited and formed into pannels ; the roof is covered in the same way, and had a beautiful effect. At the end of the wings are two towers, one a Greek church, and the other a museum of china. The unfortunate Peter III built a Lutheran chapel here, where he and his Holstein soldiers used to pray, instead of going to the Greek church ; this indiscretion furnished a terrible weapon against him in the hands of the late empress.

In the gardens we saw the celébrated flying mountains, a vast fabric of three lessening acclivities of wood, resting upon brick arches, commencing from the terrace of a lofty and spacious pavilion, and sloping to the ground; from the top to the bottom of this singular structure are parallel grooves, in which triumphal cars running upon casters are placed: when the person who partakes of the diversion is ready, the car is released, and descends with a velocity which carries it over the hills in succession. This imperial plaything is surrounded with an open colonnade, more than half a mile in circumference, upon the terrace of which there is room for some thousands of spectators. The whole is now neglected and running to decay: it reminded me of some lines in Cowper:

> " Great princes have great playthings: some have play'd
> " At heaving mountains into men, and some
> " At building human wonders mountains high."

At this sport count Orloff encreased the love which the empress bore him, by saving her life: her car had by some accident sprung out of the groove, and was descending with uncommon velocity, when the count, whose strength was Herculean, stopped it in its career, and in so doing broke his arm, for which one of the bandages applied was the *blue riband*.

In another part of the gardens, deep embosomed in wood, we were shewn to a little retired palace, consisting of a suite of rooms upon a ground floor, built by the late empress, the taste and elegance of which surpassed every thing of the kind I ever beheld. One apartment was lined with small paintings of female heads, in pannels, representing, in the most exquisite manner, the progress of love, from hope to ecstacy. All the statues, pictures, and decorations, were calculated to kindle and cherish the noble and generous flame.

As the camps for thirty thousand men were formed in the neighbourhood for the annual reviews, we found it difficult to obtain beds; our servants, who in the estimation of inn-keepers, have no higher pretensions to their notice than their pigs and poultry, were left to shift for themselves upon the floor. On our return to the capital we proceeded to the encampment, to be present at the first manœuvres, but which had been countermanded early in the morning; here a scene took place, which, as it develops a little of the low Russian

character, I may be permitted to relate: Ivan, the coachman of a
chariot belonging to the party, a most grave and reverend-looking
personage, adorned with a beard of extraordinary magnitude and
beauty, became offended with something that had been said by two
servants, the one a German, the other a Pole, named David and Ro-
minski, who were standing behind the foremost coach, in which I was
with some other friends: Ivan, who had displayed a degree of sulki-
ness early in the morning, very unusual with the Russians, retorted
their banter by endeavouring to drive the pole of his carriage against
the legs of the servants, who, incensed at his conduct, jumped down
and endeavoured to seize Ivan, who thrashed them heartily from his
coach-box: at last the Pole, who naturally abhors a Russian, succeeded
in dragging him from his seat, curled his hand round in his hair,
tripped up his heels, and laid poor Ivan flat, and in this posture administered a sound flagellation upon the back of the charioteer with
his own whip, exclaiming at the same time, " I will let him know
" that I am a Pole." If we may trace effects to remote causes it
would not be unfair to conjecture that the abdication or rather dethronement of king Stanislaus Poniatofsky rendered some of the
blows a little more severe than ordinary. When the punishment was
over, and Ivan was once more upon his legs, it appeared that in his
descent to the earth, he had cut his nose slightly against a stone, and
was bleeding tolerably freely. Ivan knew the value of this accident,
and took grea' goo   re o u. and every crimson drop, and letting
it spread and thicken upon his beard, raised a most hideous yell, and
ran and preferred his complaint to a picquet guard of cossacks of the
Don, who placed us all under military arrest, and dispatched a com-
rade to their colonel, with an account of what had happened within
the lines ; the answer returned was, that he would not interfere, and
that if any injury had been received it might be redressed at the
first town. Ivan, who, by the by, was a clever fellow, during
the absence of the cossack had prostrated himself on the ground, and
imitated tolerably well the agonies of a dying man: as soon as he was
told what the reply was, and finding that we were driving off without him, throwing aside the terrors of death, he in a moment vaulted into his box, and never drove or looked better, until we entered
the town of Peterhoff, which was crowded on account of the court
being at the palace, when he set up the most frightful yell, tore his

hair, displayed his bloody beard, and called upon the police officers
to seize us all and do him justice. In a short time we were surrounded with crowds; the police officers, seeing we were English, heard
the accuser, but shewed no disposition to detain us, so we proposed
adjourning to the garden of the palace, and in one of its recesses to
partake of the cold collation which we had brought with us. As we
quitted the carriage, our coachman whispered something to Ivan,
who, with an arch look, told our valet, if we would give him twenty-
five rubles, he would settle the business amicably: this we refused
upon two grounds; first, that he merited what had happened; and
next, admitting he deserved any compensation, it was too exorbitant
to demand twenty-five rubles for a bloody nose, when we learnt at
Cronstadt, that twenty-three had only been paid for the loss of an
eye.

We went quietly to dinner in a delightful spot, well shaded from
the sun: whilst we were enjoying our repast, a little ragged boy approached us, to whom we offered some meat, but although he looked half famished we could not prevail upon him to touch it, as it was
a fast. In one of the walks we met a lady of rank attended by a female dwarf, supremely ugly and deformed, and dressed like a shep-
herdess on her nuptial day. Whilst we were regaling ourselves
Ivan was making the best use of his time with the guards and
police officers, and upon our resuming our seats and endeavouring
to proceed, the barrier was dropped, and bayonets presented towards
our horses: we then all alighted, and attended by a great throng of
guards and police officers, proceeded to the apartments of the deputy
grand police master, whom we found in his chamber in his shirt,
fiddling before a saint who was suspended in the corner: this gentleman addressed us in German, to which one of the party, to whom it
was his native tongue, replied, during which Ivan displayed his
blood to great advantage, but was ignorant of what was passing. In
the course of the conversation, the magistrate observed, " that the
" coachman deserved to be thrashed; and that, had we beaten him
" to a *jelly*, so that *blood* had not followed, all would have been well;
" but," after a long pause, very good-humouredly said, " that we
" should no longer be detained," and accordingly ordered the guards
to let us pass. Nothing could exceed the chagrin of poor Ivan when
he heard the fate of his application : — no non-suited plaintiff ever

threw his face into more burlesque distortions. Upon the road he stopped at every kabac for a drop of sorrow's medicine, which if Ivan had apostrophized, he would have exclaimed:

" Oh thou invisible spirit of *brandy* ! if thou hast no name to be known by, let us call thee Angel."

CHAP. XIX.

RISING OF THE NEVA—ACADEMY OF SCIENCES—THE REVIEW—CADET
CORPS—PELISSES—COUNTRY PALACE OF ZARSKO ZELO—ANOTHER BUST
OF THE BRITISH DEMOSTHENES MISPLACED—CANINE TUMULI—IMPE-
RIAL PLEASANTRY—GATCHINA—PAUVOLOFFSKY—ANNIVERSARY OF A
FAVOURITE SAINT—MORE DWARFS.

A SHORT time before I left Petersburg, the inhabitants were apprehensive of a terrible inundation of the Neva, in consequence of
the wind blowing very fresh at south-south-west, which forces the
waters of the gulf of Finland against the river, and prevents the
stream from finding its level. The guns of the admiralty fired, and
in the evening four lights were raised upon its church spire, the
usual warning upon such occasions to the people, to take care of
themselves and their property; and a general consternation spread
through the city. About eight o'clock at night a part of the Galeern-
hoff was five feet under water, and the bridges of pontoons rose to a
considerable height, so that the planks which connected them with
the shores presented on each side a formidable acclivity, which carriages of every description surmounted by the uncommon skill and
energy of the drivers and horses: their mode of reaching these almost perpendicular ascents was effected by lashing the horses, at a
considerable distance, into a full gallop, and by a great number of
police officers and soldiers, who always attend at the bridges on these
occasions—to prevent accidents, running behind and propelling the
carriage, or saving it from being dashed to pieces, by its not being
able to turn the summit. Luckily the wind, the Neva, and the public
apprehensions, subsided together, without any damage being done.

The change enabled our party to visit the academy of sciences, a
noble building, situated on the north side of the Neva, in Vassilli-
Ostroff. After passing through the library, whose damp walls were
feebly lighted from above, and where there is nothing but some Tar-
tarian manuscripts worthy of detaining the attention of a traveller,
we entered the museum of natural curiosities, in which the principal
objects were various parts of the human frame, fœtuses, miscarriages,

and births, from the first impregnation to perfect birth, monsters human and animal, and a variety of most odious and disgusting *et ceteras*, in pickle. The skin of the Heyduc, or favourite servant of Peter the Great, is here, stretched upon a wooden image of his size, which shews that the man must have been six feet and a half high, and that nature had furnished him with a skin nearly as thick and impenetrable as that of the rhinoceros's hide. In the gallery above was a Lapponian dog-sledge; the habiliments of a Siberian magician, or gipsey, principally composed of a great number of iron rings and drops, placed upon a wooden statue; several presents from the undaunted and enterprising captain Cook, and a variety of stuffed birds and animals. In the room of Peter the Great was a wax figure of his height, which was above six feet, resembling him in form and face, and dressed in one of his full suits : in an adjoining cupboard were his hat, pierced with a bullet at Pultowa, breeches that wanted repair, and stockings that required darning. In another room were his turning machines, with which he used to relax himself; cupboards filled with brazen dishes of his embossing, and spoons and platters of his turning: in short, all the curiosity which the merest trifles of great genius generally excite, is, in this instance, destroyed by their abundance. In every public garden, or building, there is a profuse display of his cloaths, arms, or culinary utensils: if a twentieth part of them were burnt, the remainder would be more worthy of notice. How singular is it, that cotemporary genius never excites our attention, nor awakens our feelings, so forcibly as that which is departed! In contemplating a great man, the mind's eye reverses the laws of vision, by magnifying the object in proportion as it recedes from it. Upon the basement story is a very curious mechanical writing-desk, by Rœntengen, a German, of Neuwied, presented to the academy by Catherine, who gave twenty-five thousand rubles for it. Upon touching a spring, a variety of drawers fly out, a writing-desk expands, and boxes for letters and papers rise. A part of the machinery may be set so, that if any person were to attempt to touch any of the private recesses appropriated for money, or confidential papers, he would be surprised by a beautiful tune, which would give due notice to the owner. We were told that, in the academy are to be seen moon-stones, or blocks of native iron, which, it is conjectured by the learned, must have been cast from the volcano of some planet. They were not shewn to us: but

several of these phenomena are to be met with in different parts of
Russia. It seems hostile to the laws of gravitation, that a single atom
should be able to swerve from its planet.

. Adjoining the academy is a pavilion containing the Gottorp globe,
eleven feet in diameter from pole to pole: the concavity is marked
with the stars and constellations, and is capable of holding several
persons: as some ladies of our party ventured in, upon the exhibitor
turning the globe on its axis, we were more sensibly impressed with
the idea of the motion of the heavenly bodies.

In the evening, after the opera, a party of us set off to the camp,
and passed the night in our carriage, in order to be present at the review, which commenced the next day at eight o'clock. After getting
a comfortable breakfast in a Cossac hut, we proceeded to the ground.
The manœuvres commenced in a village about three miles off,
where a sharp cannonading took place. The contending armies,
consisting of about fifteen thousand men each, the one headed by the
emperor, and the other by general ——, began to move towards
each other in a vast valley, and halted within half a mile of each
other, when a tremendous discharge of artillery took place, and firing
of different parties was kept up all the time, at distances of five and
six miles. Here the manœuvres of that day concluded, and we returned home to a late dinner.

It was now the second of September, N. S. and the summer began
to give tokens of rapid decline: the lamps but feebly supplied that
light which, not even many days before, gave to the evening the character of a mild mid-day.

We were much gratified in visiting, by an express appointment, a
nursery of future heroes, called the second imperial cadet corps, in
which seven hundred children are educated and maintained, as gentlemen, for the profession of arms, at the expense of the country.
The governor, a nobleman of high rank, and several of the officers
attached to the institution, attended us through the progressive
schools. Every child follows his own religious persuasion, for which
purpose there are a Lutheran and a Greek church under the same
roof: the latter is singularly elegant. The dormitories, as well as
every other part of the establishment, were remarkably clean and
handsome, the pupils having separate beds. In the store-rooms each
boy's change of linen and cloaths were very neatly folded up, and his
name marked upon a tablet over them. At one of the doors we saw

some of these soldiers in miniature relieve guard. In the schools are taught mathematics, gunnery, mapping, French, German, and Russian; fencing and dancing, and every other science and accomplishment which can complete the soldier and the gentleman. We were present at their dinner, which is served at half past twelve o'clock. The dining-hall is two hundred feet long, by forty broad. Every table held twenty-two boys, for each of whom a soup and meat plate, a silver fork, knife, and napkin, and a large slice of wholesome country bread, were laid; and at each end were two large silver goblets filled with excellent quas: they have four substantial dishes three times a-week, and three on the other days. All the boys, after marching in regular order from the respective schools, appeared at the several doors of the dining-hall, headed by their captains: upon the roll of the drum, they marched in slow time to their respective tables, form three companies of two hundred each (the fuzileer company, composed of the sons of the soldiers, did not dine till afterwards); at the second roll they halted, faced, and sat down: all their dishes appeared to be excellent: their uniform was bottle-green, faced with red. Great attention appeared to have been paid to their manners, by the decorum and urbanity which was displayed at their tables. The kitchens for soup, boiling, and roasting, were remarkably neat, although we saw them just after dinner had been served up. There are several other cadet corps upon the same princely establishment, and create in the mind of a stranger a high idea of the wealth and patriotic spirit of the empire.

A foreigner should not quit Petersburg without seeing the cabinet of jewels and furs, contained in a superb building in the grand perspective: here the clocks, gilded and bronze ornaments of the palace of St. Michael, are deposited, all of which are very magnificent; there are also massy balustrades and tables of solid silver. Amongst the jewellery I was much pleased with several beautiful watches, upon the backs of which were little figures, some in the act of angling and drawing up little fish; others cooking meat, pumping, and rocking cradles; in others little cascades of glass were set in motion. There was a profusion of magnificent diamond snuff-boxes, stars, &c. for imperial presents.

In the apartments below was the museum of furs, where we saw several pelisses made of tiny dorsal slips of the black fox, valued each at ten thousand pounds. This animal, a native of Siberia, is so rare and so small, that one of these pelisses cannot be made in less than ten years, and they are then paid to the emperor in lieu of money, as tributes, from different provinces. These are generally presented upon some great national occasion to crowned heads. There are also fine collections of sables and other furs, many of which are annually sold.

As I have mentioned these tributes, it may be proper here to observe, that the imperial revenues chiefly arise from the poll tax, the crown and church lands, the duties on export and import, profits of the mint, the excise upon salt, the sale of spirituous liquors, post-offices and posting. The proprietors of houses, as well natives as foreigners, pay in lieu of all other taxes, and in discharge from the odious burthen of maintaining soldiers, to which they were formerly liable, a duty of one half per cent. *ad valorem*, upon the house; and a ground-rent which varies according to local advantages, for every square fathom.

Of course, I did not leave the capital without seeing Zarsko-zelo, the most magnificent of the country palaces, about twenty-four versts from Petersburg. The entrance to it is through a forest, under a lofty arch of artificial rock, surmounted with a Chinese watch tower; after which we passed a Chinese town, where the enormous imperial pile, consisting of three stories, one thousand two hundred feet long, opened upon us. It was built by Catherine I, embellished and barbarously gilt by Elizabeth, and greatly beautified and modernized by the late empress. Amongst the numerous rooms fitted up in the style of ancient magnificence, was the amber-room, a vast apartment, entirely lined with pieces of that valuable fossil bitumen, presented by Frederic William I to Peter the Great, but not put up till the reign of Elizabeth. One of the pieces of amber expressed in rude characters, by its veins, the year in which it was presented.

The apartments which Catherine has fitted up and embellished display the highest taste and profusion of expense; the floor of one of these rooms was inlaid with mother-of-pearl, representing a variety of flowers and elegant figures; but I was most pleased with her two celebrated chambers of entire glass, which in novelty and beauty exceed all description. The sides and cielings of these rooms were formed of pieces of thick glass, about a foot square, of a cream and pale blue colour, connected by fine frames of brass richly gilded. In the centre, upon steps of glass, rose a divan, above which was a vast mirror, and on each side were slender pillars of light-blue glass, that supported an elegant canopy. Behind the mirror was a rich state bed. Even the doors, sophas, and chairs, were of coloured glass, elegantly shaped, and very light.

From the rooms we entered a vast terrace under a colonnade, and proceeded to the baths, which are lasting monuments of the taste of Mr. Cameron, the imperial architect. They contain a suite of superb rooms, one of which is entirely composed of the richest agates and porphyry; in this saloon were two pieces in mosaic, the most brilliant and beautiful I ever beheld. Near the baths is a vast terrace upon arches, with a central covered gallery of great extent, capable at all times of affording either a cool or a sheltered promenade. Upon this terrace are a great number of fine busts of distinguished men; amongst others was a copy of that of Mr. Fox, in bronze, placed on the *left* of Cicero. As I contemplated the head of the British orator, I secretly protested against his situation, and was endeavouring to give him the *right*, when a terrified attendant and his companion ran up and me, and prevented me from performing this act of justice.

In the gardens, which are extensively and very tastefully laid out by the late and present Mr. Buah, father and son, to whom the care of these gardens and hot-houses have been successively committed, we saw the hermitage, in the first floor of which the late empress, and a select party of her friends, used to dine without attendants, for which purpose she had a table constructed of most complicated machinery, at a great expense, through which the covers descended and rose by means of a great central trap door, as did the plates through cylinders. The party was by this means supplied with every delicacy, without being seen or heard. The machinery below filled a large room, and at first made me think I was under the stage of a theatre: this was another of Catherine's play-things. As we moved through the grounds, we were struck with a rostral column raised to Feodor Orloff for the conquest of the Morea; a marble obelisk to Romantzoff, for his victories near Kagul; a marble pillar, on a pedestal of granite, to Orloff Tchesminskoi; and the Palladian bridge, formed in Siberia, and erected here over a branch of the lake: it is similar to that at lord Pembroke's. In a retired part is an Egyptian pyramid, behind which are several tombs, erected by the late empress to the memory of her favourite dogs: amongst these I copied the following, the composition of Catherine.

Ci gît
Duchesse,
la fidèle compagne
de
Sir Tom. Anderson.
Elle le suivit en Russe
l'an 1776.
Aimé et respecté
par sa nombreuse postérité,
elle décéda en 1782, agée de 15 ans,
laissant 115 descendans,
tant levriers que levrettes.

There is a small superb palace, within about two hundred yards of Zarsko-zelo, built by the late empress for her grandson Alexander. Some of the rooms are of marble, and very magnificent. At Zarsko-zelo there are no inns, but the hospitality of Mr. Bush, the English gardener, prevents this inconvenience from being felt by any foreigner, who is respectably introduced to him. In consequence of a letter from our ambassador, we were very handsomely received and entertained by Mr. Bush, in whose house, in the life-time of his father, the following whimsical circumstance occurred. When Joseph II, emperor of Germany, to whom every appearance of show was disgusting, expressed his intention of visiting Catherine II, she offered him apartments in her palace, which he declined. Her majesty, well-knowing his dislike to parade, had Mr. Bush's house fitted up as an inn, with the sign of a *Catherine-wheel*, below which appeared, in German characters, " The Falkenstein arms," the name which the emperor assumed. His majesty knew nothing of the ingenious and attentive deception, till after he had quitted Russia. A number of very laughable occurences took place. When the emperor once went from Vienna to Moscow, he preceded the royal carriages to order the horses, as an *avant-courier*, in order to avoid the obnoxious pomp and ceremony which an acknowledgment of his rank would have awakened.

From Zarsko-zelo we set off for a town near the palace of Gatchina, about eighteen versts from the former, where we arrived about
eleven at night; although so near an imperial residence, three of us
were obliged at the inn to sleep upon straw, there being only one
sopha vacant: however, the palace and gardens compensated this
little inconvenience. The former was raised by Gregory Orloff,
and, on his death, purchased by the late empress. The rooms were
superb, amongst which were two of a crescent shape, richly furnished and ornamented; and a chamber, the sopha, bed, canopy, cieling,
and sides of which were formed of white calico, whilst over the latter, projecting a little, was stretched a broad net-work of the same
stuff, with roses in the centre of each division: the effect was unique
and very beautiful. The gardens were romantic and elegant. In a
small lake were a great number of beautiful gondolas and pleasure-
boats; and on a large space of water, a frigate of twenty-two guns,
originally built to afford Paul, when a youth, some little notion of a
man of war. With a fair wind it is capable of sailing about one hundred yards. It is kept in good order for the purpose of forming an
agreeable object, and on festive occasions is illuminated.

From Gatchina we proceeded to Pauvoloffsky, another imperial
chateau, built by Paul, in 1780, and which, with Gatchina, form the
principal country residences of the empress dowager, and the
younger branches of the imperial family, who were there at the time
of our visit. Such a crowded court I never beheld; every window
seemed to be filled with faces, and every avenue with officers of the
household, servants and cooks; it was like a great bee-hive. We
took only an hasty glance at the state-rooms, which were fitted up in
a style of gorgeous magnificence. The pannels of one of the apartments contained excellent copies of some of the exquisite India
views of messieurs Daniels. In the dowager empress's cabinet was
a most elegant writing table, the top of which was lined on each side
with Chinese roses, blowing, in vases sunk to a level with the surface.

On the eleventh of September the court, and all the people of
Petersburg capable of walking, attend in great pomp the celebration
of the anniversary of their tutelar spirit, saint Alexander Nevsky.
After performing their devotion at the kazan, the court, in grand
procession, in their state carriages, proceeded to the gate of the monastery (which I have before described), where they were received

by the metropolitan and all the bishops in their full pontificals, adorned with pearls and diamonds, and by the monks and choristers, who
preceded the Imperial family, chaunting hymns, upon a raised platform, covered with scarlet cloth, to the church, where the effect produced by their entrance was very sublime. They then proceeded to
the silver shrine of the saint, which, after several prayers and hymns,
as I was informed, they kissed; for the crowd was so great, that I
could not see the whole of the ceremony; after which they returned
and partook of some refreshments at the house of the archbishop.
As soon as they had retired, some thousands of people flocked to the
shrine of saint Alexander, and to another of the virgin adjoining, to
touch them with their lips.

As the empress dowager passed, the musheeks or common boors
said to one another, " There goes our good mother." All the male
Russians, of equal degree in rank, address each other by the name of
brat, or brother: which is also used by any one speaking to his inferior. The emperor calls his subjects brats. A friend of mine
heard Paul one day say to a bearded workman, " *My brother*, take
" care; the ice is too thin to bear you." When the low address their
superiors they say, batushka moia, " my father." Very near the
monastery is the glass manufactory, where the vast mirrors, for
which Russia is so celebrated, are rolled. The establishment resembles a little town: almost all the artists are Russians, and in their
various departments displayed great taste and ingenuity.

From this place we visited the hotel of the prince Usupoff, a very
noble edifice, but, like all the great houses of the nobility, presented
a scene of uncommon neglect and dirt in the front and court yard;
for example, several of the broken windows of the basement story
were filled with hay, and in the yard lay offal-meat, bones, shells,
and horse-dung, here and there half concealed by grass growing
above the stones. The prince has a fine gallery of paintings and
statues, which he has collected at a vast expense in Italy: most of
the subjects are in the highest degree voluptuous. Over one painting the prince has extended a curtain: how little does he know of
human nature, if he wishes to pay homage to modesty by exciting
curiosity: I will venture to say there was more indecorum and peril
in the curtain than in the picture. In the library, which is very excellent, we were attended by a frightful bilious dwarf, about forty
years of age, a Polish laquais took him by his little shrivelled hand,

M M

and patting him on the head, observed to us, that he had been in a small island in the Mediterranean, which swarmed with dwarfs, many of whom he solemnly declared *were not taller than cats set upon their hinder legs ! ! !*, In the language of count Aranza,

——————" That's a lie."

A few days before I left the city I applied, through a friend of mine, to the polatch or executioner, to purchase of him a knout, to bring with me to England: upon going to his house, which seemed to be a very comfortable one, he was from home, but his wife took up one of the thongs, and in a very *gentle and tender* manner began explaining the theory and practice of this instrument of *torture*, in the course of which she observed, that it was made, not of the skin of a wild ass, as has been asserted, for, excepting a small breed of that animal in Siberia, not one is to be found in any other part of the empire, but of ox's hide soaked in milk and dried, and that her husband was so expert, that he could cut a piece of flesh from the back of exactly its size. These functionaries of justice are held in such abhorrence, that although this very executioner offered to give four thousand rubles as a dowry with his daughter to a common droshka driver, she was rejected with scorn. The merciless empress Elizabeth enjoyed the reputation of having abolished the punishment of death: she little deserved the homage which was paid to her: the fact was, knowing how hateful the appearance of death is to the Russians, she ordered a capital culprit to be knouted to such a degree, that he was only enabled to reach his prison alive, when his lacerated frame was thrown upon a bed of boards, and left to gangrene and mortify for want of medical application: such was the boasted humanity of Elizabeth! To the superstitious dread of seeing a corpse, which marks the Russian character, let me add an unconquerable aversion to receiving any thing as a *present* which has a sharp point: a gentleman presented a young Russ lady with an elegant female pocket-book, in which there was a row of needles; with some concern she took from her purse a little silver piece, and gave it to the donor as the *purchase money*.

A number of interesting objects still remained to be seen, but my time, and an alteration in my intention of visiting Italy, made it necessary to bid adieu to a city, which I shall never reflect upon but with admiration, nor upon those of its inhabitants, to whom I had the honour of being known, without respect and esteem.

In the decline of the summer, (for I now speak of it as departed from these regions) the weather was very variable; a fiercely sultry day was succeeded by a very chilly one; within thirty hours, from being scarcely able to endure my dressing-gown, I was glad to place myself before (a wonder in Russia) a blazing fire in an English stove; but the atmospheric fluctuations are certainly not so great as in our own climate, and this circumstance might, perhaps, have induced a Russ servant, who had just returned from England, to say, upon being asked whether he was soon familiarized with our country, " I understood quick all tings dere, but de climate, dat I could no " understand." The harvest in the provinces near the capital, which is generally got in by the tenth of August, N. S. had been housed for more than a month, black clouds frequently obscured the sun, the winds began to blow loud and bleak, the leaves were rapidly falling, and each succeeding day grew visibly shorter: these were sufficient warnings for birds of passage to wing their way to milder regions. As some very agreeable countrymen and travellers were setting off for Berlin, I had the good fortune of being invited to join the party: to their barouche I added a Swedish carriage, requiring only one horse, to assist in the general conveyance. As this little carriage excited uncommon delight and wonder in some countries through which we passed, and lost all its popularity in another, as will be hereafter told; and moreover as I grew attached to it in proportion as I saw its merits, and beheld them at one time acknowledged, at another derided, I must be indulged in describing it. A small body of railing with a seat for two persons, a head of canvas, and a well for luggage, mounted upon two wheels about three feet high, and a shaft for one horse, composed the whole of this redoubted vehicle. In Russia, every traveller is obliged to purchase a travelling carriage, unless he is disposed to hazard a general dislocation in a kibitka.

CHAP. XX.

IT is a great object in quitting a great city, where you have strong
ties to detain you, resolutely to set off on the appointed day for the
commencement of one's journey, be the hour what it may, and even
if you can proceed no farther than one post.   After a delay of four
hours, occasioned by the stupidity of the post-master, at eight o'clock
in the evening of the nineteeth of September, N. S. the servants of
our hospitable friends, Messrs. Venning, who had been some time
previously employed in filling every crack and corner of the carriages with bottles of port, claret, and all sorts of provisions, announced that every thing was ready.   As we all assembled in the court-
yard, my old companion Mishka, to the full stretch of her chain, stood
on her hinder legs, and seemed, in her rude way, for her voice was
not the most musical, to regret my departure, but upon my giving
her some sugar, I found it an error of vanity, for she instantly ran
into her house to enjoy it and, as in the moment of repletion neither
Bruins nor Englishmen, nor perhaps any other being, like to be disturbed, I did not say with the song—

"Give me thy paw, my bonny bonny bear,"

but left her, to shake hands with those from whom we had received
the most polite and kind attentions.   My friend captain Elphinstone
insisted upon riding to the bridge with me, in the *little Swede*, as he
called it, where we parted with mutual and genuine regret.

The moon shone very bright.   The little Russ driver, who sat on
the shaft, unfortunately for my ears and the temperature of my mind,
proved to be a great singer : his shrill pipe never ceased till we
reached Strelna, the first stage, where we proposed sleeping.

As soon as we drove up to the door of a handsome inn, which
owed its architectural consequence to the proximity of the grand

duke Constantine's country palace, the host told our servant, a German, he had no room for us; upon which a voice from the top of the bannisters, with stentorian energy, exclaimed in Russ, "By G——d "there is room; the gentlemen shall be accommodated, or by to- "morrow evening the grand duke Constantine shall blow you all to "the devil." The translation of this extraordinary exclamation we received afterwards; upon which a Russ officer, a little flushed with the Tuscan grape, came down to us, and began, according to the custom of the continent, to kiss us all round. When we had submitted to this detestable ceremony, he led, or rather drove us up stairs; lavishing upon the master of the inn all the opprobrious epithets he could collect, in bad French; ordered a handsome supper, and all sorts of wines; pressed us by the hands, swore the English were the finest fellows in the world, and again repeated his loving kindness by another salutation: when one of the party recoiling a little from the violence of his friendship, he turned round, shrugged up his shoulders, and in a most significant manner exclaimed, "My "G——d, he does not kiss like a man!" After making a hearty supper, we ordered our bill, but the officer swore he would murder our host if he presented any, and ordered him out of the room, declaring that we were his own guests, which he followed by screaming several Russ songs; after which we begged to know the name of this strange creature, and presented him with a piece of paper and a pencil; but after many ineffectual efforts, we plainly saw "that "his education had stopped before he had learnt to read or write." Finding that we could get no beds, we ordered horses, travelled all night upon good roads, and arrived early the next morning to breakfast at Koskowa. All the post-houses beyond Strelna are kept by Germans; for each horse we paid two copecs per verst. This part of Ingria formerly belonged to the Swedes. The female peasantry wear a flat bonnet of red silk and gold lace, large ear-rings, a vest without sleeves, and cloth round their legs: women, before their marriage, wear their hair plaited, and hanging down: the males are simply clad in sheep's skins, with the wool inside.

I would recommend every traveller to sleep at Jarnburg, one stage before Narva. At the former, the post-master told us he had no horses; but the magic of a silver ruble discovered six, quietly eating their hay in the stable, which speedily brought us over a wooden road to Narva, at nine o'clock in the evening, to a very comfortable inn. Here the Russ character began to subside ; most of the boors speak German.

In the morning we were much gratified with contemplating a town, which the romantic heroism of Charles XII of Sweden has for ever rendered celebrated. We passed over the ground where, on the 30th of November, 1700, Charles routed one hundred thousand Muscovites with eight thousand Swedes. History says, that upon thè first discharge of the enemy's shot, a ball slightly grazed the king's left shoulder ; of this he at the time took no notice : soon after his horse was killed, and a second had his head carried away by a cannon-ball. As he was nimbly mounting the third, "These fellows," says he, "make me exercise." His sagacity and humanity were conspicuous in the disposal of his prisoners, who were five times his numbers : after they had laid down their arms, the king returned them their colours, and presented their officers with their swords, marched them across the river, and sent them home. I have heard of the humane policy of a British general, who finding, after a battle, that his prisoners greatly exceeded his own troops in numbers, and not possessing the local facilities that favoured the Swedish conqueror, to prevent any ill consequences from a situation so embarrassing, he made every prisoner swallow a copious quantity of jalap, and then ordered the waistband of his breeches to be cut : by this aperient and harmless policy, he placed four men under the irresistible control of one.

The waterfalls are about an English mile from the town. At a distance, the trees, which hang over the valley through which the waters roll, were enveloped in mist. I should suppose these falls to be about three hundred feet wide, and their descent about seventeen. The weather at this time was delightful, resembling some of our finest days in May. In the evening we went to a play, performed by a strolling company of Germans : the hero of the piece was a young English merchant, decorated with a polar star on his left breast ; and another of the *dramatis personæ* was a drunken lady.

We left Narva at seven the next morning, and entered the province of Livonia. The roads were excellent, and the country beautiful : our horses small, plump, and strong ; and above we were serenaded by larks singing in a cloudless sky. Our drivers wore hats covered with oil-skin, and woollen gloves ; and the German pipe began to smoke. The *little Swede* excited the wonder and admiration of every Livonian boor, who had never before beheld such a vehicle. In the evening things began to assume a less pleasing aspect: as we approached the lake Piepus, the roads became very sandy, and the country dreary. At the post-house at Kleinpringern, we saw the skins of several bears hanging up to dry, and conversed with a party of hunters, who were going in pursuit of that animal, with which, as well as with wolves, the woods on each side abound. Here let me recommend every traveller to take an additional number of horses to his carriage, otherwise he will experience the inconvenience which attended us before we reached Rennapungen, the next stage. To the *little Swede* we put two horses, to the barouche six; all lean, miserable animals, wretchedly tackled, and in this trim we started at nine o'clock in the evening, and, axletree-deep in sand, we ploughed our way, at the rate of two English miles an hour: at last our poor jaded cattle, panting and almost breathless, after several preceding pauses, made a decisive stand in the depth of a dark forest, the silence of which was only interrupted by the distant howling of bears. Our drivers, after screaming in a very shrill tone, as we were afterwards informed, to keep these animals off, dropped their heads upon the necks of their horses, and very composedly went to sleep: a comfortable situation for a set of impatient Englishmen! Finding that the horses of the *little Swede* began to prick their ears after three quarters of an hour's stoppage, I and my companion awoke our postilion, and ordered him to proceed, that we might send fresh horses for the other carriage. To our surprise we jogged on tolerably well, reached Rennapungen in about four hours, and dispatched fresh horses for our friends, who rejoined us at five o'clock in the morning.

When I entered the inn at this place, two Russian counts, and their suite, occupied all the beds; so I mounted an old spinnet, and with a portmanteau for a pillow, and fatigue for opiate, went to sleep, until the travellers, who started very early, were gone, when I got into a bed, which the body of a count of the empire had just warmed. This circumstance reminded me of the answer of a chamber-maid, at an inn at Exeter, who, upon my requesting to have a comfortable bed, observed, " Indeed, Sir, you cannot have a better one than the one " I have secured for you;" and, by way of recommendation, added, " Lord B——, who arrived from Lisbon about ten days since, died " in it two nights ago."

The following day we passed through a country which, no doubt, was a perfect Paradise in the estimation of the race of Bruins ; to whom I left its unenvied enjoyment, to sit down to a comfortable dinner at Nonal, the next stage, having abundantly replenished our stock of provisions at Narva. After skirting a small portion of the Piepus lake, a vast space of water, eighty versts broad, and one hundred and sixty long, we arrived at Dorpt, which stands upon a small river that communicates with the lake. The town is extensive, has several good streets and handsome houses, and is celebrated for its university, in which there are twenty-four professors, and one hundred and forty students, one-third of whom are noble. Upon the summit of a hill that commands the town are the remains of a vast and ancient abbey, which was founded by the knights of the Teutonic order, new preparing for the reception of the university library : the palace of the grand master occupied the spot where the fortifications are building. The Teutonic order was established in the twelfth century, and declined in the fifteenth. In a crusade against Saladin, for the recovery of the Holy Land, a great number of German volunteers accompanied the emperor Barbarossa ; upon whose death his followers, who had distinguished themselves on that spot where, several centuries afterwards, it was destined that Sir Sidney Smith, with unexampled heroism, should plant the British standard before Acre, elected fresh leaders, under whom they performed such feats of valour, that Henry, king of Jerusalem, the Patriarch, and other princes, instituted an order of knighthood in their favour, and were ultimately placed under the protection of the virgin Mary : in honour of whom they raised several magnificent structures at Marienborg, or the city of the Virgin Mary, near Dantzig. Afterwards growing rich, they elected a grand master, who was invested with sovereign prerogatives : by the bulls that were granted in their favour, they were represented as professing temperance and continence ; virtues which, no doubt, were religiously observed by *soldiers*, and *travelled men of gallantry*.

The prison of Dorpt, in which a number of unfortunate creatures are immured, is a subterranean vault, damp, dark, narrow, and pregnant with disease and misery. To be confined in it is, in general, something worse than being sent to the scaffold; for a lingering death is the usual fate of the wretch upon whom its gates are closed. Hanway, in the name of justice and humanity, denounced this dungeon: to the present emperor some recent representations have been made upon the subject; they will not be made in vain to one who, gloriously reversing the ordinary habits of beneficence, listens with more fixed attention to the sounds of misery, in proportion as they are *distant* and *feeble*.

If a pebble be thrown into a standing pool, it will disturb its even surface from the centre to the extremities; but if a stone be cast into the ocean, it creates but a momentary interruption, unfelt by the succeeding wave: thus will a petty occurrence agitate the tranquillity of a small community, which would produce no sensation upon expanded and active society. A trifle, not quite as light as air, a few days before our arrival, had rudely and unexpectedly shattered the peace and harmony which once reigned in the academic bowers of Dorpt. Professors were drawn out in battle array, and vengeance assumed the mask of learning.

Two professors' ladies had had a violent dispute at cards, and unfortunately they lived opposite to each other: one of them, upon a sunny day, when all things look clear and bright, ordered her maid, a plump, brawny, Livonian girl, whilst her opponent's husband, a grave and reverend gentleman, was looking out of his window, as a mark of scorn and contempt, to turn her back towards him in her chamber, and exhibit *le derrière de sa personne, sans voile.* It was a Livonian thought: the social condition of the country, the rash infirmity of human nature, the summary projects of pique, all plead for the urbanity of the lady, who only in this solitary instance forgot the dignity of her situation. All Dorpt was at first convulsed with laughter, save the parties concerned, and their immediate friends. The most erudite civilians were sent for; and after long and sagacious consultations, a bill was filed against the mistress and her maid, to which regular answers were put in, most ably drawn up. Nothing short of penance and excommunication were expected. No doubt, this most important suit has been long since determined; and much do I regret, that ignorance of the decree prevents me from finishing the fragment of this curious event. Upon turning the corner of a street, we beheld a sight at once shocking and humiliating to the pride of man; a vast pile of skulls and bones of the terrific and ambitious knights of the Teutonic order. In breaking up some cemeteries, for erecting the foundation of a new university, these wretched remains were removed, that once formed the plumed and glittering warrior, who,

N n

" ————————————with his beaver on,
His cuishes on his thighs, gallantly arm'd,
Rose from the ground like feather'd Mercury;
And vaulted with such ease into his seat,
As if an angel dropt down from the clouds."

The students at the university seem desirous of retaining in their dress some traces of the martial founders of the town, by wearing great military boots and spurs, a common coat, and a leather helmet with an iron crest: a costume less appropriate could not easily have been imagined. The peasant women of this province are very ordinary, and wear huge pewter breast-buckles upon their neck handkerchiefs.

At Uttern, the first stage, we found the governor of the province had ordered all the post-horses for himself and suite, and was expected every hour to return from a singular species of service. It appeared that an ukase had been passed considerably ameliorating the condition of the Livonian peasants, but the nature of it having been mistaken by three or four villages in the neighbourhood of the post-house, they revolted. Two companies of infantry were marched against them, and after flogging half a dozen of the principal farmers, tranquillity was restored, and we met the soldiers returning. This spirit of disaffection detained us at this post-house all night, for want of horses.

At night a Russian, apparently of rank, of a powerful and majestic figure, and elegant manners, arrived: after a very agreeable conversation at breakfast, he departed early in the morning for Moscow, to which city he gave us a cordial invitation: the stranger proved to be count P———Z———, who took the lead in the gloomy catastrophe which occurred in the palace of Saint Michael.

In all the post-houses is a tablet, framed and glazed, called the taxe, on which is printed the settled price of provisions, horses, and carriages. Travelling still continued cheap, at the rate of ten-pence English for eight horses for an English mile; but it was painful to see the emaciated state of these poor animals. The roads still continued dreadfully sandy; we were seldom able to go above three verts an hour. The little Swede, who overturned us very harmlessly in the sand, a little before we reached Wollemar, where we dined, still preserved her popularity; and, as modest simplicity frequently triumphs over presuming splendour, she diverted all the attention of the natives from her shewy and handsome companion. Some English travellers, who followed and at length overtook us, became acquainted with all our movements from the impression which the moving wonder had excited. The post-drivers in Livonia, Courland, and throughout Germany, are called by every person Schwagers, or brothers-in-law. In the last stage to Riga we overtook a long line of little carts, about as high as a wheel-barrow, filled with hay or poultry, attended by peasants dressed in great slouched hats and blue jackets, going to market: the suburbs are very extensive. The town is fortified, and is a place of great antiquity; it is remarkable only for one thing, that there is nothing in it worthy of observation. The necessity of setting the washerwoman to work detained us here two days.

It is necessary at this place to take a fresh coin: accordingly we went to a money-changer's shop, of which there are several, where the man of money sat behind his counter, upon which were rouleaus of various coins, with whom we settled the matter, premising that one ducat was worth three rubles and sixty copecs, in the following manner:

Four ortens, or Courland guldens, make	one feinfer,
Sixteen feinfers	one marc,
Forty marcs	one ferdinger,
Eighty ferdingers	one rix dollar,
Two rix dollars and twelve ferdingers	one ducat.

As we quitted the last gate at Riga, where we underwent a tedious examination of passports, we crossed the Duna, a river which penetrates a great way into Poland, and supplies all these parts with the natural treasure of that country; part of the bridge, which is built of fir, floats upon the water, and part rests upon sand in the shallows; the whole is level and very long. A peasant driving by us with improper velocity, an officer ordered him to stop, and flogged him with a large thick whip.

The country to Mittau, which is twenty-eight miles from Riga, is very luxuriant and gratifying. As this road is much travelled, we bargained with a man, who let out horses at Riga, to furnish us with six, which were excellent, and two skilful drivers, to carry us throughout to Memel. Although this part of ancient Poland, and the pro-

vince of Livonia, constitute the granary of the north, we frequently
found the bread intolerable; it seemed as if to two pounds of rye,
one pound of sand had been added. We reached Mittau, the capital
of Courland, in the evening; the first object that announced the
town was the vast, inelegant, neglected palace of the late sovereigns
of Courland, built of brick, stuccoed white, standing upon a bleak
eminence, ungraced by a single shrub or tree. A great part of this
ponderous pile was some years since burned down; a *Dutch officer*
obtained a contract for rebuilding it; and having got drunk every
day upon the profits of his coarse and clumsy ignorance, died, leaving
behind him the whole of the southern side of this building as his appropriate monument. Courland has been for some years incorporated with Russia, a junction which was managed by force and
finesse. The late empress insidiously excited a dispute between the
Courlanders and Livonians, respecting a canal which was to transport the merchandize of Courland into Livonia; at which the Courlanders revolted, and sought the protection of Catherine: upon which
she sent for the reigning duke, to consult with him at Petersburg;
scarcely had he passed the bridge of Mittau before the nobility held
a meeting, and determined to put the country under the care of Catherine. At this assembly some disputes arose, and swords were
drawn, but the presence of the Russian general, Pahlen, instantly decided the matter: the poor duke heard of the revolution at Petersburg. Mittau is a long, straggling, ill-built town, and most wretchedly paved. On the evening of our arrival there was a great fair,
and at night, about a mile from the town, some excellent fire-works
took place, which to enable them more distinctly to see, two old ladies, who stood next to me on the bridge, brought out their *lanthorns.*
At several of the inns we saw people regaling themselves with beer
soup, a great dainty in this country and in many parts of Germany;
it is composed of beer, yolks of eggs, wheat and sugar, boiled together. We departed from Mittau the next morning, and passed
through the most enchanting forest scenery, composed of pines, as-
pins, oak, nut-trees, and larch; at some distance we saw a wolf cross
the road. Upon quitting the luxuriant fields, and rich and cheerful
peasantry, of the *ci-devant* duchy of Courland, a number of wooden
cottages with high sloping roofs, and rows of crosses, about fifteen
feet high, with large wooden crucifixes affixed to them, raised on the
road side, and peasants with fur caps and short pelisses, announced

that we were in that part of Poland which fell to the Russians in the
last partition; a mere slip of land, not broader than ten English miles.
As we did not penetrate into that interesting country, I had not a personal opportunity of ascertaining whether the Poles, now that the
first shock of separation and national extinction is over, are more
happy than they were before their final dismemberment. However,
I was assured by a very intelligent friend, who had recently returned
from a tour through the heart of Poland, that the condition of the
people, most unjustifiable as the means employed were, is considerably ameliorated: an assurance which may the more readily be believed, when it is considered that, as a nation, their constitution was
radically mischievous, and that their political atmosphere was never
free from storm and convulsion. It has been said, that the great
patriot, and last defender of Poland, has declared, since her fate has
been decided, that it was better for his country to be thus severed,
and placed under the various protections of other powerful governments, than to remain an eternal prey to all the horrors of an elective
monarchy, baronial tyranny, and intestine dissension. At Polangen,
celebrated for the amber found in its neighbourhood, we reached the
barrier of the Russian empire; a Cossac of the Don, who stood at a
circular sentry-box, by the side of a stand of perpendicular spears,
let slip the chain, the bar arose, and we dropped into a deep road of
neutral sand, and at the distance of about an English mile and a half
stopped to contemplate two old weather-beaten posts of demarkation,
surmounted with the eagles of Prussia and Russia, badly painted,
where, after we had, in mirth, indulged ourselves in standing at the
same time in both countries, we placed ourselves under the wing of
the Prussian eagle, and arrived to a late dinner at Memel.

Here we found an excellent inn. To our landlady one of the gentleman said, " I wish to change some money, and should like to
" speak to your husband." " If you do, you had better go to the
" church-yard," said his relict, who was herself apparently dying of
a dropsy. Memel is a large commercial town, lying on the shores
of the Baltic, most wretchedly paved, and for ever covered with
mud; yet the ladies figured away in nankeen shoes and silk stockings, and displayed many a well-turned angle. In the citadel, which
commands an agreeable view of the town, we saw the prisons, which
appeared to be very wretched. The men, and shocking to tell, the
women also, were secured by irons fastened between the knee and

calf of either leg. Upon my remonstrating with the gaoler, who spoke a little English, against the unnecessary cruelty, and even indecency, of treating his female prisoners in this manner, he morosely observed, " that he had more to apprehend from the women than " the men; that the former were at the bottom of all mischief, and " therefore ought to be ever more guarded against."

We waited at Memel two days, in hourly expectation of the wind changing, that we might proceed to Koningberg by water, instead of wading over a tract of mountainous sand, eighty English miles long, and not more than three in breadth in its broadest part, called the Curiche Haff, that runs up within half a mile of Memel, and divides the Baltic from an immense space of water which flows within one stage of Koningberg. During this period, I every day attended the parade and drills, and was shocked at the inhuman blows which, upon every petty occasion, assailed the backs of the soldiers, not from a light supple cane, but a heavy stick, making every blow resound. My blood boiled in my veins, to see a little deformed bantam officer, covered with, almost extinguished by, a huge cocked hat, inflicting these disgraceful strokes, that, savagely as they were administered, cut deeper into the spirit than the flesh, upon a portly respectable soldier, for some trivial mistake. I saw no such severity in Russia, where some of the finest troops in the world may be seen. I observed, not only here but in other parts of Prussia, that every soldier is provided with a sword. The river, which runs up to the town from the Baltic, was crowded with vessels; the market-boats were filled with butter, pumkins, red onions, and Baltic fish in wells.

CHAP. XXI.

DESOLATE SCENE—ENGLISH SAILOR WRECKED—KONINGSBURG—BEAU-
TY IN BOOTS—PRUSSIAN ROADS—THE CELEBRATED RUINS OF MARI-
ENBURG—DANTZIG—COQUETRY IN A BOX—INHOSPITALITY—A GER-
MAN JEW—THE LITTLE GROCER—DUTCH VICAR OF BRAY—VERSES
TO A PRETTY DANTZICKER.

AS the wind shewed no disposition to change in our favour, we embarked, with our horses and carriages, in the ferry-boats, and proceed on the Curiche Haff: by keeping the right wheels as much as
we could in the Baltic, which frequently surrounded us, we arrived
at the first post-house, which lay in the centre of mountains of sand.
Here we learned that some preceding travellers had carried away all
the horses, and accordingly our hostess recommended us to embark
with our vehicles in a boat which is kept for such emergences, and
proceed by the lake to the next stage; which advice we accepted,
and were indebted to a ponderous fat young lady belonging to the
post-house, who waded into the water, and, turning her back towards
us, shoved us off from the beech. We set sail with a favourable
light breeze, which died away after we had proceeded about seven
English miles, when we put into a creek before a few little wretched
fishing huts, under the roof of which, with cocks, hens, ducks, pigs,
and dogs, we passed an uncomfortable night: just as we were lying
down, an English sailor entered the room, with a face a little grave,
but not dejected, to see, as he said, some of his countrymen, " hoping
" no offence:" the poor fellow, we found, had been wrecked a few
nights before, on the Baltic side of this inhospitable region. After
hearing his tale, and making a little collection for him, we resigned
ourselves to as much sleep as is allotted to those who are destined to
be attacked by battalions of fleas. In the morning we could obtain no
post-horses, the wind was against us, and at least eight English miles
lay between us and the post-house. Hoping for some fortunate
change, I resolved to look about me, and after considerable fatigue,
ascended one of those vast sandy summits, which characterize this
cheerless part of the globe: from the top, on one side, lay the Baltic,

and on its beach the cordless masts and hull of a wreck, high and dry; on the other, the lake which had borne us thus far, and before and behind a line of mountains of sand, many of them I should suppose to be a hundred feet high, over whose sparkling surface the eye cannot wander for two minutes together without experiencing the same sensations of pain as are felt upon contemplating snow: below, in a bladeless valley, stood two wretched horses, almost skeletons, scarcely making any shadow in the sun: the natives of this sandy desert, we were afterwards informed by respectable authority, eat live eels dipped in salt, which they devour as they writhe with anguish round their hands. The whole of this hideous waste looked like the region of famine.

A shift of wind springing up, we ventured once more upon the lake; and after a little fair sailing, we were driven, in our little open boat, where there was scarcely room for the helmsman to steer, nearly out of sight of land; the wind freshened to a gale, and the rain fell heavily: at last, when we had renounced all sanguine expectations of ever touching land again, a favourable breeze sprung up, and about ten o'clock at night we reached the quay of the post-house called Nidden, and after supping, were shewn into a large gloomy room to our cribs, where we were surrounded by at least fourteen sleeping damsels, lying with their cloaths on, in filth and coarseness, fit to be the inamoratas of the coal-heavers of London. The next morning, as we were preparing to start, we were presented with an enormous bill, which made us feel like the clown in "As You Like It," when he exclaims, " It strikes a man more dead than a great reckon-" ing in a little room." This imposition, after much altercation, we successfully resisted.

As we approached Koningberg the country assumed a more agreeable aspect; at the inns we found better accommodations, and met with what to us was a great treat, excellent potatoes, a vegetable which has only been introduced into the north within these twenty years. It is scarcely possible to conceive the dreadful state of the roads during the last stage from Mulsen: it was a succession of pits. On the tenth of October we saw the spires of Koningberg, and after passing the place of execution, where three posts were standing, surmounted with wheels, upon which malefactors are exposed, we entered the ancient capital of Prussia Proper. As we were proceeding to the Ditchen Hause, a noble hotel, we passed a vast antique and gloomy pile of red brick; one of my companions pronounced it to be either the jail or the palace; it proved to be the latter, and to be inhabited by the governor: in the church adjoining, Frederic the Great was crowned. The city was first founded in 1255; is extensive, having fourteen parishes: the streets are narrow, terribly paved, and have no foot-path; almost every woman I saw was handsome, and wore great thick boots, and a black riband tied in a bow in the front of their caps. We were obliged to stay here two days, on account of the wheels of the *little Swede* having presented a strong disposition to renounce a circle for a square. The parade exhibited three fine regiments: previous to their forming the line we were again shocked with several instances of the severity of Prussian drilling. The king of Prussia scarcely ever visits this city. The trade is very considerable: one thousand vessels sailed last year into its ports. The river Pregel, which is here rather shallow, was crowded with market-boats, filled with fish, butter, bread, plums, and Bergamot pears. I was present at a marriage ceremony in one of the reformed Catholic churches, which was very simple: the priest joined the hands of the couple, and addressed them extemporaneously with considerable eloquence, as it was explained to me, invoking them to constancy, to love and cherish each other. The young bride and bridegroom seemed much affected, and shed many tears.

Upon my return to the inn, where it was again my fate, in common with the rest of the party, to sleep in the ball-room, I found a little gentleman with a neat bob-wig, and a narrow rim of a beard, just sufficient with his features to denote that he was a member of the synagogue; the object of his visit was to change our money for a new currency, as under:

Twenty-four groschen, or ninety kleine, or three gulder, or thirty ditchen, are equal to . . . . . one dollar.

Three dollars and four groschen . . . . one ducat.

The price of posting is ten groschen per horse, per one German mile, or four English miles and a half.

A courier having arrived to secure about a hundred post-horses for the new married couple, the grand duchess of Russia and the prince of Saxe Weimar and suite, who were on their route from Russia to Weimar, we lost not a minute to put ourselves in motion;

and the *little Swede*, who began now to be much despised, being completely repaired, we reached Frawemborg the next evening, where we stopped the carriage at the foot of an almost perpendicular hill, crowned with a vast extensive edifice of red brick, including a monastery and a Catholic church : it was dusk as I ascended this height, from which there was a fine view of the luxuriant country through which we had passed, and immediately below us a wide-spreading beach and the sea. One of the monks conducted us to the church, which is very large, and the awfulness of the scene was increased by the mysterious gloom which pervaded every part of this massy pile : we had only time to see the tomb of Copernicus, whose remains, we were assured, repose under a plain stone slab which was shown to us upon the pavement. At the last stage, to my regret, a majority of the party resolved upon seeing Dantzig.

It is impossible for an Englishman who has never left his own country, to form any notion of the Prussian roads in general, particularly of that which lay before us to Elbing: I cannot say that we moved by land or by water, but in a skilful mixture of both, through which we waded, axletree deep, over trees laid across each other at unequal distances. To complain would be useless; moreover, the most terrible of joltings, every minute threatening a general dislocation, would hazard the repining tongue being severed by the teeth.

We reached Elbing to breakfast: a very neat town, not unlike a swallow's nest, which is within very comfortable, and without nothing but sticks and mud. Considerable commerce is carried on, and the appearance of the people is respectable, prosperous, and happy. The fruit and vegetable sellers carry their articles in little pails, suspended at the ends of a curved stick, like the milk-women of London. The houses are very singular; but, as they resemble those of Dantzig, one description will be sufficient.

The post from Elbing to Marienbourg is nineteen English miles, a tremendous long stage; indeed, an autumnal days' journey upon such roads, which were precisely the same as those we had already passed, except that we had the *variety* of an endless row of shabby sombre willow pollards. Our poor horses halted several times, when they had a copious libation of water, but nothing else. The German postilions seem to think with Dr. Sangrado, that nothing is so nourishing as water; and, what is more surprising, the horses seem to think so too. I have seen a German horse drink three large

pails full, as fast as his driver could supply him. To cheer our pos-
tillions, we gave them occasionally some snaps, or glasses of excellent
brandy, that we had with us, which the fellows drank, and, with a
smile, seemed ready with Caliban to exclaim:

" That's a brave god, and bears celestial liquor."

In the evening we reached Marienbourg, a small town, once
celebrated for being the principal residence of the knights of
the Teutonic Order, as I have before mentioned, who raised a
castle, and several other structures, in a style of unrivalled Gothic
magnificence, in the twelfth century. To these hallowed remains,
so treasurable to the reflecting mind, Frederick the Great, although
a professed admirer of antiquities and of art, paid no veneration.
The hoary pile has been beaten down, to furnish materials for
building Prussian barracks, hospitals, and magazines, and scarcely
any vestige is left of this pride of ages but the chapel, in the
window of which is a colossal wooden virgin, but little defaced; and,
by her size and shape, entitled to associate with Gog and Magog, in
the Guildhall of London.

We were thirteen hours in reaching Dantzig from Marienbourg,
a distance of thirty English miles, through a country abounding with
corn-fields, in one of which we counted nine bustards, each of them
larger than a turkey. After passing several monasteries, beautifully
embosomed in trees, and the suburbs of Dantzig, extending nearly
two English miles, we reached the drawbridge, and entered the capital of Pomerania in the evening; and, at the *Hotel du Lion Blanc*,
which was very crowded at the time of our arrival, we were very glad
to resume our old quarters, to which we appeared to have a travelling
prescriptive right, a vast ball and card room.

Nothing can exceed the fantastic appearance of the houses, which
are very lofty, and have vast sloping roofs, the fronts of which are
surmounted with lions, angels, suns, griffins, &c. The windows are
very large and square; and the outsides of these edifices are generally painted with brown or green colours, with great softness and
variety: in the streets, which are wretchedly paved, and narrow, and
if the atmosphere be damp, covered ankle-deep with mud, are several noble chesnut and walnut trees. The Rathhaus, or Hotel de Ville,
is an elegant spiral structure of stone, with a variety of elaborate decorations. The prison is well arranged: on one side are felons; and,

on the other, the house of correction, where the women are separated from the men. The female prisoners, many of whom were servants, sent by their masters or mistresses for misbehaviour, to receive the discipline of the house, were employed in carding and spinning, and are obliged to produce, at the end of the week, a certain quantity of work, or, in default, receive a whipping: the prisoners looked healthy and clean.

The Lutheran church is a noble structure: in one of the towers is a gloomy well, into which certain offenders against the catholic faith, many years since, used to be let down, and left to perish: the stirrups and chains by which they descended were shown to us. The Bourse is most whimsically decorated with a marble statue of Augustus III, king of Poland, models of ships, heavy carvings in wood, and great dingy pictures. The Vistula, the largest and longest river in Poland, after springing from mount Crapach, on the confines of Silesia, and crossing Poland and Prussia, washes the walls of Dantzig, and falls into the Baltic. Upon this river a stranger cannot fail being struck with the singular appearance of the Polish grain-boats, in shape resembling a canoe, many of which are eighty feet long, by fourteen broad, without any deck, and have a single elastic mast, 'tapering to the top, fifty, and even sixty, feet high, upon which they fasten a small light sail that is capable of being raised, or depressed, so as to catch the wind, above the undulating heights of the shores of the Vistula. We saw several store-houses of salt: the only salt merchant in the Prussian dominions is the king, who has the monopoly. The exportations of corn from this city are amazing; and it may justly be considered as the grain depot of Europe. The exportation of grain, for the preceding year, amounted to thirty-four thousand one hundred and forty-nine lasts; a last being equal to eighty-four Winchester bushels: that of the year before to fifty-two thousand four hundred and sixteen. The people appear to be at length reconciled to the loss of their hanseatic sovereignty, and, having no remedy, submit themselves without repining to the Prussian sceptre. Mirabeau, one of the most brilliant orators of his age, said, "that the Dantzickers, who, according to appearances, supposed "kings were hobgoblins, were so enraptured to meet with one who "did not *eat* their children, that, in the excess of their enthusiasm, "they were willing to put themselves, without restraint, under the "Prussian government."

On a Sunday, we visited the theatre, a handsome rotunda, where we saw, the great favourite of the Germans, the tragedy of Mary Queen of Scots, between whom and the sanguinary Elizabeth the author effected an interview: there was no after-piece, as usual. The form of the theatre before the curtain was three parts of a circle; and the scenery, dresses and decorations were all handsome. The grand drop scene, used instead of a curtain, was sprinkled with gigantic heads, and had a very strange and whimsical appearance. Nothing could exceed the polite and profound attention paid to the business of the stage: if any one of the audience only whispered rather loudly, all eyes were turned towards him, and a buz of general disapprobation made him silent. In the box, next to that in which I sat, was a lady of fashion, remarkably deformed; in age, I should suppose, touching the frontier of desperation, dressed in a white robe, and a garland of artificial flowers; to attract more notice, she was knitting a rich silk purse: the whole of the party exchanged frequent glances with her; but, alas! had she known what was passing between the eye and the mind, our homage would not have proved very acceptable.

In Dantzig, every thing partakes of that petty spirit which is too often engendered by traffic amongst small communities of mercantile men. Heaven protect the being who visits this city without a commercial commission! As we were walking by the Bourse, we requested a German Jew, who had the appearance of a gentleman, to shew us the way to a commercial house to get some money exchanged; upon which he offered to accompany us. " We cannot, " Sir, think of troubling you: if you will only direct us, it will be " sufficient," said my German friend and companion. " Oh! gen- " tlemen," replied the descendant of Abraham, " I beg you will not " mention it; you will of course pay me for my trouble, and I shall " be happy to attend you."

Having parted with my friend, who proceeded to Berlin, I went to Fare Wasser, with a view of embarking for Copenhagen, which would have considerably curtailed my journey to Husum; but the wind being contrary, and blowing a hurricane, and several English captains, who were there, assuring me that it frequently continued so for three weeks and a month together, after spending three cheerless days in hopes that a change might take place, I returned to Dantzig, where, without knowing a human being, for this city was not originally included in our route, I presented myself at the counting-house of an elderly Englishman, a denizen of Dantzig, and in the presence of a host of clerks, detailed my story, and requested that he would be so obliging as to permit one of them, who spoke English, to attend me a few minutes to the post-house, that I might endeavour to overtake my friends. The hoary merchant, with an immoveable countenance, coldly looked at me, and briefly replied, " It is our post " day; and, without saying another word, returned to his accompts. It reminded me of Gadshill and the Carrier, in the first part of Henry the Fourth.

" *Gad.* I pray thee, lend me thy lantern, to see my gelding in the stable.

" *Car.* Lend thee my lantern, quotha ! Marry, I'll see thee hanged first."

This Englishman had grown old in the traffic of Dantzig, and the generous spirit of his country had been indurated into the selfishness of accumulation.

The *little Swede* was now in the lowest state of depreciation : the post-master thought her unworthy of being drawn by a Prussian prancer, and absolutely refused to put a horse into the shafts ; at the same time he offered me a ducat, that is, nine shillings and sixpence, for her. I would have set fire to her, sooner than that he should have had her. The god of gold seemed to have made this spot his favourite temple, to have constituted a bag of corn his chosen altar, and to have recorded his oracles in a leger : the rampart of the town seem preserved only to repel hospitality and generosity. The Dantzickers keep a cash-account of civilities, and never indulge in festivity without resorting to calculation. A calculating countenance under a little bob-wig, shining brushed cocked-hat that has seen good service, a brown coat, waistcoat and breeches of the same colour, worsted stockings, a pair of shining little silver buckles, and an ivory-headed cane, denote the thrifty Dantzicker : the very beggar in the streets seems to expect a double proportion of bounty for his misfortune, and for the trouble of asking relief. As I was purchasing some articles at a grocer's for my journey, his wife held a little child in her arms, not old enough to speak, to whom I gave a pear, and presently after I presented him with a gulden, a little coin, which he griped, apparently with the same instinct that would induce a young bear to rifle a honey jar, and dropped the fruit. The little grocer seemed much pleased with his son's preference ; and, in German, as well as I could understand him, exclaimed, " that he would make a brave " tradesman."

In this place, where there were so many of my own countrymen settled, accident led me to the civilities of a polite and amiable young Dutchman, who had not staid long enough in Dantzig to lose every liberal sentiment. " How strange," said I, " that amongst " the residents of this place you alone should wish to serve an un- " fortunate solitary Englishman ; and that, too, whilst our respective " countries are at war !" " It is true, our countries are at war," said he, in good English ; " but what is that to us ? every man *whom* " *I can serve is my countryman*."

Through the medium of this gentleman, I hired a man to go with me all the way to Berlin (who, on such occasions is called a fuhrman), instead of going post, to avoid as much as possible, the galling pressure of Prussian imposition. To the friendly Dutchman I sold the *little Swede* for ten ducats, which he vowed he would brush up and paint, and drive with into the country. On the day preceding my departure, my Dutch friend related the following story. Being at church one Sunday, at Alkmaar, when that town was in the possession of the English forces, previous to the sermon the preacher prayed very fervently for the long life of his Majesty George III, and the prosperity of England. Scarcely had he finished this pious compliment, before an inhabitant entered, and announced that the English forces were retiring, and that the French were about to resume the protection of the place : upon hearing which, this Dutch vicar of Bray explained to his audience, that the supplication which they had just heard was coerced ; but that now, being able to follow the spontaneous emotions of his own heart, he begged them to unite with him in offering up a prayer to the throne of grace, to bless and preserve general Brune and the French armies !

Before I met with the courteous Dutchman, the only consolation which I found was in sitting in the same room with the young *Maitresse d'hotel du Lion Blanc*, where, without knowing each other's language, we contrived to pass away the hours not unpleasantly. The beauty and sprightliness of this young woman produced the following *jeu-d'esprit* :

The sign of the house should be chang'd, I'll be sworn,
   Where enchanted we find so much beauty and grace ;
Then quick from the door let the *lion* be torn,
   And an *angel* expand her white wings in his place.

The young Dutchman translated it into German, and presented it to the fair one.

CHAP. XXII.

REFLECTIONS UPON A STUHLWAGGON—PRUSSIAN VILLAGES—MILITARY
MANOEUVRES—IRISH REBEL—BERLIN—LINDEN WALK—TOLERATION
—PRUSSIAN DINNER—CHEAP LIVING—THE PALACE—CADET CORPS.

THE traveller going to Germany will be under the necessity of changing his money as under :

Twenty-four good, or ninety Prussian groschen, are equal to one dollar, or three Prussian guilders.

N. B. Six Prussian dollars are equal to one pound English.

When the stuhlwaggon, that was to carry me to Berlin, a distance of upwards of three hundred English miles, in the stipulated time of eight days, drove up to the door, I observed that it had no springs, consequently I could not be detained on the road by their breaking ; that I should be nearly jolted to death ; but that would be an admirable substitute for want of exercise ; that I should not be able to sleep by day, consequently I should sleep the better by night ; that my driver could not speak English, nor I three words of German ; *ergo*, we should associate like a couple of dumb waiters ; and my reflections, if chance any should arise, would not be shaken. Having settled all these points in my mind, with infinite pleasure I passed the drawbridge of this seat of extortion and inhospitality, and as soon as we had cleared the suburbs and dropped into a deep sandy road, my heavy unimpassioned driver took from his waistcoat pocket a piece of dry fungus, and holding it under a flint, with a small steel struck a light, kindled his pipe, and was soon lost in smoke, and a happy vacuity of thought. Although the red leaves of retiring autumn were falling in showers from the trees, the country appeared very picturesque and rich. After we passed the town and abbey of Oliva, the latter celebrated for containing in one of its chambers the table on which the treaty of peace was signed between the crowned heads of Germany, Poland, and Sweden, called the treaty of Oliva, my driver turned into a by road, the inequalities of which I can compare to nothing but those of a church-yard, thronged with

P p

graves; we were several times obliged to alight, in order to support the carriage on one side, whilst it crawled along the edge of a miry bank. The uncertainty of a German mile never fails to puzzle a tra-veller: there is a long and a short one; the former is as indefinite as a Yorkshire mile, which I believe is from steeple to steeple, some-times it means five, six, and seven English miles, the latter I have already explained.

On the road every Prussian was at once equipped for his bed and for a ball, by having his head adorned with a prodigious cocked hat, and a night-cap under it. The Prussian farm-houses were either tiled or very neatly thatched: some of them were built of brick, and others of a light brown clay, but the favourite colour is that of vivid flesh, which were remarkably neat; the ground exhibited the marks of high cultivation, and the farmers looked rich and respectable, and perfect-ly English. Although the soil is sandy, yet from its fineness it is ca-pable of bearing all sorts of vegetables for the kitchen: out of four grains of rye sown, the tillers calculate that one will rise. By the time I reached Stolpe, I had formed a little budget of current Ger-man expressions, which at the inn in that town enabled me to under-stand a man who said to me, " pray sir, are you a Frenchman?" " No, I am an Englishman," " Ah, sir, so much the better for you,. " and so much the more agreeable to me," said he. I wondered to hear such language from Prussian lips: but I afterwards found the man who addressed me was a Dutchman.

The road to Berlin has, in one respect, a great advantage; there is a constant and rapid succession of towns and villages, but no scatter-ed cottages: upon every acclivity the traveller commands six or seven spires rising from little clumps of trees, and clusters of houses; the road to each of these small communities for about a quarter of a mile is paved with large rough angular stones, which constitute the pride of the parish, and are brought from a great distance, and with con-siderable cost. Upon my wishing them at the devil one day, which I never failed to do as often as I had to contend with them, my driver turned round and said : " Do not wish them there: do you " know that each of those *fine stones* cost four good groschen ?"

In Prussia, robberies very seldom happen: the Prussians only pil-fer in the shape of extortion,

" And for a pistol they present a bill."

Having seen many Englishmen travel through their country with a moveable arsenal of arms in their carriages, united to the received opinion that suicide prevails more in England than in any other country, they conclude that the preparation is not against robbers, but to furnish their owner with a choice of deaths, if his ennui is not dissipated by roving.

My adventures upon the road were few, and not worthy of relation, except that my driver was very fond of quitting the main road for every short cut, in which we were frequently obliged, carriage and all, to spring as well as we could over a small ditch; having repeatedly warned him that we should be overturned, at last my prediction was verified, the wheels were uppermost, and we lay sprawling in the road: as soon as I could look around me I found the driver in great agony, and concluded that he had at least shattered a rib or a leg: but the misfortune was a much greater one in his estimation, he had broken his pipe, which lay in the road by the side of scattered provisions and trunks; he lamented his loss bitterly, and frequently, as we were replacing matters, apostrophized the remains of this natural and inestimable source of German comfort. We frequently passed through the most beautiful avenues of majestic oak, stately lindens, and graceful beech and birch trees. I found the inns very poor: at Pinnow I slept upon a bed of straw. In the best room are generally the depot of the Sunday gowns, the best crockery, two or three filthy straw beds, a stove of black Dutch tiles, one or two corn chests, a chair with a broken back, jars of butter: adjoining there is generally a room for the daughter or upper servant of the host, who reclines her sweet person upon a bed placed upon a corn-bin, and surrounded by a winter-stock of potatoes. If a traveller fasten the door of his bed-room he will be under the necessity of rising to open it twenty times after he is in bed, that the master or mistress of the house may have access to something or another which is deposited in his chamber.

The winter was now rapidly setting in, and in every post-house the stoves were warmed: before one of them some peasant children were reposing upon forms, and their mother standing with her back against it, fast asleep. The peasants erect their ovens, which are made of clay, about seven feet high, in the shape of a dome, at the extremity of their orchards, removed as far as possible from any thatch. All the roads and by-lanes in Prussia are abundantly supplied with legible and intelligent directing posts, representing a negro's head, with large white eyes, and a pig-tail, whilst two long stiff arms point the wanderer on his way. The want of this species of attention to travellers in England is severely felt. It is scarcely necessary for me to observe that the universal language of Prussia is German.

The garrison towns are numerous, at which the traveller is obliged to furnish the officer of the guard with his name, condition, and motive of travelling. The soldiers looked to great advantage ; they have a favourite, and much admired manœuvre, of forming hollow squares by sections, which at present is confined to the Prussian service ; and by means of a hollow curve, at the bottom of the barrel of the Prussian musket, leading into the pan, through a large touch-hole, no priming is necessary, or rather the loading primes, by which several motions are saved. With this improvement, and a heavy ramrod, an expert Prussian soldier, even with Prussian powder, far inferior to that of England, can load and fire twelve times in one minute. A soldier who had not long been enlisted, performed these motions in my presence ten times in that period by my watch.

At Konigberg, as I was sitting down to dinner, a portly soldier, in the Prussian uniform, opened the door, an addressed me in English. With much address and respect, under the venial pretence of my not having written my name legibly at the barrier, he introduced himself to me, and enabled me very soon to discover that he was one of those infatuated Irishmen, who having incurred the displeasure of the British government, had been plucked from a station of respectability, and the bosom of a beloved family, exiled from his country, and doomed to wear the habit, and endure the discipline of a Prussian soldier for ten wretched years, five of which he had already survived. The poor fellow acknowledged the fatal delusion which had thus torn him from all that was dear to him, and reduced him to the humiliation of gladly receiving a dollar from a stranger.

Between Gruneberg and Freyenwalde I passed the Oder, which flows to the walls of Olmutz, rendered eminently familiar to the memory by the cruel captivity of La Fayette, and the spirit of British generosity which restored him and his lovely marchioness to light and liberty.

Upon our leaving Freyenwalde, we ploughed our way through the dark forests and trackless sands of Brandenbourg, the latter of which Frederick the Great highly valued as a national barrier, capable of impeding and embarrassing an approaching enemy. Of their depth and dreariness no one can judge, but those who have waded through them: we quitted them with great joy, to roll merrily along over a noble new royal road, of about ten English miles in length, lined with sapling lindens; and, early on the eighth day from my leaving Dantzig, I passed the gate of the wall which surrounds Berlin, and with forty-one ducats discharged my companion at the *Hotel de Russie*.

Having refreshed myself, I sallied into the Linden Walk, which is very broad, is formed of triple rows of the graceful and umbrageous tree from which it receives its name, and is situated in the centre of the street, having carriage roads on each side, from which it is protected by a handsome line of granite posts connected by bars of iron, and illuminated at night by large reflecting lamps, suspended over the centre by cords, stretched from corresponding supporters of wrought iron: its length is about an English mile, and presents at one end the rich portico of the marble opera-house and the palace, and at the other the celebrated Brandenbourg gate, designed by Monsieur Langhans from the Propylium of Athens, and raised in 1780. This superb monument of tasteful architecture is a stone colonnade, of a light reddish-yellow colour, composed of twelve grand fluted Corinthian columns, forty-four feet high, and five feet seven inches in diameter, six on each side, leaving a space for the gates to fold between, presenting five colossal portals, through which the park is seen in fine perspective. The wings composing the custom and guard houses are adorned with eighteen lesser columns, twenty-nine feet high and three feet in diameter: the whole is crowned by colossal figures of the angel of peace driving four horses abreast in a triumphal car, below which are rich basso relievos. This most elegant structure, and the Walk of Lindens, are unique, and would abundantly repay any traveller for the fatigues of an eight days' journey to behold them. In the walk, although the weather was very cold, several ladies were promenading without caps or bonnets, and others were riding astride on horseback, according to the fashion of the country, in a long riding habit, pantaloons, and half-boots. In the street scarcely any other objects were to be seen, than

" the soldier and his sword."

Upon ascending the gallery of the superb dome of the institution of the poor, in the grand market place, I commanded the wall of the city, the dimensions of which are small, I should not think larger than those of Bath; but having been the result of one design, and in a great measure built in one reign, it has the advantage of being regular. The river Spree runs through it, and is adorned by some handsome stone bridges. The streets are spacious, and, to the surprise of a stranger, are well paved for carriages and pedestrians, although nature has refused to furnish the country with a single stone: this denial has been supplied by the policy of Frederick the Great, who made all the vessels that came up the Elbe, the Hawel, or the Spree, take on board at Magdeburg a certain quantity of freestone, and disembark it at Berlin gratis. The houses are generally built of brick stuccoed, but some are of stone, in the Italian style of architecture. The palace of prince Henry, the brother of Frederick the Great, lately deceased, is built of stone; but, for want of ornament, possesses but little attraction for the eye: the royal palace is an enormous square pile of the same materials, whose massy and gloomy walls the reigning sovereign has wisely resigned to his courtiers, for a small plain mansion, opposite the common foundery. Mon-bijou, the residence of the queen dowager, is a palace, or rather a long gallery, nearly the whole being upon the ground floor, situated on the side of the river Spree, embosomed in a wood and gardens. The Rotunda, or Catholic church, partly designed by cardinal Alberoni, is a noble edifice, the grand altar of which was made at Rome, and is celebrated for its beauty. Soon after Frederick the Great ascended the throne, he conceived the sublime idea of building a vast Pantheon, in which every description of devotion might, at an allotted time, find its altar. Policy, if not genuine charity, induced that sagacious prince to think that tolerance was necessary to the interests as well as the dignity of a nation; and he was desirous of not only seeing his subjects and foreigners worship their God in their way, but that, like brothers, they should prostrate themselves before him in the same temple. On account of the state of the treasury, Frederick was successfully advised to drop this benign plan, and it was never afterwards resumed. The generality of the Prussians are Calvinists.

In the evening after my arrival I went to the New Theatre, a superb building, on the entablature of which the following elegant in-

scription appeared in German, " Whilst we *smile* we mend the manners." All the front of the inside was occupied by the royal box,
formed into a saloon, from the centre of the ceiling of which a rich
lustre descended, and on each side were alabaster vases. The boxes
were neat and well arranged. Over the curtain was a large transparent clock; the players were good; the orchestra very full and
fine; and the scenery, particularly the drop, or curtain scene, very
beautiful.

The statue of the celebrated general Ziethen, the favourite of
Frederick the Great, and one of the greatest and bravest generals of
Prussia, is well worthy the notice of the traveller. It is raised in
Wilhelm's Platz, or William's Place, upon a pedestal, on three
sides of which are basso-relievos, representing the hero on horseback, in some of the most celebrated campaigns, surrounded by an
elegant railing: the figure of the general, in his hussar regimentals,
is as large as life; his hand is raised to his chin, which was his usual
attitude of meditation: it is said to be a strong resemblance, and is a
fine piece of statuary. In this little square there are several other
statues of Prussian generals, who distinguished themselves in the
seven years' war, without any inscription. Upon my German friend
enquiring of some of the soldiers, who were standing near us, their
names, they told us they knew nothing about them. It is well known,
that no living creature is more ignorant than a Prussian soldier.

As we passed to the royal Opera-house, the cavalry were drilling;
the wretchedness of their horses not a little surprised me: the same
remark applied to those of every other regiment of cavalry which I
saw. The Opera-house, which is never open but during the carnival, is a superb and elegant building, raised by Frederick the Great.
The audience are admitted gratis, by tickets issued by the king's
authority: the pit is allotted to the regiments in garrison, each of
which is permitted to send so many men. In the time of Frederick
the Great, it was no unusual spectacle to see the wives of the soldiers
sitting upon their husbands' shoulders: the internal decorations are,
I was informed, very magnificent.

Berlin is justly celebrated for the excellence of its hotels: in my
sitting room, looking upon the Linden-walk, I had every article of
useful and elegant furniture, my bed-room and sopha-bed and linen
were remarkably neat and clean, and both rooms, although the frost
was set in with intense severity, were, by means of stoves which are

supplied from the passage, as warm as a summer day. It is a received opinion, that Englishmen are so accustomed to sit by their firesides, that they cannot grow warm unless they see the fire : to this remark I have only to observe, that I partook so insensibly of the atmosphere which pervaded my room, that I neither thought of heat, cold, or fire-places. At breakfast, the rolls, butter, and coffee, were delicious, and the china beautiful. The porcelain of Berlin is very fine, and nearly equal to that of Saxony. In the infancy of this manufactory, Frederick the Great granted permission to the Jews within his dominions to marry, only upon condition that they should purchase a certain quantity of this china; by this despotic policy he soon brought it into repute. At our *table d'hote* in the hotel, the dinner, with little variation, was in the following order: cold herrings and salted cucumbers, soup, bouilli, ham with sliced carrots, honey and rice pudding, venison and stewed pease. In the streets were groups of female fruiterers, sitting before tubs filled with the finest grapes, and Bergamot-pears, walnuts, &c. From those stands a respectable dessert may be furnished for the value of three-pence, English. Upon the Spree were a great number of boats, completely laden with the finest apples and pears. Living in Berlin is moderate, in the country remarkably cheap. A bachelor in Hesse Darmstadt, and in many other parts of 'Germany, can enjoy elegant society, have every day a bottle of excellent wine, and keep his horse, for one hundred and twenty pounds per annum.

In the audience-room of the great palace we were shown a chandelier of chrystal which cost 4,200*l.*; amongst the paintings, which are few, we noticed a portrait of the duke of Ferrara, by Corregio, for which ten thousand ducats were given : there is also a beautiful statue of Marcus Aurelius, drawn up from the Tiber about fifty years since; several curious and costly clocks and secretaires of exquisite workmanship and mechanism, one of which, should any one improperly attempt to open it, would betray the robber by a tune similar to that in the academy of sciences in Petersburg : we were also shewn a circular closet in a turret, from whence Frederick, in his latter days, used to contemplate the people in the streets.

The cadet corps is a noble establishment, much resembling those in Petersburg: we attended a parade of about four hundred boys, who, as they were not sized, nor ranked according to age, presented a striking instance of the progress of merit, by displaying mere

" apple-munching urchins" commanding companies of boys bigger than themselves. From the cadet corps we visited an exhibition of the Prussian arts and manufactures, displayed in a suite of rooms : the busts, models, and carpets, were beautiful : some of the draw‑ ings were pretty, but the paintings were below criticism. English manufactures are severely prohibited in Prussia.

CHAP. XXII.

POTSDAM DILIGENCE—POTSDAM—SANS SOUCI—VOLTAIRE, AND DOGS
OF FREDERICK THE GREAT—NOBLE FIRMNESS OF AN ARCHITECT—
KING AND LOVELY QUEEN OF PRUSSIA—ANECDOTES—FEMALE TRA-
VELLING HABIT—THE DUCHY OF MECKLENBURG SWERIN—RETURN
TO ENGLAND.

ON the Sunday after my arrival, namely, the third of November, I seated myself at seven o'clock in the morning, with an intelligent companion, in the Potsdam diligence, a vehicle considerably less commodious than that of Paris: it was without springs, and so villanously put together, that the biting air pierced through a hundred crevices; sliding wooden pannels supplied the place of glasses, and in the back part were two seats, the occupiers of which were separated from each other by a stout iron bar. Our companions, male and female, were clad in their winter dress of muffs and fur shoes. After passing through a country of corn-fields, and fir forests, and some small frozen ponds, at eleven we reached the barrier of Potsdam, which is situated on the river Havel, and is formed into an isle by the adjoining lakes and canals, about sixteen English miles from Berlin.

Having expelled the cold with some soup, we hired a little phæton, and immediately proceeded to Sans Souci, distant about two English miles, which, as well as the neighbouring country palaces, are so much the fruit of the great Frederick's taste, that it was like paying a visit to his spirit. As we proceeded to the gallery of pictures, we passed by his hot-houses, which he cherished with great care. So partial was his majesty to hot-house fruit, that before the buildings were erected, he who would have scantily provided for a gallant officer mutilated in his service, did not hesitate to pay a ducat for a cherry! When he was dying, his pine apples occupied his principal attention.

We entered the picture gallery from the road through a rustic door: this room, two hundred and fifty eight feet long, thirty-six broad, and fifteen high, is supported by Carrara pillars, and is superbly gilded and ornamented. The collection is very select and pre-

cious; we principally noticed the Graces, by Dominichino; Ver-
tumnus and Pomona, by Leonardo da Vinci; Titian and his wife, by
himself; Danae and Cupid, by the same artist; Venus bathing, by
Corregio; three different styles of painting, by Guido; the Holy
Family, by Raphael, which cost fourteen thousand ducats; a Cave of
Devils, by Teniers, in which his mother and wife are represented as
members of the infernal family, his father as saint Antonio, and himself in *bonnet rouge*, laughing at the group; a Head of Christ, by
Vandyke; Ignorance and Wisdom, by Corregio; a Head of Christ,
upon leaf gold, by Raphael, for which Frederick the Great paid six
thousand ducats; several other paintings by the same great master,
upon the same ground; a Virgin and Infant, by Rubens; and several other exquisite works of art.   There was once a beautiful little
Magdalen here, by Raphael, which Frederick bartered to the elector
of Saxony *for a troop of horse :* this sort of barter seems not to have
been unusual. Augustus II, elector of Saxony, purchased forty-eight
bulky porcelain vases of Frederick William I, of Prussia, for a fine
regiment of dragoons.

From the gallery we ascended a staircase, and entered a terrace,
whence a beautiful view of the river, and the surrounding country,
lay expanded before us. As we proceeded to the palace, or pavilion,
composed of a long suite of rooms upon a ground floor, the tombs
of Frederick's dogs were pointed out to us, the only creatures for
whom he entertained a cordial affection. It is well known that he
indulged the strange belief, that these animals possessed the power of
discriminating character, and that he disliked those at whom they
barked: most of these canine favourites were honoured with a royal
epitaph. It is related, that whenever he went to war, he always carried
a small Italian greyhound with him; and that when, in the seven
years war, he happened to be pursued by a reconnoitering party of
Austrians, he took shelter under a dry arch of a bridge, with his
favourite in his arms; and that, although the enemy passed and re-
passed the bridge several times, yet the animal, naturally churlish,
lay quite still, and scarcely breathed: had he barked, Frederick must
have been discovered and taken prisoner, and Prussia, in all human
probability, would have shared the fate of Poland, and swelled the
empires of Russia and of Germany. There is another story told, the
authenticity of which is indubitable: Frederick the Great, in his
dying moments, expressed a wish to be buried by the side of his dogs.

One of these favourites, another greyhound bitch, was taken at the battle of Sorr, when the baggage was plundered by Trenck and Nadasti. Regardless of *inferior* losses, the king was in the act of writing to Nadasti, to request his bitch might be restored, when the Austrian general, knowing his love for the animal, which was itself greatly attached to him, had sent it back; the bitch, unperceived by the monarch, leaped upon the table while he was writing, and, as usual, began to caress him, at which he was so affected that he shed tears: the day before he had cut off many thousands of men, and charged his *dear children* to give no Saxon quarter. The only amiable trait in Frederick's composition was of a canine nature: he possessed nothing to attach man to *him* but *his* fondness for dogs.

We saw the room where Frederick slept and died: it was plain and simple; and, upon the chimney-piece, was a beautiful antique of Julius Cæsar when a boy. After passing through several handsome rooms, we reached the dining-room. It is well known that Frederick the Great indulged in the pleasures of the table, and that English, French, German, Italian, Russian cooks, were employed in this royal philosopher's kitchen. The apartment of Voltaire, where I could not resist sitting down in his chair before his desk, dotted all over with spots of a pen, more keen and triumphant than the sword, and wondering how such a genius could associate for three years with the crafty, ungrateful, cold, ungenerous, tyrannical, rancorous, and implacable Frederick, who, if he merited the title of Great, had no pretensions to that of Good: that the wit and the sovereign should have differed no one can wonder; but every one must, that they had not quarrelled and parted sooner.

In the life of Voltaire we see the triumph of letters. The late empress of Russia courted his friendship by every touching art which, even from clever women in the ordinary ranks of life, is irresistible: she did nothing without affecting to consult him: she invited him to Petersburg, and placed the model of his house at Ferney in the hermitage. Frederick the Great sought him with avidity, bordering on abject solicitation; but the mean and ungenerous despotism of the sovereign's heart rendered him unworthy the honour of an association, which with equal meanness and harshness he dissolved. Why was Voltaire thus courted by two of the most distinguished potentates of their own, or perhaps of any other age?

Because they knew that the pen of such a genius could give any colour to their actions, and could measure out and extend their fame.

The gardens of Sans Souci appeared to be elegantly arranged;
but it was no time to explore leafless bowers and alleys no longer
green :

> " When icicles hang by the wall,
>   And Dick the shepherd blows his nail,
> And Tom bears logs into the hall,
>   And milk comes frozen home in pail."

The *facade* of Sans Souci, towards the plain, is very elegant; towards the terrace very heavy, where it resembles more a great
tasteless green-house than a royal residence. From Sans Souci, we
drove through a beautiful park to the new palace, distant about an
English mile and a half. After passing two grand lodges and out-
offices, connected by an elegant semicircular colonnade of eighty-
eight columns, we entered the palace, the front of which is adorned
with Corinthian pilasters, and the body built with the rich red Dutch
brick: the hall was a superb vaulted grotto, formed of chrystals,
branches of coral and shells, and fountains, arranged with equal elegance and novelty. Respecting the construction of this extraordinary apartment, the king and his favourite architect had a violent
dispute; the latter insisting that it should be a vestibule, the former
a grotto. The royal disputant of course prevailed, and the architect
was so disgusted, that he declined proceeding in the building. It
was lucky for him, that the tyrant Frederick had not sent him to the
fortress of Spandaw, where so many brave men who had fought and
bled for him have been immured for some error in petty punctilio,
to meditate on the superiority of grottoes over vestibules: the rest of
the rooms are very elegant. Having satisfied our curiosity, we
galloped to the little marble palace, about two English miles off,
built also by Frederick the Great, of Silesian marble and Dutch
brick: I was more pleased with it than with the *Petite Trianon* at
Versailles. The road to the pavilion is lined with small rustic dwellings, surrounded by shrubs for the household: on the left is an extensive and elegant orangerie, in the centre of which is a superb ball-
room, lined with mirrors, and opening on either side into alleys of
orange and lemon trees: on the right are the kitchens, externally
resembling the ruins of an Athenian temple: a lake, lined with ele

gant groups of trees, pleasure-houses, cottages, and mills, washes the terrace of the little palace, the apartments of which are small but singularly elegant, and were adorned with some exquisite anti-ques. Upon our return to our hotel the clock struck four: just as we had begun to thaw ourselves with some soup, attended, as the Saxon kings of old were, by a wandering harper at our door, just as he had sweetly and wildly run over the first division of a German air, by which time my intelligent companion and I had settled it, that had the palaces been covered with rubies, and the trees of the royal gardens dropped pearls, we should return discontented to Berlin, un-less we had beheld the lovely queen of Prussia; in truth, she was the principal object of our excursion: the son of our host ran into the room, to tell us the queen's carriage was just drawn up to the great palace, which our window commanded. From a little private door of this vast pile she descended, leaning upon the arm of a page, and attended by an elderly lady of the court; upon seeing us she stopped, and moved to us in the most gracious and enchanting man-ner. She is very fair, her face sweet, elegant, and expressive:

> " ———— Whose red and white
> Nature's own sweet and cunning hand laid on."

Her hair is light, her figure exquisite; and, as she stepped into her carriage, she displayed a foot and ankle which at once convinced us that the most perfect symmetry reigned throughout her frame. Her charms were heightened by her situation; she was expected, in a few days, to augment the illustrious house of Brandenbourg. At a party at the British ambassador's, Mr. Jackson, I was regaled with the most enchanting account of her amiable virtues; but to look at her is sufficient:

> " There's nothing ill can dwell in such a temple."

She is very fond of retirement, and devotes herself to the educa-tion of her children. As my stay in Berlin was too short to admit of my being presented, I was much gratified in seeing a princess of whom every one speaks with rapture. The manner in which her marriage occurred was interesting: At a grand review, which took place at Francfort on the Maine, monsieur Beathman, one of the richest bankers upon the continent, appeared at the parade, with a superb equipage: struck with his appearance, the king enquired his name, and monsieur B. was introduced, who invited his majesty to a grand *fête* he intended giving that evening at his chateau; which invitation the king accepted, and there met the lovely princess of Mecklenburg Strelitz; to look upon and love her were the same.

About eighteen months after their marriage, they paid a visit to monsieur B; and, as they entered the room where their first interview occurred, the king caught his royal bride in his arms, kissed her, and, with tears of sensibility, exclaimed, " It was in this very " room, my dear Beathman, that I found the treasure of my happi- " ness." The royal couple are remarkably domestic, and largely taste of those endearing and tranquil enjoyments which are seldom seen in the neighbourhood of a throne.

The great palace at Potsdam, in which the royal family principally reside, has a few elegant state rooms: in one of which was a half-length portrait of Bonaparte. The queen had displayed her taste by decorating one of her little cabinets with engravings from some of the exquisite productions of Westall.

The next morning (Sunday) we attended the two parades, which take place on this day within two hours of each other. I should suppose about ten thousand men were upon the ground; they presented a very noble appearance. The King, attended by several officers, was present. In roving through the city, we observed that its size and buildings resembled those of Berlin, and that it was equally gloomy.

Upon our return, a soldier mounted the coach-box of the diligence at the gate at Berlin, and as we passed close to our inn, we called to the driver to let us out, but the soldier refused, and upon our attempting to get out, jumped down, drew his bayonet, and called the guard, upon which, with some little surprise, we submitted to be taken to the post-house, at the further end of the city, where we were suffered to alight without further molestation. This regulation is a part of the military police of this despotic government, which converts every city into barracks, and palaces into head-quarters. Upon regaining our hotel, cold and hungry, and ordering our dinner, we found that the cooks, it being *dimanche*, were all gone to the theatre: however, one of them was soon found, and our appetites soon satisfied.

On the fifth of November, at eleven o'clock in the morning, as I wished to see a little more of the manners of the people, I mounted the Hamburg diligence, and proceeded in it as far as Grabow, and afterwards travelled post to Husum: this machine was much inferior to its Potsdam brother; it was a leather tilted waggon without springs, filled with rows of seats, separated from each other by iron bars; behind was a basket for hay: there were neither glasses nor wooden pannels in the sides, but two hard leather curtains were dropped and buttoned down, when it rained or was cold. The passengers consisted of two Prussian ladies, a girl servant, an Hungarian officer, myself, and one *conducteur*, an old wrinkled gentleman of sixty-five at least, who lost all his vivacity when he set down the girl, between whom some tender touches of the hand, and gentle whispers, passed during one of the most bitter nights I ever experienced. The ladies, who were neither handsome nor aged, and were, as I learned, very respectable women, made no hesitation in tying up their garters, *sans ceremonie*, and, in other matters of travelling comfort, displayed as little restraint as the French ladies. All night, it being dark, and the roads very deep and sandy, we moved at a funereal pace. The next evening I bade adieu to the Hamburg diligence, and having convinced myself of the danger of attempting to push through that spit of Hanover through which the direct Hamburgh road lies, in consequence of the ruffian-like perfidious violation of the law of nations, exhibited in the seizure of our ambassador, sir George Rumbold, at that city; I ordered a stuhl-waggon at Perlberg, and travelled post to Swerin, the capital of the duchy of Meckleburgh Swerin, which commences on this side at Grabow. In this petty state, luxuriant in corn-fields, posting, which constitutes one of the revenues of the duchy, is very dear; for five German miles I paid seven dollars and two groschen. To avoid this extortion, I recommend a traveller to hire a furhman at Perlberg to carry him through to Lubec: he will save considerably by it. A little beyond Grabow I passed a superb country residence of the reigning duke, situated in a beautiful country, and surrounded by a very neat village. Swerin is a large and respectable town, where the inns are very good, and well supplied with French spies. The palace is a vast and very ancient building, forming an oblong square, presenting galleries, balconies, and turrets, without end. The sol-

diers on duty were fine-looking fellows; the forces of the duke
amount to fourteen hundred men. I could not help smiling when,
upon discharging my driver at this town, he presented me, with
great ceremony, a government receipt, to shew that he had paid
two groschen for permission to pass over a nearer and better road,
which led from the country palace of the duke. The Malaga wine,
of which a great quantity is brought to this duchy, is excellent and
reasonable.

The approach to Lubec was through a noble road, lined with stately lindens, extending four English miles: it was dusk when I entered
it, and early in the morning when I left it; but, if I may judge by
its avenues, gates, and streets, I should pronounce it to be a very
beautiful, extensive, and wealthy city. It has a small surrounding
territory, and is at present independent; but strong fears may be entertained that, following the example of Dantzig, its sovereignty is
nearly at a close, and that it will speedily be incorporated with Hanoverian France. Through every town to Husum I was obliged to
give my name and quality. An English humourist, who had, by
virtue of his freehold, a parliamentary vote in the municipal county,
upon being stopped at the gate of a town in some part of Germany,
throughout which empire an elector is considered as a personage
only inferior to the emperor, and upon his name being demanded,
replied, *" Je suis un electeur de Middlesex ;"* upon which the captain
ordered the guard to turn out and salute him, and sent a company to
follow the carriage to the inn, and attend him there, and paid him all
the honours due to an electoral prince. The delusion was easily
carried on, for princes, even crowned heads, in Germany and various
other parts of the continent, trouble themselves but little about equipage. The venerable and gallant prince de Ligne, whom I have
before named, a prince of great rank and dignity, under the pressure
of seventy years, travelled from Vienna to Berlin, a distance of seven
hundred English miles, in an open common stuhl-waggon. After
waiting a few days at Husum, where, like the hunted hare, I returned to the spot I first started from, during which two French spies
dined every day at our *table d'hote*, and gave regular communica-
tions of the arrival of every Englishman at the nearest Hanoverian
posts, I went on board the packet, which narrowly escaped being
frozen in the river, and after encountering a severe gale, during
which our only consolation resembled that of Gonzalo in the tem-

pest, who observed of his captain, " That he seemed to have no
" drowning mark upon him," we crossed the north seas in forty-six
hours, and landed upon the shores of that beloved country which,
uneclipsed by any superior in arms, in arts, or in sciences; and
without a rival in commerce, in agriculture, or in riches; possesses
more religion and morality, more humanity and munificence, more
public and private integrity, is more blest with freedom, more enlightened by eloquence, more adorned with beauty, more graced with
chastity, and richer in all the requisites to form that least assuming,
but first of earthly blessings, *domestic comfort*, than any nation upon
the globe.

If, my reader! after having paid our homage to the merits of other
countries, we return together, with more settled admiration, to that
which has given us birth, I shall the less regret my absence from
her, and from those who are the dearest to my heart, and to whom I
am indebted for all my present enjoyments.

Having felt most sensibly, in the hour of my return, those prime
distinctions of my country, which eminently and justly endear her
to all her children, I close the volume with an ardent wish, that
heaven may graciously render those distinctions perpetual.

FINIS.

DR. REES's

NEW CYCLOPÆDIA.

SAMUEL F. BRADFORD

IS PREPARING TO PUBLISH BY SUBSCRIPTION

THE NEW CYCLOPÆDIA;

OR,

UNIVERSAL DICTIONARY

OF ARTS AND SCIENCES,

IN TWENTY VOLUMES QUARTO.

Formed upon a more enlarged plan of arrangement than the Dictionary of Mr. Chambers.

COMPREHENDING THE VARIOUS ARTICLES OF THAT WORK, WITH ADDITIONS AND IMPROVEMENTS, TOGETHER WITH NEW SUB-JECTS OF BIOGRAPHY, GEOGRAPHY, AND HISTORY, AND ADAPTED TO THE PRESENT IMPROVED STATE OF LITERATURE AND SCIENCE.

BY ABRAHAM REES, D. D. F. R. S.

EDITOR OF THE LAST EDITION OF CHAMBERS'S DICTIONARY;

With the assistance of eminent professional gentlemen.

Illustrated with new plates, including Maps, engraved for the work, by some of the most distinguished artists.

The whole improved and adapted to this country, by gentlemen of known abilities, by whose aid it will be rendered the most complete work of the kind that has yet appeared.

CONDITIONS.

I. The work will be printed in large Quarto, with new types, cast for the purpose, and on a superfine woven paper.

II. It will be comprised in about Twenty Volumes, from eight hundred to a thousand pages each.

III. An half volume, in boards, will be regularly published every two months, price Three Dollars, payable on delivery. No advance will be required.

IV. Any subscriber, who, upon the receipt of the first half volume, does not approve of the work, shall be at liberty to withdraw his name.

V. Between six and seven hundred Plates, engraved in a superior style of elegance, will be comprised in the course of the publication; by far a greater number than is to be found in any other Scientific Dictionary. At the close of the publication will be delivered an elegant Frontispiece, the dedication, preface, and proper title pages for the different volumes.

VI. The work will be put to press as soon as a sufficient number of subscribers are obtained.

VII. A list of the names of those who subscribe will be published in the last volume, as the patrons of this great and magnificent work.